From Boots to Business

From Boots to Business

Transitioning from the Service to a Career in Business

Jillian Ventrone, Robert W. Blue Jr.,
Roxanne Rapske, and Julie LaCroix

ROWMAN & LITTLEFIELD
Lanham • Boulder • New York • London

Published by Rowman & Littlefield
An imprint of The Rowman & Littlefield Publishing Group, Inc.
4501 Forbes Boulevard, Suite 200, Lanham, Maryland 20706
www.rowman.com

6 Tinworth Street, London SE11 5AL, United Kingdom

British Library Cataloguing in Publication Information Available

Library of Congress Cataloging-in-Publication Data

Names: Ventrone, Jillian, 1973– author.
Title: From boots to business : transitioning from the service to a career in business / Jillian Ventrone, [and three others].
Other titles: Transitioning from the service to a career in business
Description: Lanham : Rowman & Littlefield, [2020] | Includes index. | Summary: "From Boots to Business is designed to help guide service members interested in pursuing a career in the field of business post-military service on their journey by guiding them through the maze of possibilities and assisting them in maximizing their available choices"— Provided by publisher.
Identifiers: LCCN 2019059428 (print) | LCCN 2019059429 (ebook) | ISBN 9781538126943 (cloth) | ISBN 9781538126950 (epub)
Subjects: LCSH: Veterans—Employment—United States. | Business—Vocational guidance—United States. | Career changes—United States. | Veteran reintegration—United States.
Classification: LCC UB357 .V335 2020 (print) | LCC UB357 (ebook) | DDC 650.14086/970973—dc23
LC record available at https://lccn.loc.gov/2019059428
LC ebook record available at https://lccn.loc.gov/2019059429

♾️™ The paper used in this publication meets the minimum requirements of American National Standard for Information Sciences—Permanence of Paper for Printed Library Materials, ANSI/NISO Z39.48-1992.

Contents

Preface

While people are driven to join the military for different reasons, many opt for military service specifically so they can earn a debt-free education through the Post-9/11 GI Bill. But navigating higher education and the world of work can be complicated, especially for those who are unsure how to begin. *From Boots to Business* offers service members and veterans accessible information that will guide them through the maze of possibilities and assist them in maximizing their available choices.

From Boots to Business was written for those interested in pursuing a career within the business realm, whether in corporate America or in business/franchise ownership. Since business degrees, at both the bachelor's and master's levels, are the most sought-after degrees by veterans using the Post-9/11 GI Bill—and according to the Small Business Administration, 9 percent of all businesses in the United States are veteran owned—the authors recognized the need for information to be more readily available. Compiling their expertise in the areas of higher education, career counseling, and franchise/business ownership, they developed *From Boots to Business*.

The information on veteran business ownership was compiled with data from the U.S. Census Bureau's Survey of Business Owners (2017): https://www.sba.gov/sites/default/files/advocacy/435-veteran-owned-businesses-report.pdf.

Introduction

The military builds the initial platform leading to a lifelong career pathway for individuals interested in serving for one contract or those who stay on active duty for a full career. However, most service members will someday need to prepare for a post–military service career. While the skills learned during military service can carry through into the civilian sector, oftentimes further preparation will be required. *From Boots to Business* is designed to help service members interested in the field of business on this journey by guiding them through the maze of possibilities and assisting them in maximizing their available choices.

In many cases, education and training may be necessary for those interested in pursuing a career in business. In other cases, information may be key. Learning about the possibilities can be difficult, and deciphering the world of higher education and navigating available veterans' benefits is challenging. Incorrect choices can mean extended periods of time backtracking later on or running out of payment options for funding higher education. Reading this book will help you make well-informed choices and reinforce your confidence in the decisions you make.

If service members never receive counseling regarding their education or benefits, this book will guide them through preparation, help them navigate their funding options, and enable them to outline a pathway toward a civilian career. Many service members have already achieved successful educations and careers through the advice of the authors and the programs and services outlined in this book. Additional, free resources are included that have proved useful for the service members we have worked with over the years and might enhance a veteran's education or career viability.

Some of these programs and services are even offered on military bases where readers may be stationed or live close to.

The military does not have a manual that service members can reference for all of their academic and career needs; this book fills that gap. *From Boots to Business* is meant to be a long-term reference manual and is a valuable asset for readers in collecting necessary information and learning how to manipulate available resources while preparing a plan of attack so that they will feel more capable of planning and executing the necessary steps to begin their transitions.

Some of the information delivered in this book is reprinted from the Marine Corps version, *From the Marine Corps to College: Transitioning from the Service to Higher Education.* Much of the information provided is applicable to service members from each military branch. It is also highly relevant to individuals who are considering entering the military and might be looking for more information regarding the available benefits.

Chapter One

Is a Career in Business Right for You?

Since this book focuses on the field of business, it is important to determine if this type of work is a good fit for you. This chapter is designed to help you go on a fact-finding mission about yourself: to learn if your personality and interests align with others in the field and to determine if business will be a long-term and comfortable fit for a career. Now, even if you have already made this decision, it's still important to read this chapter as business is a broad field, and many different types of positions exist. Follow along with the detailed assessments and learn about your interests and goals. Take a detailed look into your military experience to see if any parallels exist, then integrate them into your new career. The following topics will be addressed in this chapter:

- Assessments
- Occupational Data
- Military Skills Translated for the Job Market

INTRODUCTION

Are you a self-motivated, driven, organized person who is in tune with his or her strengths and weaknesses? Do you know how these traits will help you in the business world? How about the traits you have that may demonstrate an aptitude for entrepreneurship? Most of you probably are not sure of the answers to these questions, and most likely this is because you need more information about yourself, including your work interests, abilities, skills confidence, work values, and income and lifestyle goals, in order to answer them. This is the time when career assessments can be a beneficial tool in your civilian career planning.

Once you are done taking the assessments and learning a bit more about yourself, you need to consider factors specific to jobs in the world of business and entrepreneurship. Some of these positions will require long hours including weekends, frequent travel, high demands and fast deadlines, and public speaking coupled with the ability to communicate often and confidently. You need to consider the job demands as well as your aptitude and interest in taking on these demands. Much of this information will be covered throughout the book, but keep it in mind while following along with the assessments and tools listed in this chapter.

All the factors listed in the previous paragraph can also be an attribute of business ownership. Even those of you who are multitalented will still need to fill in the areas in which you find gaps. Taking the assessments will help you uncover these gaps; then you can strategize about fixing them or finding people or strategies to support you. This way, you can make better and more informed decisions. Ignoring the information you gather won't make it go away, it will just make you ill prepared.

ASSESSMENTS

You have decided that you are separating/retiring from the service and are ready to pursue a future civilian career. You are interested in the field of business, but you don't know where to start or whether it's a good fit. Some of you may have recently separated from the service and participated in the weeklong Transition Readiness Seminar (TRS); others may have separated before TRS was developed. Those of you who completed TRS may be familiar with one of the assessments we are going to go through in this chapter. Now, for many years, two of the authors of this book taught the two-day higher education track that is a follow-on course to the weeklong TRS program. They spent quite a bit of time reviewing the assessments that students were supposed to have completed during the weeklong program; however, many did not take them as required and, in most cases, they were not reviewed in the one-week, mandatory TRS class, anyway. The two authors who facilitated the groups made sure to give students time during class to complete the assessments as they are integral to students learning more about their personality traits, career interests, skills confidence, and work values. Basically, this will tell you what you enjoy, where your confidence is, and what values and skills you hold for the workplace environment. While the assessments won't tell you which career track you should ultimately take, understanding these traits will give you a springboard from which you can launch your career planning.

Now, whether you realize it or not, you have all taken a vocational assessment before. The Armed Services Vocational Aptitude Battery (ASVAB)! Little did you know at the time, but that test was going to follow you around for the rest of your military career, for some more than others. As to those of you who stayed in the military for more than one enlistment, many attended specialty schools, submitted officer packages, or wanted to change Military Occupational Specialties (MOS) or ratings. Most of these options required minimum scores on the ASVAB, and often in specific areas. The test is different from other vocational assessments in that it also measures aptitude, that is, how well you have developed your skills and their potential for further training.

The ASVAB incorporates theories from John Holland, who served in the Army during World War II. After separating from the service, he went on to get a master's degree and a PhD and to develop a career theory that is prevalent in the world of career counseling. When the old transition program was initially redesigned about a decade ago, the Holland Self-Directed Search (SDS) paper-based assessment was used by those who taught the education portion of TRS. This was during the time that everyone attended the education or vocational portion, as it was built into the week that was mandatory for every service member to attend. One of the authors of this book knows this as she was a part of the process of developing the materials and launching the new course aboard a base in Southern California. As TRS evolved, the SDS was replaced by a digital version, Defense Activity for Non-Traditional Education Support (DANTES) Kuder Journey's assessments (https://dantes.kuder.com), which is also based on Holland's theory.

Holland's theory is based on the idea that peoples' career choices are an extension of their personalities, and that people express themselves, and their interests and values, through their work choices. His theory assigns both people and work environments to specific types or themes. He believed that in our culture, people are strongest in one personality type, that all professions might require people who fit all personality types to a degree, and that people who work in a profession and environment that are a fit for their type of personality tend to be more successful and to find more satisfaction in their work. Think back to your ASVAB test results: this may also prove true for those who enter the military. However, I should state that this is true for those who entered the military and were assigned positions based on their assessment results, as many are assigned simply based on the needs of the particular service branch they entered.

Holland believed that most people can be categorized into the following six types, and each person may be characterized by one, or some combination, of these types:

- Realistic (R)
- Investigative (I)
- Artistic (A)
- Social (S)
- Enterprising (E)
- Conventional (C)

Occupational environments can be divided into the same six types, and each environment is dominated by a particular type of person. People search for environments that let them:

- exercise their skills and abilities;
- express their attitudes and values;
- take on problems and roles they find stimulating and satisfying; and
- avoid chores or responsibilities they find distasteful or formidable.

At this point, you should register for an account or retrieve your user name and password to the DANTES Kuder Journey's website as much of the following information will require you to have an account and follow along. A little hint for military spouses who may be reading this book: the accounts are not free for you, but I have had spouses use their active-duty husband's/wife's account before. Once you gain entry, scroll down on the left-hand side, and click on the "Take an Assessment" button. On the next page, you will see the option for three assessments, "Career Assessments," "Skills Confidence," and the "Work Values Inventory." They will take approximately thirty minutes to complete in total. Take them before moving on in this chapter.

Now let's move on to explore the detailed results. Scroll down further on the left-hand side, and click on "My Assessments." You will notice that you will pass by "Explore Occupations." We will return to this section at a later point to review occupations that are recommended by your assessment results. On this page, you will see links to the following:

- Work Values
- Skills Confidence
- Career Interests
- One-Page Summary Report
- Interests and Skills Composite Report

Click on the "One-Page Summary Report" link. On this page, you will get your three-digit Holland Code. My codes are SAE for my career interests and SAA/E for skills confidence, which I found to be exactly the opposite of the codes of most of the service members I assessed/placed. Take a minute to review your charts listed on this page.

The University of Louisville's Career Center has a Holland Hexagram (figure 1.1) on its website that visually depicts these categories.

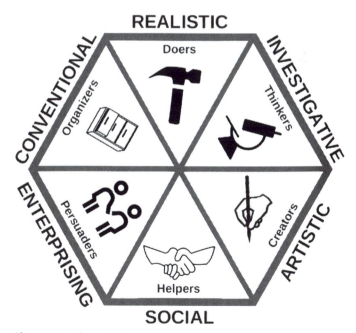

Figure 1.1. Career Hexagon
https://louisville.edu/career/images/holland/holland-hexagon/view

According to the University of Wisconsin's Career Center:

> Each letter of the Holland Code occupies a section of the hexagon. Letters that are next to each other tend to have more overlapping traits, making it easier to find careers with both of those letters. For example, Social and Enterprising both usually enjoy working in careers with a lot of social interaction. Letters that are opposite each other on the hexagon have little in common. For example, Conventional individuals enjoy structure, while Artistic individuals prefer more freedom in their work. While it is possible to find a job with both these elements, it is more challenging. Sometimes individuals find that two of their letters are most important to them in a career while the third letter is pursued as a hobby.[1]

Basically, this means that the closer two letters are to each other, the tighter the relationship, the more consistency, the more compatible the interests, and the more similar the job duties. Opposite letters on the hexagram equal less consistency and compatibility.

While I didn't keep statistics on the results I received (I'll never make a good researcher and I'm not good with numbers!), typically, most service members I worked with over the past ten years assessed into Conventional, Realistic, and Investigative. Notice that these categories are exactly the opposite of my own code of SAE. Of course, there were always the exceptions. As we progress through this information, you'll begin to understand that there is a reason why many service members assess into the same or similar categories.

Before we go any farther with the assessment's results, let's take a look at what these different categories mean. Keep in mind that a career choice represents an extension of a person's personality. Let's explore the six types of personalities further.

Realistic (R)

- Enjoy working with animals, tools, or machines
- Generally, avoid social activities such as teaching, healing, and informing others
- Are skillful when working with tools, mechanical or electrical drawings, machines, or plants and animals
- Value practical things you can see, touch, and use, such as plants and animals, tools, equipment, or machines

• See selves as practical, mechanical, and realistic

People who fall into this category are doers. They are:

• Practical
• Athletic
• Straightforward
• Mechanically inclined
• Nature lovers
• Stable
• Self-controlled
• Independent ambitious
• Systematic
• Persistent

They can:

• Fix things
• Solve problems
• Play a sport
• Read a blueprint
• Operate tools or machinery

They like to:

• Tinker with objects
• Work outdoors
• Be physically active
• Build things
• Train animals
• Work on equipment

Jobs they are good at:

• Air Traffic Controller
• Archaeologist
• Athletic Trainer
• Cartographer
• Commercial Airline Pilot

- Commercial Drafter
- Corrections Officer
- Farm Manager
- Fish and Game Warden
- Landscape Architect
- Mechanical Engineer
- Petroleum Geologist
- Property Manager
- Recreation Manager
- Service Manager

Investigative (I)

- Enjoy studying and solving math or science problems
- Generally, avoid leading, selling, or persuading people
- Are good at understanding and solving science and math problems
- Value science
- See selves as precise, scientific, and intellectual

People who fall into this category are thinkers. They are:

- Inquisitive
- Analytical
- Scientific
- Observant
- Precise
- Cautious
- Reserved
- Broadminded
- Independent
- Logical

They can:

- Think abstractly
- Solve math problems
- Understand theories
- Do complex calculations

They like to:

- Explore
- Use computers
- Work independently
- Do lab experiments
- Do research
- Be challenged

Jobs they are good at:

- Actuary
- Anesthesiologist
- Anthropologist
- Archaeologist
- Biochemist
- Biologist
- Chemical Engineer
- Chemist
- Computer Systems Analyst
- Dentist
- Ecologist
- Economist
- Electrical Engineer
- Geologist
- Horticulturist
- Mathematician
- Medical Technologist
- Meteorologist (IRS)
- Research Analyst
- Statistician

Artistic (A)

- Enjoy creative activities such as art, drama, crafts, dance, music, or creative writing
- Generally, avoid highly ordered or repetitive activities
- Have good artistic abilities in creative writing, drama, crafts, music, or art

- Value creative arts such as drama, music, art, or the works of creative writers
- See selves as expressive, original, and independent

People who fall into this category are creators. They are:

- Intuitive
- Imaginative
- Unconventional
- Emotional
- Independent
- Idealistic
- Creative
- Sensitive
- Nonconforming
- Expressive

They can:

- Sketch
- Draw
- Paint
- Play an instrument
- Write stories, poetry, music.
- Sing, act, dance
- Design

They like to:

- Attend concerts
- Read
- Take photos
- Express themselves creatively

Jobs they are good at:

- Advertising Art Director
- Advertising Manager
- Architect

- Art Teacher
- Artist
- Copywriter
- English Teacher
- Fashion Illustrator
- Intelligence Research Specialist
- Journalist/Reporter
- Medical Illustrator
- Music Teacher
- Writer

Social (S)

- Enjoy doing things to help people such as teaching, nursing, giving first aid, or providing information
- Generally, avoid using machines, tools, or animals to achieve a goal
- Are good at teaching, counseling, nursing, or giving information
- Value helping people and solving social problems
- See selves as helpful, friendly, and trustworthy

Those who fall into this category are helpers. They are:

- Friendly
- Helpful
- Idealistic
- Insightful
- Outgoing
- Generous
- Cooperative
- Forgiving
- Persuasive

They can:

- Teach others
- Express ideas clearly
- Lead
- Plan and supervise
- Cooperate with others

They like to:

- Work in groups
- Help people
- Volunteer
- Play team sports

Jobs they are good at:

- City Manager
- Community Organization Director
- Consumer Affairs Director
- Hospital Administrator
- Insurance Claims Examiner
- Real Estate Appraiser
- Recreation Director
- Volunteer Services Director

Enterprising (E)

- Enjoy leading and persuading people, and selling products and ideas
- Generally, avoid activities that require careful observation and scientific, analytical thinking
- Are good at leading people and selling things or ideas
- Value success in politics, leadership, or business
- See selves as energetic, ambitious, and sociable

Those who fall into this category are persuaders. They are:

- Self-confident
- Assertive
- Sociable
- Persuasive
- Enthusiastic
- Energetic
- Adventurous
- Impulsive
- Ambitious

- Inquisitive
- Optimistic

They can:

- Initiate projects
- Convince
- Sell
- Give presentations
- Lead a group, manage people
- Organize activities

They like to:

- Make decisions
- Be elected to office
- Discuss politics
- Participate in activities
- Lead others

Jobs they are good at:

- Advertising Executive
- Advertising Sales Rep
- Banker/Financial Planner
- Branch Manager
- Business Manager
- Buyer (ESA)
- Customer Service Manager
- Education and Training Manager
- Entrepreneur
- Insurance Manager
- Lawyer/Attorney
- Office Manager
- Public Relations
- Sales Manager
- Tax Accountant

Conventional (C)

- Enjoy working with numbers, records, or machines in a set, orderly way
- Generally, avoid ambiguous, unstructured activities
- Are good at working with written records and numbers in a systematic, orderly way
- Value success in business
- See selves as orderly and are good at following a set plan

People who are in this category are organizers. They are:

- Well organized
- Accurate
- Numerically inclined
- Methodical
- Conscientious
- Efficient
- Conforming
- Structured
- Ambitious
- Persistent

They can:

- Work well within a system
- Keep accurate records
- Do paperwork well

They like to:

- Receive clear directions
- Use data
- Work with numbers
- Organize things
- Play card or computer games

Jobs they are good at:

- Accountant
- Administrative Assistant

- Budget Analyst
- Business Manager
- Business Programmer
- Business Teacher
- Claims Adjuster
- Cost Accountant
- Credit Manager
- Financial Analyst
- Insurance Manager
- Insurance Underwriter
- Internal Auditor Tax Accountant
- Tax Consultant

The information listed previously can be found on the University of Wisconsin website: http://www.wiu.edu/advising/docs/Holland_Code.pdf. This is a good site to use to reference a wide range of occupations.

What Holland is trying to say is that people with similar personalities tend to find themselves drawn to the same type(s) of work. Consider the military. Generally speaking, you share similar traits with those around you. For an extreme example, consider infantry Marines. Those of you who know and love them, or are them, understand what I'm saying. I'm married to a recently retired infantry Marine. After twenty-six years of service, does he share traits similar to all of his infantry friends? You know it! Do infantry Marines think they excel over all others? Yes, yes, and yes. So, based on Holland's theory, when people of the same personality type work together, they create an environment suitable and rewarding to themselves. Are you starting to see a pattern?

Now, let's return to the DANTES Kuder Journey's website and review the purpose of each of these categories and explore the other information offered within the links. Remember we are currently on the page titled "Work Values Rankings."

Work Values

Work Values measures areas such as (1) core values: Are you looking for respect, independence, or achievement? (2) Work environments: Do you prefer a workplace close to home, a fast-paced environment, a diverse environment, or an environment where you can have a flexible schedule? (3) Work activities: Are you most comfortable in an environment that is challenging or creative or that offers variety? Keep in mind that working in an environment that contradicts your values may lead to dissatisfaction. Try to connect to the values you find in yourself throughout this section to better identify occupations that reflect these values. Your results will show on a graph that demonstrates, from high to low, the categories you most identify with. Categories listed include workplace, innovation, accomplishment, prestige, and income. When I took the assessment, I scored high in the first three, then prestige, and lowest in income. This means that I favor a position that offers a more comfortable workplace, leaves room for innovation, and helps me to feel a degree of accomplishment. When I reviewed these assessments with the active-duty population I worked with, I found over the years that most service members scored on the lower scale in "workplace." I once asked a Marine why he thought the results kept turning out that way for the those I assessed. He stated that, in his case, he thought it was because he was already working in the worst environment that he could possibly imagine, so anything else has to be a step up! Point taken, Marine.

Notice the other tab next to "Assessment Results" labeled "Occupations to Explore." This page lists occupations that align with your assessment results in the "work values" category. Take a minute to review a few of the occupations that sound interesting to you. Notice if any of them have a sun next to them. The sun means that the occupation is experiencing growth. Pick one of the occupations. When you arrive at the next page, you will see that there is quite a bit of more information to read about: tasks, interests and skills, education and experience, salary information, and related occupations. Don't ignore the last tab, "Additional Information." If the job requires licensing or certification at some point, this section will list the credentialing agencies and give you the websites where you can research the credentialing agency, state government site, or affiliated associations. I'm always especially interested in the "Salary & Outlook" link. I want to know if the occupation I'm researching is experiencing growth. However, this is just one place to look for this information. I prefer using Projections Central for more detailed state-based information: https://projectionscentral.com/. More information on this site can be found in chapter 5.

Skills Confidence

Now, go back to the main assessment page, and click on the next tab down, the "Skills Confidence Assessment." You will work through this section just like the last. The "skills confidence" section tells you about your current skills and interests. This section may also highlight areas you might want to develop. If the assessment demonstrates an area of weakness for you that you know is necessary for a particular occupation, then you know you need to work to improve upon it. You will notice that there is a third tab in this section, "Majors to Explore." In this section you will need to adjust the filter for the level of education you are interested in pursuing. I would recommend that you always search one level of education above the level you believe you need or are interested in pursuing. It may demonstrate more available options, more income, or more specialized positions that may come with more advancement opportunities.

Career Interest

The next section is the Career Interest Assessment. There are four tabs to explore in this section: "Assessment Results," "Occupations to Explore," "Majors to Explore" and "Person Matches." You already know what the first three tabs explore. The fourth tab gives you a group of jobs where the people currently in them share similar traits with you. One of the occupations listed under my scores was "psychology professor." When I click on the link, I arrive at a page that, in somewhat of an interview style, gives me more, hands-on, information regarding the daily doings of this occupation. This helps the job seem more realistic and attainable to me as I'm gaining practical application-based information. Make sure to click on each tab to expand the information.

Let's return to the main navigation panel on the left-hand side of the website, and click on "Explore Occupations," then "Occupations Suggested by Assessment Results." Read the explanation of the page. The jobs are matches based on the areas you tested strongest in for your interests, skills, and values. Spend time looking through the occupations that you are interested in learning more about.

These are the main tools I use on the DANTES Kuder Journey's website. Be careful using the "Find Schools" link as it doesn't differentiate between good schools and schools that are less than reputable. The "My Job Search Tools" link does have an easy-to-create résumé section. The tool is one of the easiest to use that I've found so far. The downside is that you need to already know the type and scope of information you should be addressing in your résumé. This is a complicated task. Read more about résumés in chapter 5, "Preparation and Resources for Career Planning." One link that I have found to be a resourceful tool is "My e-Profile." This section enables you to create a digital portfolio about yourself. You can publish the link when you are done creating it. Put it on your résumé so if potential employers are interested, they can find out more about you. This may help personalize the experience for those involved.

So, we have spent a bit of time learning more about ourselves and occupations that may be a good fit. Now let's explore business-based occupations more deeply. Some of you were classified as Conventional and Enterprising (CE), Investigative and Conventional (IC), and Realistic and Enterprising (RE). Many fields of business align under the Enterprising (E) and Conventional (C) designations, which house such fields as finance, manufacturing, public administration, marketing, sales, transportation (including distribution and logistics), and business (including management and administration). People who score high in enterprising tend to be good at talking. In fact, the Utah State Department of Workforce Services states: "Enterprising people are good talkers and use this skill to lead or persuade others. They also value reputation, power, money and status, and will usually go after it. They like to work with people and data."[2] But other fields, such as marketing and sales, also fall under the Social (S) designation. Let's not forget those who were classified under Realistic (R) and Conventional (C), where STEM (science, technology, engineering, and math) majors reign supreme. Many in STEM fields also want to own their own businesses. If that is you, consider the type of business you want to own. Do you want to become a civil engineer? Follow that goal first, as a bachelor's degree in this field will be challenging and may take a bit longer than other non-STEM fields, and a bachelor's degree in the field is the minimum qualification for these positions. Many of the qualities STEM majors have are also good for business ownership. Consider that those in the engineering field often must collaborate with others to complete projects, and they often must problem solve on a complex level, taking unrelated topics to create one coherent solution. Make note that having multiple areas with high scores just diversifies the areas that you might find satisfying.

If you are interested in more information regarding the categories of occupations that align under the different Holland Code categories, visit the following websites:

- Minnesota State University: https://careerwise.minnstate.edu/guide/counselors/counselorclustersholland.html
- California State University, Stanislaus: https://www.csustan.edu/sites/default/files/groups/Career%20Services/2017-Postings/other/majors_by_holland_code.pdf

After learning a bit about yourself and the types of the careers that may be a good fit, you can search for occupations that align under your Holland Code using O*NET Online and conduct more in-depth reconnaissance on particular occupations. I know many of you used O*NET during TRS, so you know how to look up particular occupations by going to the main O*NET website, https://www.onetonline.org/, and typing in an occupational title in the "Occupation Quick Search" bar. This method is fine to use if you already have particular occupations in mind, but what if you don't? O*NET also allows us to search by Holland Codes. On the main page, click on "Advanced Search." This page has the following methods you can use to search for occupations:

- O*NET Data
- Skills
- Technology, skills, and tools
- Related DWA Search (detailed work activities)
- Related Tasks

We are going to use the options under "O*NET Data" to search for occupations that align under your Holland Codes. We'll use the three categories outlined immediately preceding this category: work values, skills confidence, and interests. For example, I can select the "Interests" tab, then, from the drop-down menu under the first choice, select the code that I assessed highest in. On the next page, I can select the job zone I'm most interested in pursuing. An overview of job zones can be

found here: https://www.onetonline.org/help/online/zones. For the purposes of this book, I'm going to select job zone 4, as it usually requires
a bachelor's degree for minimum qualifications for the occupation. Then
I can select occupations from the list that I'm interested in learning more
about. Peruse the following pages as needed.

OCCUPATIONAL DATA

Most people don't consider checking occupational data before starting
their academic program. This is a major area of career counseling that
should be researched prior to using your GI Bill. You only have one
shot to maximize your benefits, so preparing up-front may save you
time and money.

Wages and employment trends are important factors to consider
when selecting a future occupation. You can view these items at the
bottom of each occupational page on O*NET, and directions on how
to use the site are detailed in chapter 5. The National Association of
Colleges and Employers (NACE), which states that it is the "leading
source of information on the employment of the college educated, and
forecasts hiring and trends in the job market; tracks starting salaries,
recruiting and hiring practices, and student attitudes and outcomes;
and identifies best practices and benchmarks,"[3] projects the following
starting salaries for the highest paying business majors at the bachelor's
degree level for 2019:

- Management information systems: $61,697
- Economics: $59,480
- Finance: $58,464
- Accounting: $57,511
- Business administration/management: $57,133[4]

NACE also projects the following starting salaries for the highest paying business majors at the master's degree level for 2019:

- Business administration/management: $84,580
- Management information systems: $76,106

- Human resources: $75,792
- Finance: $74,201
- Accounting: $69,605[5]

   Business majors were not the highest paying bachelor's degree majors, however. They came in fourth behind engineering, computer science, and math and sciences. Business majors were also not the highest paying master's degree majors. They came in third behind engineering and computer science master's degrees, but they did pass the math and science majors. Don't forget that you can be a STEM major and also be a business owner. For example, my brother-in-law is a civil engineer, but he is also part owner in an engineering firm. This means that he has to define the services being sold, generate business, maintain clients, hire personnel, determine pricing, and keep track of all expenses related to the business. These are topics learned in business programs, not typically during engineering studies. Some engineering programs do incorporate business topics into their curriculum, but, in most instances, this is information engineers will need to find elsewhere. If this is you, consider taking some classes through the local community college. Many of these schools, including the school I work at, MiraCosta College, offer entrepreneurship-based classes or full entrepreneurship associate degrees. Also, consider taking courses through a program such as Coursera. Sometimes these classes are offered for free, but, if you need a certificate of completion, then often there is a cost involved.

   Wages are not the only aspect of a particular occupation that you should consider. Occupational growth is just as important. If an occupation you are interested in attaining is experiencing negative or stagnant growth, you may want to consider something different. After all, completing the required level of education doesn't guarantee employment. So you need to determine if you will have a good chance at securing employment in the field that you're going to be spending time and effort on—in education/training and in pursuing GI Bill benefits. More information on this topic will follow later in this book.

   There are many competencies that employers look for in employees. NACE publishes articles that may assist you in better preparing for your civilian career. For example, a recent article, "The Four Career Competencies Employers Value Most," discusses the results of a recent survey the organization conducted with employers. The highest listed competencies for the past three years were:

- Critical thinking/problem solving
- Teamwork/collaborations
- Professionalism/work ethic
- Oral/written communicatons[6]

Service members learn many of these traits througout their time in the miltiary. Consider the time you spent in training, through PME requirements, and in leading others in your charge. These four competencies were required for you to be successful. So, as you plan for your next career, begin to consider how you can maximize these traits in gaining employment, in demonstrating your worth when already employed, and in creating upward momentum for your career trajectory.

Lately, I have had many veterans I worked with over the years reach out to me to ask about obtaining certificates that demonstrate computer-based knowledge and computer-application competencies. I found it interesting that in the article mentioned earlier, NACE stated that digital technology was ranked fifth in essential competency skills employers are looking for from potential employees. I have referred many of those who reached out to me to the computer services and information technology (CSIT) departments of the local community colleges. Faculty in these departments typically know which certifications are beneficial for businness workers and which classes may lead to industry certifications. Gaining these certificates can help to demonstrate your strength as an employee in terms of your ability to learn and manipulate a diverse breadth of knowledge.

I referred one student veteran that I have worked with for several years, Antwan Gibson, to a professor in the CSIT department of a local community college for advice. Antwan, a former sergeant in the infantry in the Marine Corps, had just secured employment with a major U.S. management and information-technology consulting firm as a financial data analyst. He had completed a bachelor's degree in economics and was working on a graduate degree when he was hired. He stated that the courses the CSIT professor recommended to him, and that he subsequently took through Coursera, helped him secure employment with this company. The courses he took covered SQL, Python, and Tableau. He stated that after eight years on active duty and two more in the Reserves, his military information was the smallest section on his résumé. Since it wasn't directly related to the position he wanted, he felt that it wasn't an area he should overemphasize, as he didn't want his résumé to get lost in the pile of all of the other newly graduated applicants. Antwan offered the following advice:

> I would emphasize that my military experience really helped me in my interview when answering open-ended questions on conflict resolution. That being said, my military experience was an added bonus. I had to bring something tangible to the table and that was my analytical experience, relevant education, and certifications. People will tell you that certifications don't matter. Here's my take; it depends on the profession. The data science/analytics industry, for example, has many certification programs that can positively impact your chances of getting the job you want or even boost your salary. At the end of the day, you have to do your homework to see if the benefits outweigh the costs. I spent hours pulling data from all data analytic job applications over the past year to see what hiring agencies are looking for. I looked at the trends for different coding programs to see what is the current market demand for analytic software programs. Once I narrowed them down, I received additional guidance from various SME's and I enrolled in those courses. Like a degree, some companies are looking for that check in the box. Do you have training in that field or not? If so, prove it. That can be expressed through your current work history or through having certifications. For my applications, I've had to use a combination of both.[7]

MILITARY SKILLS TRANSLATED FOR THE JOB MARKET

Some of you held MOS and ratings that have some counterpart in the civilian section, such as those in the fields of logistics, embarkation, mobility, aviation logistics, maintenance management, operations, civil affairs (which includes diplomats and workers in specialized fields in business/international business), information security (like IT management), and so on. The military has some unique job titles that are not automatically understood by civilians. In the civilian world, the term *engineer* is usually associated with someone who has completed a bachelor's degree in a field of engineering (mechanical, electrical, civil, etc.) and is employed in a profession requiring those skills. In the military, the term *engineer* usually means some type of mechanic (i.e., engine mechanic), as was the common usage in the late eighteenth and early nineteenth centuries. Another example is *yeoman*, the job title of an administrative assistant in the Coast Guard and Navy. *Yeoman* is a term more commonly used in past centuries to refer to a farmer with a small landholding or someone who performed a loyal service (https://www.merriam-webster.com/dictionary/yeoman). So how do you translate those skills when looking into occupations in the world of business? There are tools that can assist, including:

- O*NET Online: https://www.onetonline.org/crosswalk/MOC/
- My Next Move: https://www.mynextmove.org/vets/
- DANTES Kuder Journey: https://www.dantes.doded.mil/Education Programs/PrepForCollege/Kuder.html

The last website is for DANTES Kuder Journey, which has many tools including a section for finding occupations relating to a military specialty.

Let us try to look up a few military skills using some of these resources. We will start by looking up a few military specialties on the O*Net Online Military Crosswalk Site: https://www.onetonline.org/crosswalk/MOC/. Let's review a few MOSs and ratings and find out if any of them translate into civilian careers in the business and business-related sectors:

USMC

- 0521, Military Information Support Operations: logistics managers
- 0491, Logistics/Mobility Chief: administrative services managers, storage and distribution managers
- 0679, Data Systems Chief: computer and information systems managers, information technology project managers
- 0699, Communications Chief: information technology project managers
- 3043, Supply Chain and Material Management Specialist: administrative services managers, logistics managers, storage and distribution managers

- 3044, Operational Contract Support Specialist: logisticians, market research analysts and marketing specialists, property managers, purchasing managers, technical directors/managers

Air Force

- 3D0X2, Cyber Systems Operations: computer and information systems managers, information technology project managers, information security analysts
- 1A2X1, Aircraft Loadmaster: administrative services managers, document management specialists, supervisors of office and administrative support services, operations managers, logistics managers
- 2G0X1, Logistics Planner: administrative services managers, business intelligence analysts, logistics managers, management analysts, purchasing managers, transportation managers
- 2S0X1, Materiel Management: administrative services managers, storage and distribution managers, purchasing managers
- 3E9X1, Emergency Management: emergency management directors, operations management, risk management specialists, training and development managers
- 4A0X1, Health Services Management: medical and health services managers, clinical data managers

Army

- 79S, Career Counselor: human resources specialists, training and development specialists, administrative services managers
- 120A, Construction Engineering Technician: construction managers
- 140A, Command and Control Systems Integrator: computer and information systems managers, emergency management directors, general and operations managers, training and development specialists
- 14A, Air Defense Artillery Officer: security managers, emergency management directors
- 37F, Psychological Operations Specialist: human resources managers
- 38A, Civil Affairs: public relations and fundraising managers

Coast Guard

- YN, Yeoman: administrative service managers, financial managers, human resources managers, labor relations specialists, and compensation, benefits, and job analysis specialists
- DC, Damage Controlman: emergency management managers, construction managers
- IS, Intelligence Specialist: computer and information systems managers, operations managers

Now that we have a sampling of related occupations, we can take our research to the next level at My Next Move for Veterans: https://www.mynextmove.org/vets/. There are three options to choose from in the search for new careers. Option 1 allows a search for careers with key words. Option 2 has a section for browsing careers by industry. Option 3 is for finding jobs like those of your military career.

For the Army MOS of 79S Career Counselor, human resources occupations appear in the O*Net Online Military Crosswalk Site. Using the first option in My Next Move for Veterans, conduct a career search with the key words "human resources." This brings up all human resources related jobs through a connection with O*Net. Job titles that come up include human resources managers and human resources specialists. Click on the job title to find the knowledge, skills, and abilities associated with the job. Information on the type of personality qualities associated with the job and the technology employees in the field need to be familiar with is also listed. Information is also available on education levels and certifications associated with the career field. Salary information is included by national average, state average, and local average. Similar and related job titles, and even a job-search link where one can plug in a zip code and see a display of local job postings for the job title, are provided. In this fashion, you can begin to broaden your search for career fields that share similarities with your military career.

Chapter Two

Informed Decisions

People are driven to join the military for many different reasons; oftentimes, education and career skills are at the top of the list. Many consider going to school while they are on active duty to study business, at the undergraduate and graduate levels, to be better prepared to transition when the time rolls around. Some prefer vocational skills-building programs. And others combine both pathways to get the knowledge they need to practice certain types of business or trade and, at the same time, begin building the skills and knowledge they need to run a business. For example, I worked with a marine several years ago who wanted to start his own welding business. I sent him to the local community college to take business and entrepreneurship classes, then, just before his EAS (end of obligated service) date, I sent him to complete the free Veterans in Piping (VIP) program aboard our base. This way he learned his trade but also learned how to run a profitable business.

But what if you are not sure where you should start? That is a statement I hear almost daily from the active-duty and veteran population I counsel. This chapter is designed to give you a glimpse into the different options available to pursue. The following topics are discussed:

- College to Work, Entrepreneurship, and Franchise
- Training for Vocational-Technical Small-Business Owners
- Direct to Franchise
- Career Strategy Stages

INTRODUCTION

There are so many options for employment, entrepreneurship, and educational pathways that sometimes the choices feel overwhelming. Make an informed decision, and know that a large part of making the right decision comes from simple concepts that are hard to measure: What do you want to do? How can you direct your education and instincts into a product or a service? What will your family tolerate in terms of risking money, time, resources, or relocation?

This chapter outlines the basic information for obtaining additional education in commonly transferable pathways while translating military experience to high-paying, high-in-demand jobs. The review of options is not comprehensive, of course but is a place for you to begin to understand the common pathways that your peers may be taking. They are not prescribed or recommended pathways, so be sure to reflect on your own desires and abilities before choosing a program.

Self-confidence and risk tolerance are concepts to consider before making a strategic move to buy a franchise or start a business. There are ways to calculate and mitigate risk, but in any move toward franchising and entrepreneurship, there will be financial, family, and career risk involved. Most entrepreneurs thrive on taking well-calibrated risks, and if you are of this type, then this chapter is for you.

Some service members find businesses that they feel confident starting with the knowledge they already hold. Some even start while on active duty, even after calculating the risks. My old neighbor, a staff sergeant in the Marine Corps, went on recruiting duty and was sent to a suburban location outside of Chicago. When he got there, he commenced buying as many rental properties as he could afford. This was a strategic move on his part. He thought it through after he was assigned to a recruiting station, and once he knew where he was going, he began his market research and contacted a real estate agent to begin to get a better idea of the area, property types, and cost of the property. He has already targeted a management company to use when he is reassigned, which will allow him to leave the area but maintain ownership of the properties.

As another example, while author Robert W. Blue Jr. worked aboard a federal installation, an active-duty service member visited the base education center to find a way to start a business with a skill he had acquired in the military. His unit was often assigned to areas without access to barbers, so he bought a set of barber clippers and scissors, watched YouTube instructional videos, and taught himself to cut hair in the military style. As he approached the end of his enlistment contract, he enrolled in a state-approved barber school and used his savings to open a small barbershop. The service member was able to transition into a career and small-business ownership, and it all started with providing haircuts to his fellow service members.

COLLEGE TO WORK OR DIRECT TO ENTREPRENEURSHIP/FRANCHISE

There are many pathways to becoming an entrepreneur or franchise owner. The pathway you take needs to be tailored to your employment goals and your life. To start, you need to explore what will work best for you. This means exploring your options and commitments. For example, if you have a large student-loan debt upon graduation, getting money from a bank to invest in your business or to buy a franchise might not be immediately viable. This may force you into a job working for someone else. If so, don't waste your time while you are there. Learn about everything relevant to your future business. Keep a notebook where you write down anything that may assist you in your own endeavor. Ask lots of questions. Learn about the different departments and employee functions, and consider how the infrastructure might be duplicated for your company. And, of course, network as much as possible. Keep in touch with your new contacts as they may become clients or resources when you are in business for yourself.

Some of you reading this book already have a bachelor's and maybe even a master's degree, but others will not have attended or completed college before joining the military. Now, if you are a separating/retiring senior enlisted person or officer, you may feel that you have already learned the skills necessary to make you successful, such as personnel and equipment management, budgeting, logistics, team building, and leadership. If you are separating after one enlistment, and haven't attended college, you may want to consider attending school and gaining some experience first. Of course, this also depends upon your pre-service experience and the type of business you are interested in starting or buying into. Being an owner of some businesses (e.g., accounting firms, real estate companies) or a provider of some services (e.g., private therapy practices) will require you to have a college degree, license, or some form of personalized training. Even those of you who have completed college and have significant management experience may want to consider some type of schooling, especially if you are still on active duty. Consider looking into a graduate program or an in-demand certificate program to make you more competitive as you enter the civilian workforce or more knowledgeable regarding the business you want to own. See the section on certificates in chapter 5 for more information on certificates that may help you round out your business knowledge. And, obviously, don't forget you have a GI Bill that can offer a very nifty way to gain cost-free information!

College isn't for everyone, but if you are new to the business field, it may be a good idea to consider. Many colleges and universities offer entrepreneurship classes, bachelor's degrees in entrepreneurship, or business degrees with concentrations in entrepreneurship. The latter means that the majority of your coursework will be in more general business classes with usually around five to seven classes specifically tailored to entrepreneurship. Let's take a look at some differences in the programs.

Babson College in Massachusetts specializes in business and related fields. It is a private school so, if you consider it, remember to check whether it is participating in the Yellow Ribbon Program (YRP). Refer to chapter 7, "Cost and Payment Resources," for more information on paying for private schools. Babson does not offer the traditional academic pathway that a large state university does. The school specializes in business and entrepreneurship, and students select two concentrations to focus on during their studies. This may be appealing to those of you who are interested in entrepreneurship but also want an education in a subject area that will support a career within a specific business field. Being able to concentrate on two business-related subject areas offers students flexibility in their learning and potentially diversifies the areas of business they can consider for careers.

Babson prepares students for their studies by immersing them in a group of core classes that all students take. The classes form the foundation of the business program and include First-Year Seminar, Arts and Humanities/History and Society Foundation, Foundations in Management and Entrepreneurship, and Coaching for Leadership and Teamwork. More information on the program can be found here: https://www.babson.edu/academics/undergraduate-school/core-experiences/.

First Year Seminar is designed to help students acclimate to college life by assisting them in finding an identity, communicating with others, and learning about the academic and co-curricular resources available to students to support their success. The Arts and Humanities/History and Society Foundations platform of courses helps students diversify their knowledge base and stimulate complex thought. Students engage in a learning theme. "Themes include Nature and the Environment, Justice and Inequality, Memory and Forgetting, and The Self in Context."[1]

Foundations of Management and Entrepreneurship is a yearlong course that introduces students to managing a real business venture. Students work together to develop the entire process, from creation, to launch, to managing the startup. This way they learn about key areas that must be included, such as communication, leading a team, and overcoming obstacles. Coaching for Leadership and Teamwork is held two times, in different years during your stay at Babson. It offers students one-on-one coaching in interpersonal and leadership skills. Coaches observe your team interactions and then offer follow-up advice.

Entrepreneurship classes include, but are not limited to, the following: Entrepreneurship and Opportunity; Future Trends and Entrepreneurial Ventures; Great Entrepreneurial Wealth: Creation, Preservation, and Destruction; Managing a Growing Business; Entrepreneurial Finance; Entrepreneurial Innovator Marketing for Entrepreneurials; and Crowdfunding. Management classes offer students a wide selection of classes that place emphasis on both working for someone and creating and maintaining your own business. Classes offered are: Global Leadership Development, Business Presentations, Human Resources Management, Business Writing, and Arts and Entertainment Management. Since the school is hyper-focused on business, the subject permeates almost every aspect of the learning. Many of the professors are even successful entrepreneurs themselves.

Babson also offers an intensive, one-week entrepreneurial boot camp titled "The Entrepreneur's Bootcamp: A Deep Dive for New Ventures," which is housed in the open-enrollment programs found here: https://www.babson.edu/academics/executive-education/open-enrollment -programs/. The program helps participants learn the skills essential to becoming successful entrepreneurs. It also helps business owners and managers promote an entrepreneurial mindset in their employees to encourage innovation at the company. Techniques such as the art of customer discovery, pitching to investors, and hypothesis testing are reviewed, as well as traditional business concepts such as financial modeling and marketing and selling. Other notable programs at Babson include: The Entrepreneurial Family, Women's Leadership Program, Leadership and Influence, and Growing a Business and Family across Generations.

The University of Wisconsin, Madison, offers entrepreneurial options at undergraduate and graduate levels and even as a doctoral degree minor. The institution also offers an entrepreneurial certificate program that is open to all non-business majors. The website states:

> Students pursuing a career in entrepreneurial management develop a broad range of skills in preparation for roles as business owners and managers, venture capitalists, and consultants. Our entrepreneurship degree programs and experiential opportunities help students to effectively navigate new venture creation, the financing of new ventures, the strategic management of emerging technologies, the legal and regulatory influences on innovation and venture creation, and related policy issues. Students and faculty have earned national attention from publications and blogs ranging from *Businessweek* to *Inc.* magazine.[2]

The undergraduate major in entrepreneurship is pursued in tandem with another focus area, either management or human resources. Courses include: New Ventures in Business, the Arts, and Social Entrepreneurship; Introduction to Entrepreneurial Management; Entrepreneurial Finance; and Arts Enterprise: Art as Business as Art. The undergraduate certificate program, which non-business majors can elect to complete, is for those "undergraduates interested in starting a new venture, working for young new ventures soon or later in life, and tackling new ventures inside existing organizations."[3] The program is designed with a "distinct bundle of courses that span business entrepreneurship courses and the curricula of several colleges and schools at UW–Madison. It emphasizes skills in entrepreneurship, creativity, and innovation along with the ability to analyze the role of entrepreneurship in society."[4]

The business-related master's degrees at UW–Madison are diverse, offering students a selection of specialty areas of study, especially for those of you who need/want something more specific. UW–Madison has an MBA program. MBAs are nifty, and some allow for small areas of specialization, but what about those who need something more targeted, such as one of the following graduate degrees the school offers:

- Business Analytics (master's of science): This master's degree is designed for those who are interested in learning how to sort, understand, visualize, and apply data. Students also have opportunities to learn through hands-on consulting projects. Topics such as the following are taught:
  - Data acquisition, analysis, and visualization
  - Machine learning, experimental design, and optimization
  - Descriptive, predictive, and prescriptive analytical approaches
  - R/Python/SQL/Tableau[5]
- Finance (master's of science): This master's degree has a focus on applied security analysis and is geared toward those interested in investment research and portfolio management. Students have the opportunity to manage over $20 million in equities and fixed income assets during their studies.
- Real estate (master's of science): For those of you interested in pursuing work or business ownership within real estate, this master's degree program covers topics such as brokerage, development, leasing, finance, and investment. There are hands-on learning experiences provided through conference attendance, a unique student-managed real estate investment trust fund, and case competitions.
- Master of accountancy (master's of science): There are two options to this master's degree, one for students currently pursuing an accounting undergraduate degree at the school and one for those without an accounting background, the Graduate Master of Accountancy (GMAcc) This program qualifies students to become a certified public accountant (CPA) and is a viable option for those of you who are separating from the service, already have a bachelor's degree, and are interested in becoming a CPA, especially for those who are considering owning their own accounting firm at some point.
- Supply chain management (master's of science): This is a one-year master's degree program, so it will be short but intensive. A range of subjects, such as operations, marketing, and risk management, are covered.

Upon completion of the degree, students will be prepared to meet the current demands of global industry, which require "integration of analytics tools, information systems, manufacturers, suppliers, inventory management and distribution to seamlessly meet customer demand."[6]

So, at this point, we should take a deeper look at how these programs may better prepare you to be an entrepreneur. Remember, we are trying to determine if you should go to college first or directly to business ownership. The first step I'm going to look at is the curriculum both schools offer to students. An in-depth look at the courses will give me an idea of the topics I will learn about while attending one of these schools, and a peek at the background of the professors will tell me about the experience they bring to the learning environment. I also want to keep my eyes open for any other special programs in the business departments.

I'm going to peek at the faculty biographies first before I take a look at the types of classes they teach. It doesn't matter which order you look in, just that you take the step to delve deeper into the investment you are making. You only have one GI Bill, so you need to conduct as much reconnaissance as possible before committing your benefit to a particular institution. I noticed the "Faculty" tab on the left-hand side of the Babson websites I was searching and gave it a whirl. You may need to use the search bar on the website of the school you are searching. Next, I clicked on "Faculty Profiles." Then I filtered by division and selected "Entrepreneurship." I was rewarded with a section of the website that houses the bios for all of the professors currently lecturing in entrepreneurship at Babson. I found, upon review of their bios, that many of the professors have PhDs from institutions such as Princeton, Boston College, the University of Southern California, the University of Colorado, and Cornell. And there are master's degrees from institutions such as Boston University, Notre Dame, Harvard University, and Syracuse University. This tells us that the professors bring a wealth of diversity in educational backgrounds to Babson, which is important for students looking to gain a broad scope of knowledge from their degree programs.

Now, let's take a look at the practical experience these experts bring to the students at Babson. One feature that I like about the faculty profile section is that listed below each professor's level of educational attainment are their awards, courses taught at Babson, presentations, and publications written. As I perused the information, I found that several of the professors teach classes that appear to take place in foreign locations. I made a note to check into this further later. This may offer students at Babson foreign-country immersion options. For those of you hoping to develop a company that operates with or in a foreign country, this may offer you on-the-job learning opportunities that would otherwise be impossible to get. Doing business in foreign countries and/or with foreigners often entails understanding foreign cultures so that you have at least a bit of insight into their attitudes, behaviors, and practices. A foreign immersion experience through your college is a perfect chance to get started building this knowledge. For more information on study-abroad options and international business, see chapter 4, "International Business Degrees and Study Abroad."

The professors' area of expertise, the programs they are affiliated with, and the areas in which they are considered subject-matter experts (SMEs) are listed. These areas are important as they demonstrate the depth of experience the school is offering and the areas in which the professors specialize. Publications are important for professors as publication, especially in peer-reviewed journals, is verification of subject-matter expertise, and several entrepreneurship professors at Babson have completed research that has been published. Many of the professors have written books or chapters for others' books, act as consultants to major companies, worked with executive education programs around the world, and presented at conferences and seminars in numerous foreign countries.

The University of Wisconsin professors also collectively hold degrees from many highly reputable universities such as the University of California, Berkeley, the University of Pennsylvania, Stanford University, Dartmouth College, and Brigham Young University. They have presented at many industry conferences and published many journal articles and books collectively. Many also have worked on a global scale and even served as the chair of the World Economic Forum's Global Agenda Council on Real Estate.

Now, let's take a more detailed look into the coursework offered by both schools. After all, we are trying to determine if you should go straight into business ownership or go to college first. Now, coursework alone shouldn't make this decision, but it is a good place to start. You need to get a glimpse of the types of classes offered and the curriculum imparted by the professors.

Babson University

EPS3501 Entrepreneurship and Opportunity

> This course concentrates on identifying and evaluating opportunities for new business. The primary purpose is to investigate concepts tools and practices associated with identifying or creating new venture opportunities. Students will explore ways to shape and evaluate the viability of these opportunities by understanding key industry factors, market and competitive factors and customer needs. Students will gain a better understanding of personal entrepreneurial capacity, team building and management, and lectures are augmented with readings, guest speakers, videos, and software simulations. Student teams will do at least two opportunity feasibility assessments.[7]

This course sounds especially interesting for those of you who want to own your own business but are unsure of which business or whether your business idea is competitive and sustainable.

EPS4510 Entrepreneurial Finance

> This course focuses on the various aspects of funding and managing entrepreneurial ventures through the various stages of business growth. The class will utilize videos, cases, simulation and experiential learning techniques to explain how to finance the entrepreneurial firm, investment analysis and decision making, and managing company finances through growth, crisis and harvesting. Frequent guests ranging from entrepreneurs, venture capitalists, banking and legal professionals will bring the entrepreneurial experience to life in this course which utilizes the flipped classroom methodology of teaching.[8]

Now, many of you will have finance experience from your time in the military, but can you already relate it to business ownership, or do you need help in making that transition? This course offers students the ability to peek inside the system and learn how those who are already in business manage the finance aspect. If you don't have finance experience, you will learn it. If you already have finance experience, you will learn how to approach it from a different perspective. Remember that managing money in your business is very different from managing the money allocated to you for purchases, large or small, in the military.

EPS 3580 Marketing for Entrepreneurs

This course provides an in-depth study of entrepreneurial marketing strategies for the 21st century. It examines how start-up and small/medium-size companies reach the marketplace and sustain their businesses, within highly-competitive industries. Recognition is given to the need of management to operate flexibly, make maximum effective use of scarce resources in terms of people, equipment and funds, and the opportunities that exist within new and established market niches. Classes focus on a combination of brief lectures, extensive case study analyses and a term-long group assignment involving student-generated entrepreneurial product or service offerings.[9]

So, how do you intend to market your brand? Where do you intend to market your product? How do you intend to pay for it, and where are your customers? This class will help you determine these answers.

University of Wisconsin, Madison

Let's move on and take a look at the courses offered at the undergraduate level at the University of Wisconsin, Madison, to see about the types of subjects the institution covers. Remember as you look through the information that you are trying to determine the benefits of completing an education before launching your entrepreneurship venture.

MHR 365 Arts Enterprise: Art as Business as Art

Artists and other creative workers have long balanced their expressive work with business realities—marketing, contracts, funding, financing, patronage, and public engagement. Whether as independent contractors, sole proprietors, company founders, contract artists, project collaborators, board members, or volunteers, successful artists have wrestled with the life of an entrepreneur in a complex and ever-evolving industry. But what if the business side of artistic expression wasn't just an inconvenience, but an integral part of the expressive palette? What if the tools of business were used with a craftsman's hand to advance an artistic vision in more elegant and connected ways? This course will explore the dynamic interplay between artistic life and business strategy, and will feature compelling national figures who cross that line everyday. It will offer new perspective and foster new connections for an interdisciplinary group of students, and advance the role of "arts enterprise" on the UW–Madison campus.[10]

Artists are often not thought of as small-business owners, but many work in this capacity. Entrepreneurship classes that are designed with the artist in mind are not common. Artists are entrepreneurs as they have a product to sell and need to define their brand, price it appropriately, get it into the marketplace, and make sales. This class will help with these strategies.

MHR 434 Venture Creation

This course is designed for students interested in the entrepreneurial process, with a special emphasis on creating a new venture. Students will learn how to test the viability of new business opportunities and conduct a feasibility study of their own idea. Students will present their concepts to a panel of professionals who will evaluate their analyses. Students are also strongly encouraged to participate in the WI School of Business Burrill Business Plan Competition. The course prepares students to launch a new venture in several different forms—a traditional for-profit start up, a social nonprofit enterprise, or virtual organizations. The course is not focused on buyouts, franchising, or launching new ventures within larger organizations. Many of the concepts discussed in the course, however, can easily apply to these scenarios.[11]

Have you considered being an entrepreneur or do you have a product to market? This class will help you learn the foundations of the process and give you direction to get started.

MHR 321 Social Entrepreneurship (StartUp Learning Community)

For the student interested in creating socially-engaged businesses and using entrepreneurial approaches to non-profit ventures. Activities include developing mission statement, assessing social impact, seeking funding from varied sources. Guest lecturers, cases, role playing. Course grounded in management theory.

Many veterans have started nonprofit programs designed to help support their community, such as those who started the Student Veterans of America and the Iraq and Afghanistan Veterans of America. Maybe you have an idea that will help further promote the needs of the population.

This was just a small example of the types of classes that Babson and the University of Wisconsin, Madison, offer students. For those of you who know they need to attend college first, make sure that you thoroughly research the types of classes offered at the school you are interested in attending. Take a hard look at the bios/profiles of the professors. If the professors don't have experience in the field, how will they relate the information embedded in the curriculum to real-life practicality? If the curriculum seems lacking, how will it support your endeavors? If you are not satisfied with either, it may be time to look into a different school.

One of the reasons I picked the University of Wisconsin, Madison, to review in this section is that the institution offers two unique programs that drew my attention:

- Residential housing that is based on mutual student interest: Labeled "residential learning communities," UW–Madison has taken the school learning experience and integrated it into its dormitories. Select dormitories are designated for students who share common goals. The StartUp learning community is geared toward those students who have an interest in entrepreneurship. The community is not limited to those interested in business degrees and, since it was launched almost fifteen years ago, has had students from over seventy majors reside within it, including engineers, writers, designers, musicians, and biologists. These students come together to network and develop startup ideas, even competing for grant money to help their ventures get started.
- The Morgridge Entrepreneurial Bootcamp (MEB) course: This is a one-week-long course that gives graduate students in the sciences, engineering, and math training in technology entrepreneurship. Students learn how to explore connections between tech and business and "imagine, create, and assess opportunities using multiple lenses; develop resources for an organization by forming teams and seeking funding; and use accounting and finance as language and assessment tools."[12] Attendees must currently be students in a graduate program at UW–Madison.

Considering schools that offer extra and nontraditional learning activities may offer you extra and nontraditional learning opportunities. Learning to be an entrepreneur, or to be competitive in a global market, requires people to think outside the box. Taking advantage of opportunities like those offered at UW–Madison may help you broaden the scope of your knowledge or diversify the way in which you view business, including in areas such as problem solving and growth, which are important regardless of who you work for.

So, let's consider the benefits of attending college, working with highly educated and trained professors and taking advantage of school-based programs versus eschewing higher education to get started directly on your entrepreneurship. Let me start by stating that I will do my best to keep the following relevant and short, but it will be difficult as there are so many benefits to choosing college first and very few drawbacks.

Failure Rate

The failure rate of entrepreneurships is a hard-to-pin-down statistic, and you will find different numbers on every website you visit. One thing that all the stories, data, and knowledge being passed around have in common is that the failure rate is significantly higher than the success rate. This is a fact you should keep in mind as you prepare for your venture. Knowing that the odds are stacked against you doesn't mean that you should quit before you begin; it means that you should prepare a plan B just in case. If your aptitude falls in the business area (remember the vocational assessments we discussed in chapter 1), then preparing for a career in a business sector means completing a college degree. It is mandatory for almost every sector of the business world, and, keeping in mind how competitive the business market is nowadays, you will greatly boost your chances for employment by completing formal education.

Skills

Completion of higher education gains you skills you might otherwise not have known you needed. Consider the courses we discussed earlier. Were you aware that you could learn about these topics at college? Completion of coursework such as this helps you widen your horizon, gain invaluable knowledge in a multitude of areas important to attaining employment in the field, and nurtures the skills you already attained in the military. Consider being faced with a complex business situation; having had formal business training through higher education, you will better understand the pros and cons of any action you take or decision you make.

Consider the bachelor's degree to be verification of your expertise. It acts as quality control for companies interested in hiring you. It endorses your skills and knowledge and proves competency in the field. Consider a company that publishes a job announcement that requires a bachelor's degree within its minimum-qualifications section. If this is a coveted position, the human resources department may receive hundreds of résumés. How will yours stand apart from the rest? Well, human resources will use a list of qualifications to determine who, of those who applied, is eligible for the position based on the parameters of the announcement. In most cases in the field of business, a bachelor's degree will be part of these qualifications. If you don't have one, your résumé will never make it to the hiring manager's desk. This means you will be disqualified at the first review, which is usually done by a computer program. Even if a bachelor's degree is not listed, if the position is competitive, then a degree will be one way for the hiring manager to weed out résumés. This way the hiring manager can narrow down the list of people he or she would like to interview. Because a bachelor's degree is considered a minimum qualification to work in business, a job posting that does not demand a degree will not be common. Plus, more advanced degrees, résumé-enhancing certificates, and formal training are often preferred nowadays, especially if your intent is to secure a position as a manager.

Part of your skill set in business is having and demonstrating self-confidence. Imagine speaking to a hiring panel, going to the bank to ask for a loan, or networking with successful businessmen and women, most of whom will be highly educated people. They will expect you to be educated as well. Now, we all know there are some highly successful people who dropped out of college but still achieved success in the business world. I would like to point out that you only hear and read about a few successful dropouts because the majority of dropouts who tried to create a business failed, and no one wants to write about them. A harsh reality, but a truth you must face. What is your plan B?

Financial Flexibility

Hopefully, you have saved some money from your time in the military. Now, that may help you go to college, start a business, or simply give you some time to get going. Any way you do it, you will need some extra cash to access. If you are still on active duty, you need to either keep saving or start saving. You may also be able to start preparing for your business now using the resources listed and reviewed in this book.

You will need to support yourself while you start your venture. Financial flexibility is key during the first few years. If you have a family to take care of, going to work for someone else may alleviate a bit of the financial burden during your transition from active duty. This also means that you may have to take the risk of giving up a steady income to start your venture at some point.

Nowadays the cost of the college can deter recent graduates from considering entrepreneurship right after graduation. If you decide to go to college first, hopefully, you made good decisions regarding your education and haven't taken on a load of student-loan debt. If you haven't separated yet, make sure to get help from the education-center staff aboard the base where you are stationed. If you are wise with your GI Bill benefits, you should be able to graduate with little to no student debt. This should offer you some financial flexibility. Also, you should try to work while attending school. Try to save as much as possible, and also try to work in a field that offers you some practical-application knowledge on running a business or in making business-type decisions. If you are unsure where to start for a job, check out the career-services department at your school, even if you are attending a community college. Many schools even offer college credit for internships and part-time jobs, although costs associated with this type of credit are not typically covered by the GI Bill. Read chapter 5 for more information on this topic.

Trends

Going to college first will help you stay abreast of current trends in the industry. Professors teaching entrepreneurship are often currently working in the field, or at minimum, have worked in the field recently. Sometimes, when colleges and universities hire new adjunct professors to teach entrepreneurship classes, they require that they have current experience working for a privately held company or owning one. Think about the hands-on experience you may be able to gain from someone currently running their own business.

College can help you develop or refine skills that are necessary for success as an entrepreneur or franchise owner, such as problem solving, public speaking, and networking. It will also help you learn the vocabulary and terms used within the business sector. This way, when you speak with others who are involved in your sector, you can speak from knowledge. College curriculum often requires students to work in groups, to conduct boots-on-the-ground research, and present in front of other students, professors, or working members of society. This practice will help you meet new people, network for employment or resources, and teach you how to communicate information about complex topics in a professional manner. Throughout these activities, you are learning how to research and compile data and conduct problem solving on your own of within a group. Remember, college degrees in the business sector are expected, and if your intent is to be competitive in this market, you will be expected to spend the time to get a formal education in business; then you will have earned the right to be taken seriously.

There are some exceptions to these standards. Some of you may require training but not need a bachelor's degree. If your intent is to become an entrepreneur, you really need to consider the area in which you want to build a business. For example, if you intend to own a plumbing business, then getting trained as a plumber should be at the forefront of your plan of attack. Do you need a business degree to build a plumbing business? No, but taking business classes at your local community college could only benefit you in the planning, building, and maintaining phases of your company. Now, if you want to develop a tech startup, do you need a formal degree? Most likely, yes, as almost all tech fields require formal training. In this case, should you also consider business classes? Yes, formal learning of a computer-based trade is important, but running a business is usually not part of the training. Note that I state that it is usually not part of the training. Many colleges are beginning to include business coursework into IT and computer science pathways, and master's degrees in IT project management are readily available. Read more about the Project Management Professional (PMP) certifications in chapter 3, "Education and Training." Maybe you are considering working in IT management before starting your own company. If this is the case, you will need formal education in information technology and business, but it may not mean a bachelor's and a master's degree. Chapter 3 also has information on certifications that can enhance your bachelor's degree and can make you more marketable as a manager.

Regardless of which career path in business or business ownership you decide to pursue, training in accounting, marketing, data analysis, advertising, and management will be beneficial. Then, gaining experience using the knowledge you learned by working for someone else first will help you apply the formal training to practical-application purposes. You will also witness other employees' tactics, which will diversify your problem-solving skills and broaden your scope of practical knowledge. All of this gives you more tools to put to use at a later date. And, remember, practicing the practical application of these skills at someone else's business means you learn from experience without risking your own company nor your own dollars. So, it is much less risky!

TRAINING FOR VOCATIONAL-TECHNICAL SMALL-BUSINESS OWNERS

You may have the opportunity to become a franchise or small-business owner in a field that you may not be an SME in. In this case, attending a training program will be helpful. For example, fast-food franchise owners may benefit from learning basic information about sanitation, hygiene requirements, and safety (think OSHA). A new owner of an auto repair center, without previous automotive-mechanic experience, will benefit from vocational training in basic automotive repairs in order to better understand the business.

So, where can you find this training? Let's consider the example of an individual who wants to own an automotive shop. A basic internet search for automotive technology training reveals many programs across the United States, including low-cost state-supported public school options (community college!). A sampling of the training opportunities that turn up in a search includes:

MiraCosta College, Oceanside, California
http://www.miracosta.edu/instruction/automotivetechnology/index.html.

MiraCosta College offers several automotive-related certificate programs and an associate of arts degree in Automotive Technology. Certificates include: Automotive Electronics, Computer, Emissions, and/or HVAC, California Smog Check Technician, and Master Technician. The certificates vary in the length of time they take to complete and in units required (between thirteen and forty-three). Classes include information on preventative maintenance and engine performance, electronic engine-control systems, automotive brake service and repair, and hybrid fuel vehicles. But the school also offers classes that focus on other areas of skill that are necessary to run a business, such as customer service and personal selling.

These programs were designed to prepare students for entry-level positions and to offer training for those already working in the field. Curriculum was purposely designed to prepare students to take Automotive Service Excellence (ASE) exams. ASE is the organization that provides quality control oversight on those individuals working in the automotive repair industry. Hence, gaining ASE credentials for yourself, and making sure that those you hire are ASE credentialed, gains you and your business credibility.

MiraCosta College also offers an associate degree in entrepreneurship. Combining these two training pathways may be your best way forward, as you will also learn about subjects directly related to business ownership, such as budgeting, marketing, and human relations in business.

Honolulu Community College
https://www.honolulu.hawaii.edu/amt

Honolulu Community College offers an automotive technology program where participating students can earn a certificate of achievement in one year or an associate of applied science degree in five semesters, approximately two and a half years. An associate of applied science degree typically does not require a full load of general education units but will require a few, including math and English courses. According to the website, the program is "certified in all eight ASE areas: engine repair, automotive transmission and transaxle, manual drive train and axles, suspension and steering, brakes, electrical/electronics systems, heating and air conditioning, and engine performance."[13]

Western Kentucky Community and Technical College
https://westkentucky.kctcs.edu/education-training/program-finder/auto motive-technology.aspx

Western Kentucky Community and Technical College offers an associate degree in applied science in automotive technology and numerous certificate programs including for positions such as automatic transmission technician, air-conditioning mechanic, brake and engine repairer, and front-end mechanic. The programs are taught by ASE-certified master automobile technicians. The program is Master School–accredited by ASE, and the courses are designed to prepare students to become ASE certified. This particular program uses a selective admissions process. This typically means that prospective students must attend an open house, submit a high school or GED transcript, and often, pass a basic skills, math, and English test.

Many automotive companies have begun to partner with community colleges across the country to offer specialized training on their vehicles. Companies such as Honda and Tesla have created curriculum and hands-on training specifically for community colleges. The programs help students become familiar with their brands, and some of the programs result in factory training certifications. A few of these programs may result in employment with the company, and others are more geared to helping students develop niche-market skills.

Recently, several community colleges in California were approved to offer specialized bachelor's degree programs on their campuses. One such school is Rio Honda College in Whittier, California. The program, for a bachelor of science degree in automotive technology, has two tracks, business and marketing and technical studies. These two tracks offer students the ability to choose which route will best fit their future career needs. For the purpose of this book, we are focused on working within the business sector or small business/franchise ownership. Well, for those of you interested in working in the business sector, were you aware that there is an entire sector of automotive business management and support? The business and marketing track of the Rio Hondo bachelor's degree program prepares students to work in after-sales automotive business and support. Students in the junior and senior years of the program learn skills that will help them secure positions as customer relations specialists, sales and service marketing experts, service operations managers, and fleet-operations managers.[14]

Consider your military service. Many of you worked in operations that involved vehicles, such as marines with the MOS 3537, Motor Transport Operations Chief. The Marine Corps COOL definition of this MOS states:

"A Motor Transport Operations Chief supervises crew/operator level maintenance, planning and execution of motor transport operations."[15] A search on Indeed.com produced several fleet-operations manager, operations training manager, and fixed operations manager positions that require a bachelor's degree. Here are some of the job responsibilities outlined:

- Schedules and trains all regularly assigned personnel and establishes the budget, planning, and systems required to achieve objectives
- Prepares goals and objectives
- Executes fleet strategies
- Performs periodic inspections of all network vehicles
- Manages safety
- Collaborates with planning to meet business needs
- Plans for appropriate staffing levels and corrects when necessary
- Ensures proper equipment utilization
- Works with planning to establish contingency plans when needed
- Utilizes transportation management systems
- Provides world-class customer service and sales
- Participates in the creation of content and messaging
- Collaborates with other departments to select vendor partnerships to ensure business goals are achieved

You can see that these positions require business, leadership, and training skills, but remember that these are automotive-industry positions and will also require general automotive knowledge. I'm also sure that many of these responsibilities sound familiar to you from the job you did or currently do in the military, but all of these jobs listed a bachelor's degree as a requirement for employment.

Some of you already have general automotive skills training that you received for your MOS, or rating. A specialized bachelor's degree such as this will help you round out your skills and prepare for the business side of the automotive industry. For those who haven't learned general automotive skills through military service but are interested in working in or owning a business in this field, consider an associate degree in automotive technology as your gateway to a specialized bachelor's degree in the field. Bachelor's degree programs in automotive technology with an emphasis in business and marketing are not easy to find, and not everyone can stay in or move to California, but associate degrees in automotive technology are more common. If you are unsure which pathway to take, but are interested in getting started, local community colleges are usually the safest bet. Once you are enrolled, work with the career-services department and your counselor or advisor to begin forming a pathway tailored to your needs.

Here are a few more options for automotive programs across the country:

- Eastfield College in the Dallas-Ft. Worth metro area: https://www.east fieldcollege.edu/cd/dcc/trans/autotech/pages/default.aspx
- Mount Wachusett Community College in Massachusetts: https://mwcc .edu/academics/degree/automotive-technology/
- Western Dakota Tech in South Dakota: https://www.wdt.edu/degree -programs/automotive-technology
- Georgia Piedmont Technical College: https://www.gptc.edu/programs/ automotive-technology/

These state-supported schools have automotive technology certificates and also have options for applied-technology associate degrees. There are private institutions that offer training in this field, but they are usually more expensive because private programs are not taxpayer subsidized. Also be careful with private schools as they often do not hold regional accreditation. This means that you may have difficulty transferring units at a later date.

Many entrepreneurs decide to go into hospitality-industry businesses, including bed-and-breakfast lodges and hotels and restaurants; many community colleges and universities offer degrees in hospitality management or in a related field. Many of you held positions in which you managed many other service members and worked in a field related to hospitality management, such as Navy personnel holding the rating of CS—culinary specialist. The Navy COOL rating description is as follows:

Culinary Specialist (CS) operate and manage Navy messes and living quarters established to subsist and accommodate Naval personnel; estimate quantities and kinds of foodstuffs required; assist Supply Officer in ordering and stowage of subsistence items and procurement of equipment and mess gear; check delivery for quantity and assist medical personnel in inspection for quality; prepare menus; plan, prepare, and serve meals; maintain food service spaces and associated equipment in a clean and sanitary condition, including storerooms and refrigerated spaces; maintain records of financial transactions and submit required reports; and maintain, oversee, and manage quarters afloat and ashore.[16]

This information is from https://www.cool.navy.mil/usn/enlisted/cs.htm. So, outside of managing quarters while afloat, most of the skills listed will also be required of you if you consider a business in one of these disciplines. Note, if you review this website, that there are several certifications in management, including the Project Management Professional credential, which we review in chapter 3, and also several Microsoft certifications. Gaining computer skills that will assist you in running your business will help you manage the detailed information you must document for most businesses. Gaining a civilian education on top of any COOL credentials you are able to earn will arm you with the knowledge and credentials you need to be reputable and successful.

A search of hospitality-management training yields training programs throughout the country. Here are a few examples:

- Mission College in Santa Clara, California: https://missioncollege.edu/depts/hospitality-management/
- Cornell University: https://www.ecornell.com/certificates/hospitality-and-foodservice-management/hospitality-management/
- Cuyahoga Community College in Cleveland: https://www.tri-c.edu/programs/hospitality-management/index.html
- Northern Virginia Community College: https://www.nvcc.edu/catalog/cat2018/academics/programs/programdetail.aspx?prog_id=2700&subprog_id=0&level=1
- Casper College in Wyoming: https://www.caspercollege.edu/hospitality-management
- Coastal Carolina Community College: https://www.coastalcarolina.edu/academics/programs/aas/hospitality-management/

These programs consist of certificates and associate degrees and even include bachelor's degree programs. Consider how much time you are willing to commit to pursuing education, as the amount of education you attain is directly related to the level of the position you will be able to attain. Completing an associate degree will prepare you for supervisory positions, and completing a bachelor's degree will prepare you to attain advanced leadership roles, which will lead to earning more money. Many people in a field such as hospitality management want to work within the industry to gain practical, hands-on experience to better prepare them for business ownership. Completing one of these programs will arm you with the credentials you need to secure a position.

Military cooks who desire to open restaurants, in addition to business-management programs of study, can earn many types of certifications. The military often offers funding options for required exams through the COOL program mentioned previously. Here are a few offered through the American Culinary Foundation (ACF):

- Certified Culinary Administrator
- Certified Chef de Cuisine
- Certified Culinarian
- Certified Culinary Educator
- Certified Executive Chef

More information on these exams can be found here: https://www.acfchefs .org/ACF/Certify/Exams/WrittenExams/ACF/Certify/WrittenExams/.

There is also an option for a Certified Dietary Manager certificate through the Certifying Board for Dietary Managers (CBDM) for those interested in positions such as personal chef or meal planner or in opening restaurants focused on healthy eating. Information on this credential can be found here: https://www.cool.navy.mil/usn/enlisted/cs.htm and https:// www.cbdmonline.org/.

Some personnel in the military do career counseling or career planning and would like to continue to do a civilian version of the job upon returning to civilian life. One possibility is to become a certified career counselor and set up a consulting business. There are several ways to become one.

One pathway is the National Career Development Association (NCDA) program to become a certified master of career services. A bachelor's degree in any disciplines and 7,000 hours of work experience or a master's degree in any discipline and 5,000 hours of work experience are required

for this program. More information can be found here: https://www.ncda
.org/aws/NCDA/pt/sp/credentials_cmcs.

Another option through the NCDA Certified Career Counselor program
requires a minimum of a master's degree in counseling education, counseling psychology, or a closely related counseling degree. It also required
a minimum number of documented hours in career counseling under the
supervision of a career counselor. More information can be found here:
https://www.ncda.org/aws/NCDA/pt/sp/credentials_ccc.

Military recruiters can consider setting up their own civilian recruiting
firm or "headhunter" shop. Many civilian recruiting firms concentrate on
particular professions, for example medical professionals. Author Robert W. Blue Jr. briefly worked at a civilian firm that recruited physical
therapists and respiratory therapists. The company that employed me was
a small business set up by a former hospital administrator who had just
retired after a career with a large health-care company.

Some branches of the military offer recruiters the opportunity to receive
funding to become a certified professional services marketer through the
Society for Marketing Professional Services. The certification program requires eight years of experience in marketing for high school graduates, six
years of experience for associate degree holders, and four years of experience for bachelor's degree holders. More information can be found here:
https://www.smps.org/learning/certification/how-to-become-a-cpsm/.

Business training and guidance are essential for setting up a successful business, and there are many resources available for assistance. Many
local community colleges offer business management, small-business,
and entrepreneurship courses and certificate options. Universities often
offer business-certificate programs through continuing education and
extension departments, often with options for online training. Whatever
business you decide to enter into, local community colleges and extension
programs at state universities offer a wealth of training opportunities for
many types of businesses.

Free information and referrals can be found through web resources
and referrals offered by the U.S. Department of Labor and the U.S. Small
Business Administration (SBA). The new business entrepreneur will especially find the section on planning and launching a business helpful in
turning an idea for a business into a reality. It can be found here: https://
www.sba.gov/business-guide/plan-your-business/calculate-your-startup

-costs. There is also information on writing a business plan, researching a location for your business, launching your business, registering your business, getting federal and state tax ID numbers, and managing and growing your business. Free business counseling is available from a variety of organizations, including SCORE mentors, Small Business Development Centers, and Women's Business Centers. Visit this website for more detailed information: https://www.sba.gov/business-guide/launch-your -business/register-your-business.

Many people find success by buying a franchise. The SBA has advice on buying a business versus buying a franchise. The SBA points out some pros and cons of buying a business versus buying a franchise. The buyer of a franchise buys a brand and receives guidance but has less control due to conditions imposed by the organization providing the franchise opportunity. Buying a business offers more control but no guidance from an experienced corporation. Read on for more information on becoming a franchise owner.

DIRECT TO FRANCHISE

You can start your new, post-military life and begin earning a living right away without having to attend school to obtain a degree. The life and work experience you gained during your period of service may set you up to be successful in owning a business. You should, however, be aware that taking this route usually does not lead to a routine nine-to-five job. Being a business owner means that you are directly responsible for the success of the venture, and you must understand that it will require great responsibility. This can mean many hours away from family and friends while experiencing great stress and sleepless nights. Starting a business usually requires owners to make a significant financial commitment as well, so ask yourself if this is the right time, if you are the right person, and if this is the right business before you commit to the venture.

The following is advice offered by Frank Garner, retired marine:

> My recommendation to anyone looking to get into a franchise, or any business, for that matter, would be to first determine what sort of lifestyle you want with respect to work and then target a business that can provide it. . . .

Do as much research as possible on the type of work you'll be doing. Will your business run five days per week, seven days per week? How many hours per day? What will you be doing? What about your manager, if it's not an owner-operator concept? Are you willing to do your manager's job indefinitely should the need arise? Can you do their job?[17]

Mr. Garner found that being in the QSR (quick service restaurants) industry as a business owner did not fit with the lifestyle that he wanted for himself and his family, although he does intend to become a business owner again in another capacity.

My experience was that it was very difficult to find quality talent in the QSR industry that could run the restaurants with an acceptable level of competence or efficiency. That means ownership gets sucked back in to working in the business instead of on the business, which is not where you want to be. . . . That impacts everything else, including growth and margins. In the end, I was burned out. It put a big strain on my family and my health that quickly outweighed the potential benefits, and I decided to walk away.[18]

The last bit of advice Mr. Garner offered was that the struggles he mentioned are not exclusive to the QSR industry, as they can also be found in other industries. This means that finding a good fit is imperative and not just with the product or service offered. Consider other aspects also, such as Frank's example that it can be difficult to attract quality employees in certain industries, which can have a detrimental effect on your capacity to operate.

Have you heard the expression "The business owns you, you don't own the business?" Proper planning and research will help you create a work-to-life balance so that you will not feel owned by your business. Next, if you decide that you are prepared to tackle the franchise venture, conduct the following outlined steps to make sure you are choosing the right business for your skill set, lifestyle, and income goals, as well as to determine your ability to invest and support your household while ramping up your new business.

Step One

Take a personality profile. Think about the Myers-Briggs or Holland-based assessments that we cover in chapters 1 and 6. These tests help you gain a better understanding of your interests, skills, and aptitudes. The assessment used by one author of this book to support those looking to franchise is based on the science of the DiSC (dominance, influence, steadiness, and conscientiousness) profile. This particular version has been massaged for business ownership. It was created by a behavioral psychologist who specialized in psychometric profiling. These tests help franchise consultants get to know a person better, as far as their strengths and weaknesses. They also help determine whether a person is task or people oriented and reserved or active. Certain personality types fit certain businesses better than others, and this assessment helps determine the best fit for a potential business owner. Just because someone enjoys doing something (for instance, coaching and training) does not mean they have the ability to go out and land clients. Usually, it is best to work with someone who has experience interpreting the results of these tests to gain greater depth and meaning in interpreting the results; otherwise, it can be confusing to decipher the meaning behind the results.

Step Two

Step two requires the potential entrepreneur to create a business model that includes clear outcome goals. In other words, what is he or she trying to accomplish? The following questions should be answered during this stage.

1. What is the individual's wants and needs from a business?
2. What are the individual's personal goals?
3. How much money would the individual like to make? Consider that he or she will most likely not make any money during the first year. Year two should be better, but it will be the third year of ownership before he or she will begin to see a payoff.
4. How much money (liquid cash) is he or she willing and able to invest? (See "Financing a Business" in chapter 6.)
5. What size loan is the individual willing and able to take out? The loan and cash combined equal the total project amount you have available. Business owners should never invest more than they can afford to lose should it all go south. Research and planning will mitigate some risk, but not all of the risk involved in starting a business.

6. How much can the individual afford to lose without losing his or her financial stability? But remember that the number one reason a business will fail is undercapitalization. The business needs to have enough working capital built into the total project amount to sustain it until it reaches the point where it can pay for itself or break even.
7. What is the exit strategy?
8. How long does the individual want to own this business?
9. Does he or she want to grow something and sell it for a profit?
10. Does he or she want to slide a manager in place and continue to draw an income into retirement?
11. Does he or she want to create a legacy for his or her children?
12. The potential business owner should create a rating scale of weakest to strongest, on a scale of one to three, in the following areas: sales, management, and operations.
13. Next, he or she should create a rating scale of least interested to most interested, on a scale of one to three, in the same areas: sales, management, and operations.

When considering the last two questions, determine if there is any difference between what you are most skilled at and most interested in. If so, this may require additional research or training. For starters, google "sales training" or "management training" in your area to determine the available resources. Check out programs at local community colleges (usually cheap!) or universities. Local organizations, like the Small Business Development Centers (SBDC) and SCORE, may also have programs or training available in the area.

14. How do you fill in the gap to gain additional knowledge or skills in the area you have the most interest in, but are not most skilled at?
15. When considering product sales, do you prefer to go out and find your customers or do you want them to come to you?

| 1-Proactive (Hunter) | 5- Mixed | 10-Reactive (Gatherer) |

Out in the Community Initiating Relationships – OR – Stay Put and the Business Comes to Me

Figure 2.1. Responsiveness Scale

16. Where are you on the scale of 1 to 10, in figure 2.1, and what are some conclusions about your answer?

  - Proactive: Home based, low cost, ability to go out and get clients. Don't need a location. Lots of personal time and effort required to drive business.
  - Reactive: Higher investment, buy into a recognized brand, lots of expenses as it relates to marketing, building out a site, may be able to hire a manager initially or over time. Less personal time and effort required in some cases.
  - Mixed: An office location that would require a little personal effort and possibly some paid marketing and/or advertising.

17. Do you prefer *business to business* (B2B) or *business to consumer* (B2C), or are you open to both?

Think about who you would like your customer to be for your business. Do you prefer to work with a business as your customer (B2B) or directly with a consumer (BTC)? If you prefer B2B, think of things that can help another business operate, grow, or save money, for example. You may want to provide small- to medium-sized businesses with IT services. These size businesses usually do not have the funding to staff a full-time IT department, and they rely on outside vendors to help them when needed. You may want to focus on helping businesses gain more business by designing websites or helping with social media and creating an online presence.

If you prefer working directly with the public, then your business falls into the B2C model: business to consumer. You may have excellent customer service skills (Were you ever a recruiter?) or enjoy providing a product or service to the end user. In this model, business owners would typically have a location that people can come to for the service/product you are offering. This model can have longer hours and is open six to seven days a week. It also provides the business owner with the opportunity to hire a manager to run the business for you, either initially or over time. A benefit of this model is that when you can hire a manager, the business could become semi-absentee or semi-passive run, requiring you to spend maybe ten to fifteen hours per week managing your manager and overseeing the business versus working there on a daily basis. This would free you up to either expand your business or focus on other areas of it.

18. Do you prefer to offer a product or a service?

19. Do you have a strong preference for repeat customers and relationship building, or is a one-and-done model okay for you?

    - Examples of repeat customers: IT services for small to medium-sized businesses where clients come back. Massage Envy is a membership-based model in which you sign up X number of members, and that covers your rent, then X more members, and now your payroll and rent are covered.
    - An example of a one-and-done business might be a restoration business where you may respond to a flood or smoke damage in a home or business.

20. Is there anything else unique to you about sales or customer acquisition?

The primary answer received is "I have to believe in the product or service I am offering," but it is important to separate the function of the business from the function of you, the business owner. Clients should be aware of misplaced passion. You want to avoid turning your passion into your job. You may find you lose your passion once it becomes work. You may also find yourself spending too much time working in your business, doing the part you like, versus working on your business, which may be less appealing to you. This type of structure may not set you up for success.

21. Would you like to have employees? If so, how many and what kind?

22. Are you open to all demographics of employees?

    - Hourly minimum wage?
    - Hourly skilled?
    - White-collar salaried?
    - An artsy or creative employee like a hair stylist or graphic artist?

23. Are you a hands-on manager (love to mentor) or a hands-off manager (just get it done)? You should have an idea of the type of manager you would be from your military service. Do you like to mentor soldiers, sailors, airmen, and marines who are new to the fleet, or do you prefer they learn on their own time?

24. What hours do you want to be available to your customers and employees?

- Rate yourself on the scale of 1 to 10 in figure 2.2 on willingness to take a risk.

Figure 2.2. Risk-Taking Scale

- This rating will help you decide if you prefer a business that offers what people want or what people need, a 7 or above means you will usually be attracted to what people want, a 5 or below means you will typically only be interested in offering what people need. An example of what people want would be a business such as Massage Envy. An example of what people need would be a restoration business that responds to flood or smoke damage.

25. Define for yourself why you would want to start your own business. Is it based on quality of life, passion, money?
26. Rank *quality of life*, *passion*, and *money* in order of least important to most important for yourself.
27. Write down what that ranking looks like for you. For example, if the most important is quality of life, what does that mean? If it's money, how much do you need to survive and what amount would make you feel like a success? If it is passion, your passion can also come from: mastery, autonomy, or purpose.

Addressing these factors in advance will give you the best chance for success. Most people definitely don't start looking online for a business based on what you like to eat or what attracts you. For example, let's say you love eating Subway sandwiches, and you are attracted to their popularity. Does that mean you can be a successful Subway franchisee? Depends. Do you like managing high school students or a constantly revolving staff? These employees can make managing the store difficult.

Now that you have answered these questions, you should have a good idea of what you would like your day to look like, how much you are willing to spend, where you want to be located and how far you might be willing to commute, but considerations do not stop there. You also need to match your skill set to the business so that you will enjoy the experience. Veterans have learned leadership skills that many civilians never learn. Use these skills wisely in managing staff, product, and expenses.

James Hawthorne, branch manager of ABC Supply Co., Inc., has the following advice regarding leadership and management skills service members learn while on active duty and business ownership:

> After retiring from the military, I was fortunate enough to get recruited by ABC Supply Company to manage and operate a Branch in San Diego, with the entrepreneurial spirit in mind. While managing my Branch and day to day operations, I am completely P&L (Profit and Loss) responsible. Being P&L responsible means, I am accountable for making my business a success or failure. You have the opportunity to use your military training and excellent leadership skills, while learning new and amazing things as well. Most servicemen and women can't imagine the amount of talent that they truly possess and how those talents will assist them in starting their own business, or working for a company. The military taught me structure and discipline, which is how I train my staff, and how I run my business. I have visited several similar businesses and can immediately tell when a team lacks structure. There are many other things the military taught me that are still prevalent in my business today such as leadership, team building and morale, the ability to handle multiple problems at one time, adapting and overcoming adverse situations and being decisive when making business decisions. The one thing that I believe sets us apart from the rest is strength in leadership. When running a business, you must be the leader, and you sometimes have to be able to make unpopular decisions. You also need to inspire and motivate your employees, just as you would in the military, deliver on your promises and keep your word. We are trained to do just that. The military has prepared me very well, and given me the necessary tools to be a successful businessman.[19]

As you move forward with the business-ownership process, remember that creating a business is about meeting your income and lifestyle goals. These two factors should be in sync. Thinking through these factors before beginning your search will help you find a business model that you will enjoy and can be successful owning. The military taught you how to manage workflow, eliminate distractions, and lead with vision. Take these skills and apply them to the structure of your business, and you will find that you will be in command of the management process.

CAREER STRATEGY STAGES

Everyone finds themselves at a different place when it's time to reevaluate career options. These places are based on our age; experience, training, and confidence levels; and opportunities to pursue education or work. In general, there are three stages of a career to consider: early career, mid-career, and late career. Understanding where you are on your own career timeline is a sure way to get more oriented to the right career strategy for you at that time.

The early-career phase happens roughly from the early to mid-twenties through the mid-thirties. Usually, these are the first ten skill-building years across your career arc. This is the time, just after or including the years of building your education or military foundation, that you should pursue a few occupations, and get a feel for what you enjoy and where your skills fit or are needed. This is a great time for career exploration, and making a few attempts at establishing a career in different fields is normal. These attempts should provide you with a better understanding of the world of work and how you fit into it. The focus on strategic career moves at this stage should be on the type of industries, projects and career paths that spark your interest, and then, as you establish yourself in these early jobs, it is important to focus on building skills you enjoy using and that you feel confident using and demonstrate strength in. You usually enter this phase with less clarity and direction, but with more potential. These years are critical to taking career risks, investing in your education, and beginning to define your skills-development potential. In interviews, be sure to convey your academic or military background, a little about your skills and work-related experience, and a lot about your potential and what you still want to accomplish.

You will transition into the mid-career stage in your mid-thirties with a solid base of employment and skills, and still quite a bit of potential. Your job in interviews and in assessing your next strategic career moves should be based on what you can offer and what you have yet to become. Usually, by this time in your career, you have made a few career changes and are beginning to settle into a field or even develop an area of expertise. Think about moving from E3 and E4 to E6 and E7. It is the same concept. Strategic career moves at this point should be made to further develop skills, while still keeping an eye on the type of work that is most interesting and fulfilling to you. If you find your skills falling behind and you want to amplify them, or activate a new set of learning, this is the ten-year window to go back to school to get a master's degree in the field you have chosen or earn a professional credential. These second ten skill-building years usually bring new beginnings and begin to shape and sculpt your overall path, to reveal what you excel at, and to leave behind the work activities you don't enjoy.

The late career stage begins in the mid-forties, when we start to develop a feeling that we have an expertise. This is the stage in a career to drive forward opportunities to teach, give back, consult, start a business or partnership, or settle into a niche. These are also usually the highest earning years and it's important to assess any ideas of leaving your career for simple misalignments in a role or workplace. Many individuals at this stage feel they have not reached that level of mastery, and if that is the case, then a thorough inventory of the work activities, skills, and jobs you have enjoyed the most must be done, and those areas must be ignited, activated, and developed. In interviews at this stage of mastery, the right strategy is to present your expertise and value as an employer, versus your potential and where you want to be in five or ten years. You are being looked at as the expert and as a worker; this is your twenty-year phase to maintain, grow, and strengthen your contributions to our society through work without shifting too far off course.

Whether someone joins the military for one enlistment or stays for a career of thirty years, eventually there is a transition back to civilian life. Many young veterans make plans to use military education benefits to go to college or vocational training. Author Robert W. Blue Jr. talked to many veterans getting out of the service after one contract who want to go home and help with the family business or start their own businesses. Older veterans have to think about second careers, how to prepare for them, and how they can translate their military experience into something a civilian can understand.

Blue found himself going through the transition twice. The first time, I was an unprepared young man with an incomplete education returning to civilian life. Things did not go smoothly, and I eventually ended up returning to active duty to buy myself more time. My second transition came after finishing out a twenty-four-year career in the U.S. Navy. This time I left with a plan to find work in the field of education, and I had completed a bachelor's degree before leaving active duty. By the time my second transition came around, workshops were offered for transitioning service members, and I took full advantage of these new resources. Some of the workshops I attended included résumé writing, networking, and job interviewing.

My own life stages during my early years in the military were often unexpected, unplanned, and all too typical. I entered the Navy because I was having difficulties paying for college. At the end of my fourth semester, my financial situation was dire. I would not have a way to pay for another semester. After talking to a Navy recruiter, I enlisted in what seemed to me to be the most exotic branch of the military because of all the time spent on ships and visits to foreign ports all over the world. At the end of my four-year enlistment, I really had no viable plan for going back to college, and I ended up reenlisting for a guaranteed four-year tour in the Republic of the Philippines.

My first return to civilian life came at the end of my second enlistment. I separated after eight years of active duty in the U.S. Navy. I planned to use veterans benefits to return to school. I had a family to support, so I planned to work full time while attending school part time, and we would live with my relatives to save money. I also planned to stay in the U.S. Navy Reserves to earn money by training one weekend a month and being activated for two weeks of annual active duty for training. Other than that, I did not have much of a plan. This was in the days before the Department of Defense had programs to assist veterans with the transition back to civilian life. At the time, I had no understanding of the importance of having health insurance. I had received health care through my parents' insurance policies or through the military all my life. I was clueless about health-care costs and did not think about researching which companies offered good health insurance benefits.

It was a very rough first year. We had an expected medical expense due to a required surgical procedure. That wiped out a good portion of our savings. Next, we had an unplanned pregnancy, and the expenses ate up what was left of our savings. More difficulties occurred during that first year as

I soon learned that the civilian community had very little understanding about what people do in the military. At job interviews, I would explain about the many responsibilities I had in the Navy, including maintaining records for a travel program funded with hundreds of thousands of dollars. But most prospective employers only seemed to see a very young-looking face and no college degree. I found out too many civilians only saw the military through Hollywood stereotypes, including the typical boot camp drill instructor that was often portrayed as abusive. I was asked surprising questions, including one interviewer who wanted to know if senior enlisted people just got things done by screaming at the troops.

Most civilians don't understand that many veterans have had great success in the military, advancing through the ranks and accepting great responsibilities not long after graduating from high school. Even a twenty-one-year-old service member may find himself (or herself) leading many service members, even into combat. By the time someone reaches senior enlisted rank, or gets promoted to higher rank in the officer corps, a service member can be responsible for hundreds, even thousands, of people.

As I advanced through the ranks during my eight years of active duty, I felt supreme confidence in my abilities and my management skills. After returning to civilian life, I was being interviewed by people who seemed to regard me as nothing more than a character out of an entertaining Hollywood show. At another job interview, I was even asked if I had ever killed anyone with my bare hands during my military service. Totally shocked by such a question, I stared at my interviewer for a few minutes, then answered, "No." The interviewer looked disappointed. I soon faced disillusionment and disappointment. I was not prepared for the experience of interviewing for jobs where twenty-one-year-old candidates with college degrees, but no real work experience, were valued more than someone with eight years of military experience, working in some of the most demanding work environments imaginable.

To catch up, I enrolled in evening college classes, but I was not prepared for many of the experiences I soon faced. We weren't far out of the Vietnam War at this point, and anti-military bias was still fairly prevalent. At college, I had one professor who had been active in the antiwar movement during the Vietnam War, knowing that I was a veteran, once told the class that people who served in the military were drifters wasting years of their lives. I did not think about joining veterans' organizations, where fellow veterans could have helped me determine how to deal with this instructor.

The economy turned sour one year, and I lost the job I had held for three years after my employer declared bankruptcy. I decided to request a transfer from the Navy Reserve to the regular Navy. In other words, I would return to active duty. As part of my return to active duty, I had to learn a new skill, and I chose to became a Navy Career Counselor. I finally had the opportunity to start the mid-career phase of my working life and felt a renewed sense of purpose. Part of my new job was helping sailors seek out new career opportunities within the Navy's many occupations and geographical assignments. A big part of my new Navy job was helping sailors pursue higher education. After my first, and very rough, landing in the civilian world, I became a super advocate for higher education. Over the years, I helped many sailors earn college degrees, some of whom went on to move from enlisted status to commissioned officer ranks. I encouraged everyone to use their educational benefits for college or vocational training as part of a plan for returning to civilian life. For those who wanted to help with family businesses back home, or start their own businesses, I talked about business degrees and exploring business certifications.

I took many opportunities to better myself for my Navy career and for opportunities after the Navy. I learned all I could about the field of higher education, including andragogy (adult learning). I also had the opportunity to complete a Department of Labor apprenticeship in counseling, through the United Services Military Apprenticeship Program (USMAP). For information on USMAP (for members of the Navy, Marine Corps, and Coast Guard) visit your local base education center. Over time, I put my college credits together to first attain an associate degree, then a bachelor's degree. I was now over forty and ready to move on to the next phase of my life. I retired from the U.S. Navy and started working for military education programs, first as a contractor then as a federal civilian employee for the Department of Defense. I developed college-education plans for ships of the fleet and counseled many sailors on both shipboard and shore activities—and I felt supreme confidence as I entered the late phase of my military working life. I used my GI Bill to earn master's degrees in human resources management, and education. I moved from Navy education to the Marine Corps education program and had great success and fulfillment by giving back to the military that had helped me find my own success in life.

Chapter Three

Education and Training

If you have not completed or started your education, this chapter will get you started on planning and offer you guidance pertaining to higher education. Attending college should include more than just academics. Schools often offer services to help you gain experience and prepare for the workforce, such as programs found through the career-services department.

The following topics will be covered in this chapter:

- Accreditation
- Schools, Degrees, and Programs
- Base Education Offices
- Community Colleges
- School Resources
- College Navigator
- DANTES College and Career Planning Counseling Services, Kuder Journey
- Military Digital Library Program
- Internships and Job Shadowing
- Business-Based Certificates
- Syracuse University Institute for Veterans and Military Families (IVMF)

INTRODUCTION

There are many options for education and training for you to consider. Make the wrong choice, and you could find yourself with a worthless diploma or certificate and a huge amount of student-loan debt. In the world of business, education, and training, expensive training does not necessarily mean better training and employability. No one wants to enter the workforce with a big student-load debt to repay, so it is important to know the differences between public, private, and for-profit schools.

Make sure that you research the type of training and education required for your business occupation before committing to a program. For example, in human resources management, certain certifications can be more valuable than a master's degree. Many colleges have excellent certification programs offered through the extended studies or continuing education departments. Most programs will have classroom and online options.

In this chapter, we cover information that teaches you how to explore and research the appropriate education and training required for different occupations through using websites such as the Bureau of Labor Statistics "Occupational Outlook Handbook" and "Projections Central," which can break down labor statistics by state. These tools will help you determine factors such as whether your chosen occupation is experiencing a period of growth or decline, which will help you make educated decisions for your future. For example, if you find out that your chosen occupation is experiencing a period of decline in your state, are you mobile? If so, these resources will help you find a state in which the occupation is experiencing growth. Or, if you are not mobile, you may need to consider a different occupation. These sites will also help you search similar occupations that may have greater expectations for growth. Sometimes, a small shift in planning may be all it takes; sometimes, a large shift may be necessary.

Are you academically prepared to begin your education and training? If not, the military's Online Academic Skills Course (OASC) and prep programs offered through military digital library services are programs you can take part in to improve math and English skills before starting college or a training program. If you intend to pursue a college degree, is a big university right for you, or would you thrive in the smaller classes found at community colleges or private, nonprofit universities? This chapter also reviews resources for assistance in researching school and training options including base education centers and the College Navigator search tool.

It is important to know about options for gaining practical experience through internships, job shadowing, cooperative education, and more. Support for finding a job is another consideration. Many schools offer career services, such as résumé-writing assistance for entering the job market. Many schools offer career advice after graduation through alumni programs. These networks are great for future career moves because most Americans change jobs several times over their productive working years. Having these resources available to you may make a difference in your ability to gain employment upon graduation. Do not make the mistake of simply attending school after separation from the service. There are many options for you to consider to help you build your résumé and gain experience and make connections in the field while still attending school. Some of these options will even pay you!

In this chapter, we will cover all of the previously mentioned topics and more. Your success requires careful preparation, planning, and good choices. This chapter will give you the information you need to be successful with these selections and entry into the world of business.

ACCREDITATION

Accreditation is an often-overlooked topic that service members need to consider prior to making a final selection of an institution of higher learning. Most service members receiving counseling services are not aware of the different types of accreditation that schools may hold and should take the time to research the topic. Selecting a school with the wrong type may cause significant backtracking at a later date.

The United States does not have a formal federal authority that oversees higher education. Each individual state exercises some level of regulation, but generally speaking, colleges and universities have the ability to self-govern. Accrediting organizations were born to supervise and guide institutions of higher learning to assure students that they were receiving valuable educations. The organizations develop and maintain specific standards for participating schools that hold the institutions accountable for the quality of education they are delivering. The standards "address key areas such as faculty, student support services, finance and facilities, curricula and student learning outcomes."[1]

Accredited schools adhere to the accrediting bodies' standards. Having accreditation is like having quality control for higher education, and when you are searching for schools, it should be an important factor to consider.

Students who attend accredited universities and colleges have a greater chance of receiving a quality education and benefiting from their degrees.

If a school does not hold accreditation, you will most likely not be able to apply for federal or state financial aid. Credit hours earned from non-accredited schools will not usually transfer into accredited institutions and will not be recognized for entrance into most master's degree programs. Ultimately, attending an accredited institution means that "a student can have confidence that a degree or credential has value."[2]

Typically, students need to look for institutional accreditation and possibly programmatic accreditation. *Institutional accreditation* means that the college or university as a whole is accredited. This enables the entire school to maintain credibility as a higher learning institution. Only regional or national accrediting agencies can give institutional accreditation.

The degree you chose will dictate the type of accreditation you will need. Traditional degrees, such as business and all business-related subjects, require regional accreditation. Nontraditional education encompasses subjects that are more vocational in nature, such as welding and electrical work and may or may not be offered at schools with regional accreditation.

Every state school (state community colleges, state colleges, and state universities) in this country holds regional accreditation. The Post-9/11 GI Bill is used most efficiently at a state school. Why? Because as long as you attend the state university within three years of your end of obligated service date (EAS/EAOS), and finish your degree in the allotted thirty-six months (nine months per year times four years), you will not pay any tuition for your schooling. Free school—what's better than that? Do not panic if you are intending to pursue a private school education; other options do exist.

Regional accreditation is the most widely recognized and transferable (credit hours) accreditation in this country. There are seven (the West Coast has two) regional accrediting bodies in the United States. The regional accrediting bodies are the:

- Middle States Association of Colleges and Schools: http://www.msche .org/
- New England Association of Schools and Colleges: http://cihe.neasc.org/
- North Central Association of Colleges and Schools: http://www.ncahlc .org/

- Northwest Commission on Colleges and Universities: http://www.nwccu.org/
- Southern Association of Colleges and Schools: http://www.sacscoc.org/
- WASC Senior College and University Commission: http://www.wascweb.org/
- Accrediting Commission for Community and Junior Colleges: https://accjc.org/

Regional accrediting organizations can review public and private and two- and four-year schools. Holding regional accreditation should allow credits to transfer smoothly between different member schools, depending upon the established transfer criteria at the receiving institution. Remember that ultimately the college or university you are trying to transfer to has final say on credit transferability.

Schools that hold national accreditation typically offer educational pathways that are more vocational (nontraditional) in nature. This type of education might lead to a completed apprenticeship program or certification. Vocational education is a means of training future workers with skills more directly relevant to the evolving needs of the workforce. These types of career fields are more hands-on and technical in nature. Many nationally accredited schools can offer students successful pathways to promising careers. The programs are designed to get students into the workforce as soon as possible and can usually be completed in two years or less, significantly faster than a four-year bachelor's degree.

Students do not need to attend a nationally accredited institution to receive vocational training. Many local state community colleges offer nontraditional education and often have apprenticeship or on-the-job training programs in addition to the educational classes. This might be a better pathway if you are unsure of your future career demands. Credits from a state community college are more widely transferable than credits from a nationally accredited institution because local colleges hold regional accreditation.

A few months ago, a service member who wanted to open a small welding business when he retires from the military came into the office. He was referred to a local community college that offered both welding certifications and an associate degree in business that had a concentration in entrepreneurship. The associate degree in business requires a full load of general-education classes. This grants him greater flexibility later on if he decides to continue on with his education.

Sometimes, institutional accreditation is insufficient and programmatic accreditation is also necessary. Programmatic accreditation is specific to a department within an institution, and is often needed above and beyond the institutional accreditation for certain degrees, such as nursing, business, and engineering. Programmatic accrediting organizations focus on specific courses of study offered at a college or university. Attending a program that maintains programmatic accreditation can help your degree be more effective (as in getting you a job!) or make earned credit hours more transferable. If you are not sure whether your degree requires programmatic accreditation, search CHEA's (Council for Higher Education Accreditation) website (http://www.chea.org/Directories/special.asp) for further information.

Choosing a school with the right type of accreditation is important. Credits from a regionally accredited institution usually transfer into a nationally accredited institution, but credits from a nationally accredited institution almost never transfer into a regionally accredited institution. The exception would be if a student was transferring into an institution with dual accreditation, but there are very few in the country. This means that you must make a rigorous search for qualifying information in order to determine the proper academic pathway for your selected career.

In these cases, looking at programmatic, or specialized, accreditation may be more important than institutional accreditation, or in other words, regional or national accreditation. The Association to Advance Collegiate Schools of Business (AACSB) is considered the premier accreditation for business schools. Arizona State University's website states that "AACSB has become the gold standard of business-school accreditations, and is the most prestigious, longstanding, and internationally recognized accreditation available for schools of business."[3]

Pepperdine's website states that "AACSB International is the longest-serving global accrediting body for business schools" and that "Fewer than 5% of business schools worldwide have earned this distinguished hallmark of excellence in management education."[4] AACSB accredits business and accounting schools across the world. If you intend to attend school abroad, you may want to conduct a quick search to see if the foreign institution you are considering has gone the distance in achieving AACSB accreditation.

To check for AACSB accreditation, visit the following website: https://www.aacsb.edu/accreditation/accredited-schools.

To check foreign schools that are approved for GI Bill benefits, visit the following two websites: https://inquiry.vba.va.gov/weamspub/build SearchInstitutionCriteria.do, https://www.va.gov/gi-bill-comparison-tool.

So, let's say I was interested in attending graduate business school in Turkey. Using the AACSB website search for accredited schools page, look up programs in Turkey. The list shows three schools with AACSB-accredited programs: Bilkent University, Istanbul University, and Sabanci University. Use the links listed to go to the school's site and determine whether the institution offers any English-language-based programs. Bilkent University's website is in English and easy to navigate. Istanbul University's page has a tab in the upper right-hand corner that will translate the page into English. After the translation, the page that lists any programs taught specifically in English cannot be found. You should take a pass on this institution, but, if you are still interested at this point, find an email address of an individual within the business department and send an email inquiry. Sabanci University's website has a tab in the upper right-hand corner labeled "EN" for the English translation. If you cannot find information regarding programs taught specifically in English, however, a quick search shows that the school requires a TOEFL (Test of English as a Foreign Language) score to demonstrate English proficiency in order to be admitted. The TOEFL tests English-language proficiency and is required by American colleges and universities, so, most likely, all of the programs at the school are taught in English. Again, a quick email will produce that information. At this point, you need to check to see if any of these schools accept the GI Bill; use the GI Bill Comparison Tool to check. Results show that Bilkent University is the only GI Bill–approved school of the three schools I looked up. Now, Bilkent University is in the capital city of Ankara. Ankara is about five hours from Istanbul and is not quite as cosmopolitan nor as diverse as Istanbul. It is also landlocked. You need to consider factors outside of school programs when considering foreign schools. Read chapter 4 for more information on studying business abroad.

To search for a specific school's institutional accreditation or a particular program of interest, go online (http://www.chea.org/search/default

.asp) and agree to the search terms. You can also complete a search of the national accrediting agencies that the U.S. Department of Education considers reliable at http://ope.ed.gov/accreditation/ or on College Navigator (http://nces.ed.gov/collegenavigator/).

SCHOOLS, DEGREES, AND PROGRAMS

Understanding the differences among types of schools will assist you in your search for the best school. Career choice dictates most educational pathways. For example, are you taking a vocational or traditional pathway? Do you need a two-year degree or a four-year degree? If two years are sufficient, then you can eliminate most four-year universities from your search. Narrowing your search by a few key factors will help in the selection process.

Understanding the options for higher education will enable you to choose the appropriate school for your educational pathway. Technical schools, community colleges, universities, and public and private nonprofit and for-profit schools have different guiding factors and structures. This section offers brief explanations of the types of schools and how to choose the one that best suits your needs.

Two-Year Schools

Two-year schools are community colleges (CCs) or technical schools. Most are state based, but not all are. CCs offer the following:

- Associate degrees
- Transfer pathways to universities and colleges
- Certificate programs
- Vocational programs
- Open enrollment, which is especially good if you had trouble with your high school GPA
- No SAT, ACT, or essay required
- Significantly lower tuition and fees than universities and colleges

Students on a budget can start at a two-year community college before transferring to a university and save a tremendous amount of money.

Because CCs are usually found in numerous locations throughout each state, they are easy to find and often near your home. The open-enrollment policy makes for a stress-free transition from active duty and is the fastest way to start school. Most of the service members I assist opt for a CC when they are in a time crunch because of deployments or training. Sometimes it is the only pathway, especially if university admission deadlines have passed. This often happens to those who are stationed overseas.

Most CCs offer vocational programs that require an associate degree or certification process. Many of the vocational pathways also have available significant hands-on learning options. Attending a vocational program at a state CC gives you safe, regionally accredited transfer credit if you decide later to pursue a bachelor's degree at another regionally accredited school. Always check with the specific school about the program you would like to attend. Often, programs such as nursing have more students than openings available, so acceptance may be delayed.

Community colleges frequently offer internships and apprenticeships within the surrounding community. These programs may help you gain employment at a faster rate, generate work experience for a résumé, or earn credentials for a specific career.

Four-Year Schools

Four-year schools are colleges or universities. Each state has a state university system, but not all colleges and universities are state based, as you will learn in the next few paragraphs. Four-year schools can offer the following:

- Bachelor's degrees
- Research institutions, centers, and programs
- Financial aid—four-year colleges can be very expensive
- On- and off-campus enrichment opportunities, such as study abroad and guest-lecture series
- Various fields of study that offer a wide range of job opportunities
- A broader range of course offerings than CCs
- Large, diverse campuses and populations at some of the bigger universities and state schools; smaller campuses and smaller, more congenial class sizes at smaller liberal arts colleges
- Competitive admissions process

Many universities also have graduate schools where students can continue their studies to obtain advanced degrees such as an MA, PhD, MD, JD, and others. Before going to most graduate schools, however, students must finish their undergraduate coursework and another admissions process for acceptance.

Attending a university can sometimes be overwhelming. Classes can be so large that you never have a one-on-one conversation with your professor, which sometimes makes students feel anonymous. Finding your niche might take some time in a large population, but it will afford you more opportunities to interact. Large institutions usually offer numerous degrees and classes to choose from; smaller liberal arts colleges may be a bit more specialized.

Many students start at their local community college, then finish their junior and senior years at a university or college. This is an easy pathway to pursue if you are running short on time to prepare, feel like you need more individualized attention at the start of your education, do not want to take the SAT or ACT, or simply have not been to school in a long time and feel safer in a smaller, less competitive environment. Whatever the case, arm yourself with information before making a decision. Sometimes, a visit to the campus will settle the issue. The school should be a comfortable fit because you will be spending so much time there.

Public Schools (Universities and Community Colleges)

Public schools, often referred to as "state schools," are typically funded by state and local governments. In-state residents pay lower tuition charges than out-of-state students. Some schools' out-of-state tuition charges can total an extra $10,000 or more per academic year. Sometimes state schools have reciprocal agreements with schools in other states that allow for reduced out-of-state tuition charges—for example, the Midwest Student Exchange Program (MSEP) (http://msep.mhec.org/). MSEP has nine participating Midwest states with public schools that charge undergraduate students a maximum of 150 percent of the in-state tuition charges, and private schools that offer a 10 percent reduction in tuition.

State schools offer a wide range of classes, degree options, and degree levels, and state residents get priority admissions. Class size at state schools can be a concern. Sometimes, upward of 250 students may be enrolled in a lecture class. This can make it difficult to interact with professors or staff. Most states have a flagship university with smaller locations available throughout the state for easier access. In some instances, students attending state universities cannot graduate in the standard four-year time frame because mandatory classes are often full, although many institutions now offer priority registration to veterans and active-duty service members. This enables veterans to maintain full-time status while using their GI Bills so that they also rate full-time benefits.

Private Schools

Private schools do not receive funding from state or local government. They are financially supported by tuition costs, donations, and endowments. They may be nonprofit or for-profit in nature, or traditional or nontraditional. Private schools usually charge students the same tuition whether they are in-state or out-of-state residents. Private school tuition is often higher than resident tuition at a state school, but not always. Many private schools offer scholarships and grants to greatly reduce the tuition costs. Usually, private schools have smaller class sizes than public schools, which can mean greater access to your professor. Private school acceptance may be less competitive than state acceptance, but not in top-tier or Ivy League institutions. Some private schools have religious affiliations, are historically black- or Hispanic-serving institutions, or are single-sex institutions.

For-Profit Institutions

The difference between for-profit and nonprofit schools is basically in the title. For-profit schools are operated by businesses, are revenue based, and have to account for profits and losses. According to a recent government report on for-profit schools, the "financial performance of these companies is closely tracked by analysts and by investors";[5] this means that the bottom line is always revenue. For-profit schools typically have open enrollment. Open enrollment can be helpful when you are transitioning from the military and have many other urgent needs at the same time. Open enrollment means that everyone gains entry to the school. That may prove disastrous for an individual who is not ready for the demands of higher education, but if the student is well prepared, it might provide a good pathway. Be informed when choosing your school. The College Board reported average costs of four-year state-school tuition and fees for the 2018 to 2019 academic year at $10,230, and average private, nonprofit school tuition and fees at $35,830.[6]

Veterans should be concerned about private-school cost because the average for a private school for 2018 to 2019 was significantly higher than the current Post-9/11 payout of $23,671.94. Current payment rates can be found here: https://www.benefits.va.gov/GIBILL/resources/benefits _resources/rates/ch33/ch33rates080118.asp. If you decide on a private school that charges tuition and fees above and beyond the Post-9/11 payout amount, check to see if the school is participating in the Yellow Ribbon Program (YRP). The YRP, which is explained in depth in chapter 7, "Cost and Payment Resources," may help you close the tuition gap. Current rates can be found here: https://www.benefits.va.gov/gibill/yellow_ribbon.asp.

Nonprofit Institutions

According to the National Association of Independent Colleges and Universities, "private, not-for-profit higher education institutions' purposes are to offer diverse, affordable, personal, involved, flexible, and successful educations to their students."[7] Nonprofit private schools sometimes offer flexible admissions for veterans that many state institutions cannot. Offering flexible admissions to veterans is a school-specific benefit, and veterans should address that option with their preferred institution.

Private, nonprofit schools can have tremendous name recognition, such as Harvard University and Yale University. On a smaller scale, many private, nonprofit colleges and universities are well known within our own communities. For example, in Chicago, three well-known private nonprofit schools are DePaul University, Loyola University, and Columbia College. Each of these schools enjoys an excellent reputation, has a comprehensive veterans' department, and is well known throughout the Midwest. Attending this type of school is typically a safe pathway, especially on a résumé. Be aware that private schools can be very expensive, and the cost can sometimes be prohibitive. Make sure to read the section on the YRP (chapter 7) to learn how it may help you afford private school tuition that is higher than the amount funded under Post-9/11.

Vocational-Technical and Career Colleges

Vocational-technical (votech) schools and career colleges prepare students for skill-based careers in technical fields. Many technical schools are state run, subsidized, and regionally accredited. Credits from these schools are generally accepted elsewhere. Career colleges are private, usually for-profit institutions, and they mostly hold national accreditation. Credits from these schools may not be widely transferable. Programs at these schools can run anywhere from ten months to four years, depending on the skills required to finish training. Many have rolling admissions. Programs often run year-round, including the summers, in order to get students into the workforce faster.

Typically, in a votech-based program, general-education classes such as English and math are not necessary. Program completion results in a certificate of completion or an associate degree in applied science. The associate in applied science will require entry-level math and English classes. Votech schools focus directly on the task at hand, meaning training in a need-based skill and preparing students for a career. If you have decided to take a votech pathway, research the school's cost, credentials, faculty, program requirements, and student body prior to committing to a specific institution. Cost is important: remember, the GI Bill has a maximum amount it will pay for private school. Find out whether you will also be eligible to apply for FSA (Federal Student Aid), but you should be mainly interested in the Pell Grant. You can find more information regarding student aid in chapter 7. Determine whether the school is licensed by the state and which accreditation it holds. Ask about the professors' backgrounds and qualifications. Find out if you will be able to apply any military credit toward the program and if the program includes on-the-job training or internship possibilities. Visit the campus to determine what type of equipment you will be trained on and review the faculty credentials. Check the school's completion rates, meaning how many students graduate and whether they graduate on time. Last, verify that the school offers job-placement services. Find out the following:

- What is the school's rate of placement?
- Where are students being placed?
- What positions are students getting right out of school?
- How much money are students earning?

Usually, a phone call and follow-up school visit are required to fully understand the program benefits. Remember that vocational fields prepare students for specific career pathways, so transitioning later to a different pathway will require retraining.

Votech schools usually hold national accreditation. In the accreditation portion of this chapter, the authors explained the difference between regional and national accreditation. Nationally accredited programs' credits frequently cannot transfer into a regionally accredited school, although some exceptions exist at schools that hold dual accreditation. For this reason, always check the local community college for similar programs. Many community colleges offer vocational programs that can be converted later to transferable college credit.

On a side note, you are reading this book because you have some degree of interest in either working in business or in creating and running your own business. If you are interested in developing a business based on votech-type services (welding, plumbing, etc.) and you need to get trained in the field first, I would strongly recommend sticking with a state, community, or technical school. This way, you may also be able to pursue business and/or entrepreneurial classes while earning units from a regionally accredited institution. This will offer you much more flexibility if you decide to pursue traditional schooling at a later date.

Subjects

There is a wealth of subjects available to study within institutions of higher education. For the purpose of this book, I will focus on the business-related degrees. If you are interested in taking a vocational pathway but also opening your own business, you may need to work on the vocational part first, then follow with business-related coursework. If you are unsure about where to study both, make a trip to the local community college. Set up an appointment to speak with an advisor and discuss your concerns with him or her. Most community colleges offer vocational training as well as traditional college degree pathways. If the traditional degree pathway is not for you because you are not interested in completing a full load of general-education classes, ask about business certificates that the school may offer. Certificates do not require that certain general-education classes be completed, unlike associate degree programs. Certificates offer a shorter-term type of training that may help you gain the skills you need to launch your business.

There are many different bachelor's degrees that pertain to business. Subject areas include, but are not limited to, administration, economics, general management, project management, accounting, human resources, public relations, construction management, IT, aviation management, public administration, real estate, entrepreneurship, international business, advertising, marketing, logistics and supply chain management, health-care management, information systems management, and finance.

The National Veteran Education Tracker, compiled by the Student Veterans of America and other partners found that student veterans were succeeding at a rate higher than that of their civilian peers. They also found that the majority of degrees sought were categorized within the business realm.

Specialized degree programs (figure 3.1) allow students to focus in a specific area, which gives them a clearer pipeline to a future career and a business sector to target. Think about the job you had in the military. Does that field have a civilian counterpart? Pull up the COOL website for your branch of service. Look up your MOS or rating, read the MOS description, and see what types of civilian credentials align with your military

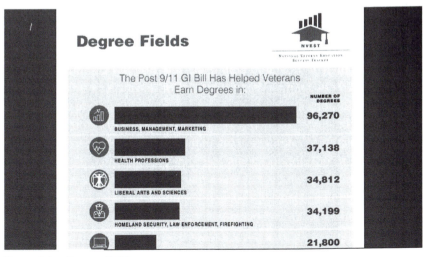

Figure 3.1. Degree Fields
https://nvest.studentveterans.org/wp-content/uploads/2017/02/NVEST_Factsheets.pdf

job. For example, I looked up the USMC 0341 Logistics/Embarkation Specialist MOS, which states:

> The Logistics/Embarkation Specialist prepares supplies and equipment for embarkation and performs various Force Deployment Planning and Execution (FDP&E) functions to support the movement of personnel, supplies, and equipment via all modes of transportation using commercial and military assets, at all levels including unit, MAGTF, and joint operations. They are trained in the application of Automated Information Systems (AIS) that are utilized throughout the Defense Transportation System (DTS) to account, track, and interface movement data with load planning programs and joint AIS to support the FDP&E process and In Transit Visibility (ITV). The Logistics/Embarkation Specialist is trained to prepare aircraft and ship load plans that meet organizational requirements. They assist with the preparation, planning, and execution of strategic mobility plans in accordance with the Time Phased Force Deployment Data (TPFDD) used to deploy and sustain forward deployed forces. The Logistics/ Embarkation Specialist also performs multiple logistics administrative duties within the J/G/S-4 section. They compile and maintain logistics support data, compute combat logistics support requirements, and coordinate combat logistics functions in support of MAGTF operations and deployments. At the SNCO level, they will also serve as Combat Cargo Assistants (CCAs) onboard naval amphibious assault ships. MOS 0491, Logistics/Mobility Chief is assigned as the primary MOS upon promotion to Gunnery Sergeant.[8]

So, let's go through the description to look for topics that may help you pick a major. We know that logistics is an option as it is part of the occupational title. The first sentence also demonstrates that the supply-chain management skill is required for this MOS. Jumping a bit ahead of ourselves, remember that most civilians won't understand the amount of equipment you were responsible for as an 0341, so when writing your résumé you will need to quantify the dollar amount. Since you are thinking about the dollar amount now, I bet you also understand at this point that as an 0431 in the USMC, supply chain management was a critical skill, as you had to account for many thousands or millions of dollars of equipment that you moved from point A to point B.

The third sentence, "The Logistics/Embarkation Specialist is trained to prepare aircraft and ship load plans that meet organizational requirements," demonstrates that an 0341 has a degree of experience as a logistician. Did you know that logisticians exist in the civilian sector and that you can study it as a major or as an area of concentration within a business bachelor degree? Here is the link to the Bureau of Labor Statistics Occupational Outlook Handbook information on logisticians: https://www .bls.gov/ooh/business-and-financial/logisticians.htm. Notice the following link "How to Become One":

> Logisticians may qualify for some positions with an associate's degree. However, due to complex logistics and supply chains, companies prefer to hire workers who have at least a bachelor's degree. Many logisticians have a bachelor's degree in business, systems engineering, or supply chain management.[9]

I'm sure you noticed that supply chain management was one of the degrees recommended.

Moving on to the fourth sentence, "They assist with the preparation, planning, and execution of strategic mobility plans in accordance with the Time Phased Force Deployment Data (TPFDD) used to deploy and sustain forward deployed forces." Sure sounds like project management skills to me. Project management is built in to many bachelor's degrees in business. Did you also know that some schools offer project management as a bachelor's degree or as an area of concentration? The Project Management Institute also offers a range of credentials that are coveted in the civilian business sector, including the Project Management Professional (PMP) and the Certified Associate in Project Management (CAPM). If you are still on active duty, you may be able to get some of these certifications paid for through the COOL program. Contact your local education center for more assistance. For the USMC and Navy COOL programs, check under the MOS rating of Leader; there are some restrictions, and you will still need to qualify through the credentialing agency even if you meet the military requirements. If you are in the Army, check under the tab "Manager Credentials." If you are in the Air Force check under "AF COOL Leadership Credentials."

Some schools may offer these subjects as a minor course of study. For example, Cal Poly, Pomona, offers a minor in logistics through its College of Business Administration, Technology and Operations Management Department. So, if you are accepted to Cal Poly, Pomona, with the intent to complete a bachelor's of science in business administration, you could also gain an academic background in logistics with a few more classes; it will help you diversify your résumé. Maybe your military background is in logistics. Rounding out your résumé with academic coursework within the subject area will give you the ability to target two areas of business instead of just one. Remember that adding a minor means you are adding classes. This means the course of study may take longer than the amount of time you have. Also, the VA will not cover minors for students using the GI Bill. If your program has elective units built into it, you may be able to use those units for the minor. The problem for most institutions is that Joint Service Transcript (JST) credit often knocks out any required elective credits. This means you don't have any elective units remaining. This information is from the school's catalog. Speak with your advisor/counselor for more information regarding minors, if and which ones the institution may offer, and forms of payment for the classes if they cannot be covered under the GI Bill. Table 3.1 is a snapshot from Cal Poly, Pomona's, Logistics Minor program. Notice that the program requires twenty-eight units to complete. This may equate to another year of study; however, sometimes minors may require classes that overlap within your major, for example, in this program, managerial statistics overlaps with the major. In this case, one class counts for two.

International business bachelor's degree programs may offer study abroad options. These programs can help you target certain areas of the world and give you the ability to demonstrate firsthand knowledge of international business practices on your résumé and during employment interviews. Study abroad programs can be as short as a few weeks over the summer or as long as a full year. Not all schools with international business-degree programs also offer study abroad options, so you must consider what level of immersion you are interested in when picking a school. For example, the University of Colorado, Colorado Springs, College of Business offers the International Business Seminar (IBS) program, which has short-term winter and summer study abroad options in Europe or China. The program focuses on experiencing the cultural, social, and political environments of the country along with the business sector. The stated purpose of the program is "to allow participants to be exposed to international business practices outside the United States."[10]

The University of Wisconsin, Madison, also offers study abroad programs. The school's website states: "Well over one third of each

Table 3.1. Logistics Minor

Offered by: College of Business Administration, Technology and Operations
  Management Department

The Logistics Minor is the only program of its kind in the California State University
  system. The Logistics Minor was developed to allow Business Administration
  majors or students majoring in non-business programs to gain the knowledge
  and skills needed to gain employment in the field of transportation, warehousing,
  logistics, planning, materials management, and physical distribution. In addition to
  the job opportunities that are available in the domestic arena, openings also exist
  in the international arena. Demand greatly exceeds supply both nationally and
  internationally for logistics managers.

Total required for program: 28 units

Prerequisites:

STA 120	Statistics with Applications (4)
IBM 301	Principles of Marketing Management (4)
TOM 301	Operations Management (4)
TOM 302	Managerial Statistics (4)

Core Requirements: 16 units

TOM 309	Logistics Management (4)
TOM 319	Transportation Systems and Traffic Management (4)
TOM 434	Purchasing Management (4)
TOM 425	Supply Chain Design, Analysis and Representation (4)
EBZ 304	E-business-enabled Supply Chain Management (4)

Directed Electives: 12 units

Select 12 additional units from the following list of courses: (Each elective must be
  outside the student's subplan department.)

TOM 350	Decision Support and Expert Systems (4)
TOM 401	Quality Management (4)
TOM 420	Operations Technologies and Strategies (4)
TOM 418	ERP-Applications in Operations (4)
TOM 436	Project Management (4)
TOM 453	Operations Management in Services (4)
EBZ 303	E-business Customer Relationship Management (4)
IBM 407	Industrial Marketing (4)
IBM 414	International Marketing Management (4)
IBM 416	International Exporting (4)
IBM 431	Management of Marketing Channels (4)

Source: https://catalog.cpp.edu/preview_program.php?catoid=4&poid=837

Wisconsin BBA graduating class studies abroad."[11] With over thirty-five programs located in countries such as France, China, and Argentina, there are options for most students interested in going abroad. In many of the programs, students who demonstrate proficiency in the native language may take classes in that language if they wish. English-language classes are available for those without foreign-language proficiency. On that note, if you target a specific region during your studies, consider studying the language(s) of the region. The study abroad experience will offer you a greater enrichment opportunity if you can use your language skills while abroad. It will also be a great benefit for you later on during your employment-hunting activities.

There are many different types of study abroad programs housed at reputable schools across the country. Some schools even offer dual-degree programs to business students. For example, the University of San Diego (USD) offers an undergraduate program in which business students can obtain a bachelor's degree from USD and another one from a partner program located at one of five schools across Europe. Current partner institutions include:

• Católica Lisbon School of Business & Economics—Lisbon, Portugal (courses abroad are taught in English)
• Dublin City University—Dublin, Ireland (courses abroad are taught in English)
• EM Strasbourg Business School—Strasbourg, France (courses abroad are taught in English)
• John Cabot University—Rome, Italy (courses abroad are taught in English)
• Universidad Pontificia Comillas—Madrid, Spain (courses abroad are taught in Spanish)[12]

The length of attendance at the foreign schools depends on which program you are participating in, as they are each tailored to the student's program of study. For example, the program at EM Strasbourg Business School is best for those in USD's BBA Business Administration program with a minor in international business or for those enrolled in the International Business degree program. Students who complete this program will also earn a Bachelor's in European Management (BEM) from EM

Strasbourg. Students in this program study abroad for their junior year. Other dual-degree business programs at USD require students to stay abroad for two years of study. For more information visit the following website: https://www.sandiego.edu/international/study-abroad/programs/ dual-degree-programs.php#accordion-panel1. Also, read more about attending school abroad in chapter 4, "International Business Degrees and Study Abroad."

You should now be getting an understanding of how you can integrate your military background into your course of studies. At the very least, you are gaining a better understanding of the different types of business-related pathways to follow.

All right, so where else do you look when so many options and statistics demonstrate that business degrees are the most sought-after degrees by Post-9/11 GI Bill–using veterans? My recommendation, beyond specializing in a certain area, is to find programs with internships and job-shadowing opportunities and other more specialized options. This may include study abroad programs, as we just discussed, programs that offer interactions with people currently in the field, field trips, or immersion activities. Speak with your school's career-services department to see what the institution offers.

If you haven't decided on a school yet, you may want to check out schools that offer combined bachelor's and master's degree programs, sometimes referred to as "4 + 1." These programs allow students to earn both a bachelor's and master's degree in less time than earning each separately. Some schools specialize in this, such as DePaul University. Check out the school's list of combined (five-year programs) business-related degrees:

- DePaul Undergraduate Degree + MS in Enterprise Risk Management
- DePaul Undergraduate Degree + MS in Entrepreneurship
- DePaul Undergraduate Degree + MS in Finance
- DePaul Undergraduate Degree + MS in Human Resources
- DePaul Undergraduate Degree + MS in Hospitality Leadership and Operational Performance
- DePaul Undergraduate Degree + MS in Management
- DePaul Undergraduate Degree + MS in Real Estate
- DePaul Undergraduate Degree + MS in Supply Chain Management

- DePaul Undergraduate Degree + MS in Sustainable Management
- Economics (BSB) + MS in Economics and Policy Analysis
- Accountancy (BSB) + MS in Audit and Advisory Services
- Accountancy (BSB) + MS in Taxation

For more information on these options, look on the school's website: https://business.depaul.edu/academics/combined-degrees/Pages/default.aspx.

Many other schools also offer combined programs, such as George Washington University, American University, the University of Florida, and SUNY, Buffalo. Some of these programs are completed simultaneously, and others are progressive but allow for a degree of overlapping classes. For more information on the programs offered at these schools visit the following links:

- George Washington University: https://graduate.admissions.gwu.edu/combined-programs
- American University: https://www.american.edu/kogod/admissions/bachelors-masters.cfm
- University of Florida: https://catalog.ufl.edu/UGRD/academic-advising/combined-degrees/
- SUNY Buffalo: https://admissions.buffalo.edu/academics/combined degree.php

Many of you may be thinking that you don't have enough GI Bill benefits to cover a combined program, and others will groan at the thought of adding on more school. Before you discount the notion, consider some benefits of entering the civilian workforce with an advanced degree:

- Gain specialized knowledge that may help you be more competitive in your initial search for employment.
- Advance in your new career more quickly.
- Gain eligibility for management-level positions sooner.
- Earn more income.
- Earn professional recognition through publication or project development.
- Make connections.

All of these factors are important in helping you gain forward momentum. Let's take a brief look at each one.

- Gain specialized knowledge: Advanced knowledge within your discipline from master's degree–level work is strictly focused on your area of study. In other words, no pesky general-education classes to complete! Some programs do require a degree of electives be completed; however, the electives are classes that either focus directly on the subject but allow you to diversify or specialize your course of study. For example, you may have a selection of classes in entrepreneurship, innovation, strategy, management, marketing, or finance. Graduate degrees require extensive research, complex thought, and the gradual bringing together of a set of ideas that correlate in some manner. This helps you to develop ideas and test your theories, thereby making you a multidisciplinary thinker. This helps make you an asset in an ever-changing business world and in an ever-evolving workforce.
- Advance in your career: Demonstrate commitment to advance before beginning your civilian career. Earning a master's degree is no easy task. It signals to potential employers that you are committed in your pursuit of knowledge to use as a platform for your, and the company you work for, growth and professional development. Maybe you are an officer and completed your bachelor's degree prior to entering the military. Earning a master's degree during your time in the service or after separating from the service demonstrates your commitment to stay current in the field and to ongoing professional development.
- Gain eligibility for management-level positions: Transitioning into a more senior position is not always easily attainable. Gaining graduate-level education helps make you more competitive for senior positions, such as management.
- Earn more income: "In 2016 the median earnings of young adults with a master's or higher degree were $64,100, some 28 percent higher than those of young adults with a bachelor's degree ($50,000). In the same year, the median earnings of young adults with a bachelor's degree were 57 percent higher than those of young adult high school completers ($31,800)."[13] This quote points out the difference in income levels for those who have earned master's degrees versus

those who haven't. Consider the years of advanced income-earning potential you may have if you complete the master's degree early in your work years.

- Earn professional recognition: Many master's degree programs require students to complete projects or submit work for publication. These practices can help you demonstrate professional expertise in your field and place you ahead of your peers.
- Make connections: Your classmates will typically come from a wide variety of industries, especially if you are in an MBA program. This may offer you connections to numerous professionals across a diverse group of disciplines. Cultivate these connections, many of whom may have already attained success in their fields, for contacts for employment, career support, and as business associates. You can never be too prepared in maintaining a list of professional contacts for support, as they may lead to a promotion, a new job, new ideas or information and a greater ability to adapt to changes in business.

This section focused specifically on factors that are important for you to consider when contemplating your pursuit of higher education, but you will also need to review chapter 7, on funding your education, before making a decision on school selection and pursuit of an advanced degree. Maybe you have decided that an advanced degree is not attainable at this point but are interested in considering other options to better prepare you in your search for employment or to make you more competitive in your current position. If so, make sure to read the final section in this chapter, which details certificates that may assist you in this endeavor.

BASE EDUCATION OFFICES

Most military base education centers can provide counseling services for service members. Base education specialists are knowledgeable about the programs available on the base, in the community, and online. If you are assigned to a small military base without an education center, locate the nearest large base to see whether there are education centers that can offer phone counseling or whether web-based counseling is available. For example, the Navy closed most of its education centers, but many of its bases are located near Marine Corps bases. While the education-center staff aboard the Marine Corps bases cannot enter sailors' TA codes (sailors must contact their Virtual Education Center for the codes), staff can counsel them regarding degree programs, colleges and universities, career-based information, and transition planning.

Many military base education centers also offer some type of remedial math and English program. Programs can vary in length and eligibility parameters. For example, the major Marine Corps bases offer Academic Skills Programs (ASP). ASPs vary in length, and some programs are TAD-based while others are offered in the evening. ASP is geared for marines who have GT scores (determined from ASVAB raw scores) of 99 and below, who want to use TA, but who fail to get the required 10.2 or higher on the Test of Adult Basic Education (TABE). If they participate in ASP and their scores improve, they may be eligible for TA. Many of the service members that attend ASP have GT scores over 100 but have not been to school in many years and would like a refresher course before attending college. Now, those with GT scores of 100 and higher can attend ASP on a space-available basis. There is no guarantee of a spot in the class. Try to attend many months before your EAS so that you are not left with just one class that fits into your remaining time on active duty. The Army has a similar program, the Basic Skills Education Program (BSEP). Both programs are often taught by professors from local community colleges.

If you prefer an online math and English program, the Online Academic Skills Course (OASC) program is free through Peterson's Online Basic Skills website: http://www.nelnetsolutions.com/dantesnet/.

Be mindful that the online version is not teacher directed. So, if you have difficulty, you will be left to your own devices to figure things out. In this case, try cross-referencing on the free Khan Academy site (www.khanacademy.org), especially for math.

COMMUNITY COLLEGES

State-supported community colleges offer college courses, certificate programs, self-improvement programs, and vocational-technical programs at lower cost. Taking even one or two courses at a community college may allow you to get a better feel for a particular career pathway. Community colleges typically have career centers where you can take personality-based career-research tests that the advisors can interpret for you. These tests can help determine what types of careers might be a good fit for you.

There are quite a few reasons to consider state-supported community colleges. State-supported community colleges have the proper accreditation. They are a good place to get back into the world of education, especially for those who need remedial or refresher English-writing and math courses. State-supported community colleges are less expensive than four-year colleges. Classes are usually smaller, allowing for more attention from professors. One of the authors of this book, who is also a veteran, completed some classes at a major state-supported four-year university with over one hundred enrolled students in each class and found it to be problematic. Doctoral students were used as teaching aides, and they were assigned the grading duties for papers and exams. Getting an appointment with the actual professor teaching a large class was often difficult.

State-supported community colleges employ counselors or advisors who commonly have master's degrees in education or counseling. The counselors are not expected to be salespeople; they are expected to be guides in assisting the students in achieving the best possible education. Community colleges are often closer to home. Many states have a network of community colleges designed so that every community will be within reasonable commuting distance from a campus. Scheduling at community colleges is often more flexible and counseling/advising sessions can often be conducted online. Also, many state-supported community colleges now offer online courses. Finally, state-supported community colleges tend to have more nontraditional students, including students returning to college after spending years in the workforce (considered adult reentry), working adults seeking career changes, and even military spouses.

SCHOOL RESOURCES

Many student veterans are not aware of the resources offered at colleges and universities. Resources may be limited or well developed, depending upon the size and scope of the institution. Resources often include career services, disability services, counseling, health and wellness, financial aid, writing centers, food pantries, women's centers, and fitness centers. Most veterans check in with the veterans' services department at the school they are attending even if they never return. But what about the other departments that may be able to offer support in your academic pursuits?

Three departments that should be on your list to recon before applying to the school are veterans' services, disability resources, and the career center. The career center is extremely important in helping you prepare for your future career, and it is where I will focus. I do want to give an honorable mention to disability services/resources. This is a department often underused by veterans. This is unfortunate as, for those who need it, many schools have well-developed departments that can offer you the support you need to create a stronger platform to support your studies. Remember when you went through the VA disability rating process when separating from the service? Think about the types of issues you discussed with the doctors or with the individual who helped you with your claim. Do you think any of these issues may create difficulty for your learning? For example, many service members have hearing or memory loss. Did you know that many schools have resources that may support you in your studies? One such option that a Marine, whom one of the authors recently worked with, received from the disability-resources department at the community college he is attending in California is a Smart pen. According to Livescribe, a maker of Smart pens, a Smart pen "capture everything you hear and write so you can be confident that you'll never miss a word."[14] Basically, you use the pen on special paper to take notes in class. When you study at home, you can tap the pen to your notes, and the pen plays the lecture from that specific section back to you. This helps reinforce the information in your memory. For those with memory problems, this can offer students a boost of support that may save them countless hours of redundant work, such as in looking up the information they can't remember from the lecture.

Let's discuss the importance of career services and take a look at three schools with well-developed departments. Remember that the breadth of resources offered will vary by institution, but most offer services such as résumé and cover-letter writing support. These are all important services that may help you make your first contact to a future career.

Let's take a look at a few schools with well-developed career resources departments. We conducted our reconnaissance by checking university and college websites.

Georgetown University

Georgetown University's career-resource site lists many services that can help students begin preparing for careers, such as career fairs; alumni panels, which are important to getting a boots-on-the-ground perspective; information sessions with companies interested in hiring Georgetown graduates and for those students interested in working abroad; an online platform (Handshake) with internship and job postings; an alumni program for graduate students (the Alumni Career Network); alumni presentations; virtual resources that support résumé and cover letter development; best interview techniques; and informative company profiles. The virtual resource Optimal Resume "is an interactive resource for resume, CV, and cover letter content and formatting. Build a document with support from the site and then download a copy that you can continue to update."[15] Then students can use Optimal Interview which is "a virtual mock interview practice website that allows you to prepare for upcoming interview opportunities at any time" to perfect their interviewing techniques.[16]

Georgetown also houses discipline-specific career centers that assist students studying specific subjects in pursuing careers. The website states:

> Each group's career center is able to cater to the specific interests of graduate students in those areas. These centers list job and internship opportunities for organizations that commonly employ graduates of those programs. They also deliver targeted skill workshops, site visits and information sessions, regular career bulletins, and more. Alumni get involved with current students through these centers to offer additional networking opportunities.[17]

Finally, the Crawley Career Center staff are available for appointments to help you review: documents, job- or internship-search strategies, and possible interview questions.

Texas A&M

Texas A&M University's Career Center offer a broad range of services to current and former students, prospective students, family members, and faculty and staff. On the main site (https://careercenter.tamu.edu/), pick the category that you identify with to gather more information. For example, clicking on the tab for current students gets students to information on the following topics:

- Major exploration (to include career assessments)
- Résumé writing
- Job shadowing
- Professional school preparation

Major exploration should be at the top of your list when targeting a future career. Many students make the mistake of picking a degree and then trying to match a career to it at a later date. Job selection should occur in the following manner: find a career, match a college major to the career, then pick a school. This requires significant career counseling prior to bachelor degree school selection. If you are a student at Texas A&M, and you are not sure about a future career field, this department offers current students self-assessments that may offer insight into a career field that matches their skills, abilities, personality type, and preferences. After reviewing the results with a career advisor, major exploration will be the next step.

Résumé-writing services are not often free. To gain access to them through a college is a great benefit. Not all institutions offer one-on-one résumé-writing appointments. Some offer classes and workshops. This is a service to consider prior to determining which institution you would like to attend. If you cannot get assistance in career preparation from your school, where else can you get it from? Most of the career services offered in the civilian sector are fee based. Costs can be overwhelming. Hence, it is important that you have support services available through your school. Also, don't forget that most major military bases house career services departments manned by a civilian workforce. These services are free, and you don't have to live next to a military base to access services. Contact the career department aboard the last base you were stationed at and request a phone-based appointment. Services can often be offered over the phone and through email. Some may even broadcast the workshops the advisors offer through Skype or another web-based format.

Job shadowing is a resource tool to use for career exploration, to demonstrate your dedication in pursuing a specific career, and to fill in blank spots (work time and experience) on your résumé. Read more about job shadowing in the next section in this chapter. Texas A&M offers students the HireAggies system, which allows you to search for internships, co-ops, and jobs. *What's a co-op, you ask?* Usually, *co-op* refers to a "multi-work term agreement with one employer; traditionally with at least three work terms alternated with school terms, resulting in a five-year degree program for what would otherwise take four years. Co-ops are traditionally full-time, paid positions."[18] This means that while you complete your degree, you also gain paid work experience to list on your résumé. A win-win situation for sure.

Interested in attending graduate school or already know it is necessary? It is an area in which most students do not begin preparing far enough in advance. Most beginning student veterans are not considering graduate school while they are in the early stages of their undergraduate programs. If you think that graduate school is a possibility, or even a necessity, I would encourage you to begin to consider tactics to prepare as early as possible and make an appointment with the career center. Texas A&M's Career Center states that staff members are available to help you research programs and schools, create timelines and personal statements, and prepare for interviews.

Even if you are currently attending a community college, you can get help preparing, as many state, two-year institutions house career centers that are capable of assisting you. Also, many graduate programs want to see that students have taken specific undergraduate courses and have gained a broad depth of knowledge. Counselors/advisors in these departments are aware of these needs and can help you create a strategy that will help you create a more competitive application packet. If you are considering applying to Texas A&M, or any other institution, you should consider the career center offerings when comparing schools.

MiraCosta College

Community colleges also house career centers. MiraCosta College is a two-year community college in Southern California, just south of the

Camp Pendleton Marine Corps Base. The college's career center (http://miracosta.edu/instruction/careerservices/index.html) offers a computer lab, resource library, and workshops. Counselors are also available for career counseling appointments. Links on the website provide student resources, faculty/staff resources, and employer resources. Also listed is a link to the college's YouTube site, https://www.youtube.com/channel/UCc2UAfZNSWOyqx0x460HM6Q, and numerous videos on career readiness and job searching: http://www.careerspots.com/newplayer/default.aspx?key=ssvpVx4VG2qC96lUO1CtVQ2&pref=

This center is even helpful for students who intend to continue on to graduate school upon completion of a bachelor's degree. You are thinking, *"Why would someone need career assistance if the career they are interested in requires, or they want to attain, a master's degree?"* Career services can help students better prepare for advanced education by making them more aware of the types of careers that are open to exploration; by helping students begin to build résumés, cover letters, and portfolios early on in their education; by teaching students how they can search for careers by arming them with resources; and by informing students of established programs that help them interact with community partners. So, by the time they are ready to begin their search for employment, students can be confident in their ability to conduct a detailed search.

On the main page, you see a window that lists career-advice videos. At the bottom of the video box, click the link to follow on to a new page that has a video screen. On this page, you can find information on career readiness, digital technology, global fluency, leadership, and teamwork. There are also two channels, Career Readiness and Job Search, that help you prepare for employment and conduct job searches. These resources can help you launch your future employment search. It is imperative that the institutions you choose to attend has resources such as these to support you in your pursuits.

Go back to the main page and click on the "Student Resources" tab to get to the bread and butter of career services at MiraCosta College. On this page are the following links:

- Take a Class or Workshop
- Find a Major or Career That Interests You
- Career Exploration Resources

- Career Resources for Diverse Populations
- Write a Resume & Cover Letter
- Prepare for Your Interview
- Get an Internship or Co-op on JAIN
- Find a Job on JAIN
- Build Online Portfolios
- Report an Internship or Co-op on JAIN
- Report a Job On or Off Campus on JAIN

You need to explore all of the links, as they each host information pertinent to preparing for a future career. Whether you intend to complete your education with an associate degree or a more advanced degree (bachelor's, master's, or even doctoral degree), you should get familiar with the resources offered at your particular institution.

The school has several in-depth resources listed for career research and preparation that are password protected. As a MiraCosta College student, you could receive access to these sites as well as book an appointment with the career counselor to learn how to use them. There are also links to free resources that host career and labor market information specific to California, such as the Employment Development Department Occupational Guides, which host information regarding types of occupations, job descriptions, and outlook and wage information.[19]

There are also links to sites that offer information on motivational interviewing. Motivational interviewing is a tactic designed to help you gain information from people who already work in the field. The three links offer information on the purpose of motivational interviewing, how to conduct it, and questions to ask during interviews (seventy-five!).

Now, many schools carry career programs over into their curriculum to better integrate classroom learning and career development. MiraCosta College offers students classes that are arranged around employment immersion opportunities. For example, the institution offers classes that are titled "Occupational Cooperative Work Experience" and "Internship Studies." According to MiraCosta College's 2018 to 2019 academic catalog, occupational cooperative work experience is:

> intended for students who are employed in a job directly related to their
> major. It allows such students the opportunity to apply the theories and

skills of their discipline to their position and to undertake new responsibilities and learn new skills at work. Topics include goal-setting, employability skills development, and examination of the world of work as it related to the student's career plans. Students may not earn more than 16 units in any combination of cooperative work experience (general or occupational) and/or internship studies during community college attendance.[20]

The school also offers "Internship Studies" classes for certain academic pathways, such as business and sustainable agriculture, for those of you interested in becoming small-business owners in the field of agriculture. The catalog states:

This course provides students the opportunity to apply the theories and techniques of their discipline in an internship position in a professional setting under the instruction of a faculty-mentor and site supervisor. It introduces students to aspects of the roles and responsibilities of professional employed in the field of study. Topics include goal-setting, employability skills development, and examination of the world of work as it related to the student's career plans. Student must develop new learning objectives and/or intern at a new site upon each repetition. Students may not earn more than 16 units in any combination or cooperative work experience (general or occupational) and/or internship studies during community college attendance.[21]

The three institutions reviewed in this section offer just a sample of the types of programs college and university career centers should be prepared to offer students. These resources can be valuable in your pursuit of a future civilian career. If you haven't settled on a particular school yet, make sure to put the school's career centers on your checklist of items that you are researching information on. If you have picked a school or are already attending, make sure to contact the career center at your institution to learn about the assistance it can offer you.

COLLEGE NAVIGATOR

College Navigator (http://nces.ed.gov/collegenavigator/), offered by the National Center for Education Statistics, is a helpful tool for both active-duty and transitioning service members. The free site enables users to search schools based upon very detailed criteria. Searches may be saved for future reference and dropped into the favorites box for side-by-side comparison. Comparing schools side-by-side enables users to determine which school better suits their needs. For example, I searched California State University San Marcos (CSUSM) and USD to determine which school would be less expensive. After dropping both schools into my favorites box, I selected the "compare" option in that section. The side-by-side comparison tool lists CSUSM's current tuition rates at $7,717 and USD's at $51,186. You still need to go directly to both schools' websites for more information, but the initial search is demonstrating the vast difference in yearly costs between the two institutions. If you understand that the Post-9/11 GI Bill will currently only cover up to $24,476.79 (as of August 1, 2019) per academic year for a private school, you know further research will be required to determine whether USD is a viable fiscal option for you as a student veteran.

College Navigator allows detailed searches in fields such as distance from zip codes, public and private school options, distance learning possibilities, school costs, percentage of applicants admitted, religious affiliations, specialized missions, and available athletic teams. This way, users can narrow down selections based upon specific needs. For example, if you were interested in attending a school with a Christian background incorporated in the learning, you could click on the religious affiliations tab at the bottom of the search section and add that criterion to your list. Beginning each search within a certain number of miles from a zip code will enable users to narrow their search parameters from the start. If the selection is insufficient, try broadening the distance a bit prior to removing all of the other parameters you deem important. Many schools offer some degree of online schooling as part of the learning environment. If you are open to online learning, you may find that you can still meet all of your search parameters comfortably even if the school is a bit further in distance. A generic initial search on College Navigator might resemble this:

1. State—Texas
2. Zip code—90290, with a maximum distance parameter set at fifteen miles

3. Degree options—business, management, marketing, and related support services
4. Level of degree awarded—bachelor's

Results demonstrate that six schools meet the search criteria: Texas Southern University, University of Houston, University of Houston (Downtown), University of Houston (Clear Lake), Prairie View A&M, and Brazosport College. Because each of these institutions met the initial search criteria, you might want to narrow the mileage to a selection closer to your home base, or conduct other, more particular searches that elicit the differences. These searches may include the student population, programs offered, and veterans' department structure, but the veterans' department may be nonexistent, which would not inspire confidence in the institution's ability to take care of an individual's unique needs.

DANTES COLLEGE AND CAREER PLANNING COUNSELING SERVICES, POWERED BY KUDER JOURNEY

DANTES College and Career Planning Counseling Services (http://www.dantes.kuder.com) is available to service members for free, whether you are still on active duty or already separated from the service. Four main areas of education and career research and planning are available on the site—assessments, occupations, education and financial aid, and jobs/job searches. Also housed on the site are inventory assessments that enable service members to see their areas of strength and weakness. This gives test takers insight into career fields that match their personality types, thereby offering a broader base of potential careers to research. Background information on the careers can be researched to determine whether users are interested in pursuing the option further. Under the education section, users can match the requisite type of education to the chosen vocation as well as find schools that offer the desired degrees.

Résumé building and job searches can be conducted through the site as well. One interesting tool Kuder offers is the ability for users to build résumés and cover letters, attach other needed or pertinent information, and create a URL that hosts the information to submit to potential employers. This allows multiple pieces of information to be housed in one place as a professional portfolio for viewing by others.

MILITARY DIGITAL LIBRARY PROGRAM

Free digital library services that offer a variety of options are available through the libraries aboard military bases. The program is available to active duty members, reservists, dependent family members, military retirees, and Department of Defense (DoD) civilian employees. E-books are available for checkout, including bestsellers, as well as audio books. The library programs offer free apps for reading and listening to books. Popular magazines with current editions are also available for checkout in digital format.

Other services include:

- Gale Virtual Research Library
- Mango foreign language training
- Ancestry Library for genealogy research
- Chilton Library for automotive repair enthusiasts
- Online encyclopedias including *Britannica* and *World Book*
- Transition services including résumé writing and career search
- Indie Flix is a service offering movies and documentaries from film festivals around the world, including Sundance and Cannes. Classic television shows and documentaries are included in the service.
- Universal Class is in a category all its own. Five hundred free continuing-education courses are available for quite a few subjects. Here is a sampling:
  - Thirty history courses
  - Forty-five finance courses
  - Forty-five psychology courses
  - Ten math courses (basic math through statistics and pre-calculus)
  - Thirty accounting courses
  - One hundred business courses
  - Ninety general-education courses
  - Fifty-five writing courses

EBSCO Learning Express has many services for test preparation for military, occupational exams, and college preparation. Other services include:

- High school equivalency center for General Educational Development (GED) preparation
- Skill building resources for classroom and homework success
- SAT and ACT preparation
- AP exam preparation
- CLEP exam preparation
- College placement exam preparation
- College admissions essay writing
- College math skills review
- Grammar and writing skills review
- Science skills review
- Graduate school admissions exams

This is just a sample of all the services available through the EBSCO Learning Express program. All branches of the military, as well as Military One Source, offer free access to this site. To sign up for the digital services, visit your base library if you have one. Some base libraries will require you to sign up for a library card. Recruiters, Navy, and Coast Guard personnel may have to visit the digital library website for your branch of the service. If you are stationed on or are near a military base for a different branch of the service, check whether the base has a library. If it does, the staff can usually assist with enrolling in digital library services for their branch of the service. If you are in a remote area far from a military base with a library, contact the library of any military base, explain your situation, and ask for assistance. Base libraries can explain how to sign up for the different programs offered, such as research databases, language training, digital books, audio books, and more. They will set you up with user names and passwords.

- Marine Corps: https://mccs.ent.sirsi.net/client/en_US/default
- Navy: https://www.navymwrdigitallibrary.org/
- Army: https://www.myarmyonesource.com/EducationCareersand Libraries/Libraries/default.aspx
- Air Force: https://libguides.nps.edu/portals/afdigital
- Coast Guard: https://www.navymwrdigitallibrary.org/

Note: The Coast Guard uses the Navy and Military OneSource Virtual Library programs.

INTERNSHIPS AND JOB SHADOWING

Military experience and a college degree are often not enough to launch a career in business. While most employers understand that training is required for new employees, any experience you can get prior to getting hired will make the learning less stressful for you and, at the same time, help you demonstrate to a potential employer that you are not a high-risk hire. Internships offer you a great way to get documented experience working in a specific area of interest. Internships give you the chance to demonstrate more than just your knowledge in the area in which you are interning. They also offer you the opportunity to demonstrate your customer service skills and your ability to interact with other employees and navigate the workplace.

So, where can you find available internship opportunities and how can you get one? Well, we have already discussed the importance of college career centers and that well-developed centers have internship, co-op, and job-shadowing experiences organized with many community-based companies. But what if you already have a degree, or are currently in the process of achieving a degree, and you don't have access to a college career center? In that case, you can look for an immersion experience the same way you would look for a job: by searching on the internet!

Internships

Indeed.com, LinkedIn, and Glassdoor, three employment sites, post internship opportunities. Other internet sites exist for searching specifically for internships, such as,

- Career Builder, https://www.careerbuilder.com/
- Idealist, https://www.idealist.org/en/?type=JOB
- Internship Programs, http://www.internshipprograms.com/
- College Recruiter, https://www.collegerecruiter.com/
- After College, https://www.aftercollege.com/

There are even some internships offered abroad. Be careful with these as they often cost you money. It may be significantly cheaper for you to complete a study abroad program using your GI Bill than paying for an internship in a foreign country. However, consider the current work environment. It is competitive and global. This means that you may not just be competing with other Americans. Participating in an internship in a foreign country, or attending a study abroad program, along with your military service may be just what you need to stand apart from the rest of the field.

Now, back on track. Think about the military service you have completed and the types of work experience you have listed on your résumé. If at this point you realize you don't have a résumé because you were intent on going to college after separation from the service and didn't think you needed one, think again. You do. You need to build one early on in your academic pursuits and continue to add to it while you attend school. This will help you to be better prepared upon graduation, and also be prepared to apply for internships, as most require a résumé to be submitted for consideration. On another note, having a résumé handy will help you find a job while attending school. If possible, be purposeful in the type of work you do and where you do it while you are a student veteran. You need to begin to build experiences relevant to the civilian career you intend to pursue. Practical experience is even more important if you intend to be an entrepreneur. Finding internships that allow you access to others who have already blazed the entrepreneurship path will be informative in helping you create your own business plan.

The U.S. Chamber of Commerce (https://www.uschamber.com/about/careers/internship-program) offers an extensive internship program during which, if you are selected, you can either receive payment or college credit for your work. Housing is not included, and housing in some areas can come at a high cost. Check out the following site for more information: https://internsdc.com/. Positions in areas such as research, writing, database management, webpage maintenance, communications, and event preparation are available. This internship offers a few unique events to participants. For example, interns participate in several "Lunch and Learn" sessions during which interns have the opportunity to sit down and speak with and gain advice from senior-level Chamber executives. Also included are résumé-writing and interview workshops, sporting events, and even a tour of the White House.

Check with your local Chamber of Commerce to see if any community businesses offer immersion experiences. They may have organized internship experiences with the local community college, provide them through member businesses, or have job shadowing possibilities. For example, the Los Angeles Chamber of Commerce (https://lachamber.com/about/employment-internships-with-the-chamber/) offers spring-, summer-, and fall-term internships. Areas of interest you can apply for include:

- Public policy
- Global initiatives
- Marketing and communications
- Southern California Leadership Network
- Education and workforce development

For more information or to apply, visit https://lachamber.com/forms/apply-for-an-internship-with-the-l.a.-area-chamber/. A quick Google search will help you find your local Chamber of Commerce. Typically, internship opportunities are posted on their website but I would recommend calling because, even if they do not have an organized internship program, the staff may have information on local area businesses interested in supporting students or veterans.

Job Shadowing

Job shadowing offers you a chance to observe an individual employed in a career you have an interest in learning about and to perform his or her daily work duties; it provides an opportunity for you to see the job from an insider's perspective. Job shadowing for career exploration can help you gain information on a particular career, from strategies for getting hired to the different types of jobs in the field. Consider it to be a sneak peek at the job. Job shadowing commitments may last as long as an entire summer or just one day or simply be an interview. Make sure to prepare in advance, especially if you only have a one-time opportunity available. Research the company, and the positions the company offers, and prepare a list of questions you are interested in having answered, such as education-level and qualification requirements, career trajectories, and job responsibilities and/or a list of subjects you would like more information on. Throughout this process, remember to search for information regarding the employees' personal perceptions. Consider how many years you will be working in this field. Finding a career in which you also find personal satisfaction is important in achieving a higher quality of life.

I encourage you to find time in your schedules, maybe during summer downtime, to find job-shadowing opportunities (Hello college career center!) and commit to putting aside time for job shadowing experiences. You may even find that during the early stages of your educational pursuits, job shadowing helps you decide which jobs you may not be interested in pursuing, narrowing down the field of choices to a more manageable list.

BUSINESS-BASED CERTIFICATES

Gaining a college education is the first step on the way to employment in the business sector. The business field is traditionally white collar, and white-collar fields usually require bachelor's degrees. Business and business-related degrees are the most sought-after degrees by veterans using their GI Bill. The Student Veterans of America (SVA), in its "National Veteran Education Success Tracker," states that veterans (using their Post-9/11 GI Bill) have earned 96,270 business, management, and marketing-related degrees. The next highest category, health professions, totaled 37,138 degrees.[22] So, how can you set yourself aside from an already packed playing field? Well, many veterans pursue advanced education (graduate degrees) to make them more marketable and more competitive on a broader scale. Certificates offer another option to help supplement résumés and diversify skills, especially if you are trying to demonstrate expertise in a specific area or a commitment to professional development. They may also help employees increase their earning potential.

There are several professional business certifications that are widely recognized in the business world. Remember that many different disciplines fall under the business umbrella, and there may be certifications specific to these fields. Some of these certifications are possible to tackle while you are still on active duty. For other certificates, you will need to meet civilian-sector work-experience requirements and/or specific education levels before being eligible to test for the certificate, which may mean transitioning from the service first. In this case, try to get all of your academic goals completed before separation as it will save your GI Bill benefits for graduate school and help you gain faster access to the workforce.

Check with the education and transition departments aboard the base where you are stationed. Some bases offer programs that are specific to certain locations and may help you gain translatable credentials. These programs might be sponsored through command dollars, promoted through transition programs, or provided through nonprofits. For example, there is a nonprofit (www.veteranstransitionsupport.org) at the Camp Pendleton Marine Corps Base in Southern California that offers free courses that can be great additions to résumés, through Wounded Warrior Battalion West and the Base Education Center located at the School of Infantry. Two of the courses offered, the OSHA ten-hour general safety course and the Lean Continuous Improvement Certification, are valuable civilian-sector certifications. The Lean course is a "system of tools used by the Toyota Motor Company to minimize waste in processes" and is "designed to help you explain to interviewers, employers, and employees how to use Lean methods to observe, document, problem solve, implement and sustain continuous improvement in Lean terms and Lean tools that companies value."[23]

If you are still on active duty, check with your local education center about the Credentialing Opportunities Online (COOL) program. The program covers the testing costs, but not the preparation costs, for the credentials. Each branch has a COOL program, but available opportunities, funding levels, and eligibility depend on the branch. Some of the credentials will be beneficial for those interested in pursuing business and business-related fields. For example, on the Marine Corps COOL site under the MOS of Leader, there are several valuable civilian-sector credentials that can boost your résumé, such as the Lean Six Sigma Green Belt, the Project Management Professional (PMP), and the Microsoft Office Specialist. All enlisted marines can test for certificates listed under the MOS of Leader but must also make sure that they meet the individual requirements of each credential. The Army has the MOS of Manager, under enlisted occupations, which holds these same credentials. Enlisted soldiers must have reached the rank of E-5 or above to be eligible, and soldiers must meet the requirements of each individual credential.

Now, on to the purpose of the COOL program. COOL aligns civilian-sector certificates to military occupations (MOS, rating, AFSC). The program has multiple purposes. For example, it helps service members during career counseling. If a service member is interested in staying within his or her military specialty after transitioning into the civilian sector, the site can be used to see which types of jobs fall within their realm of knowledge and skill base. Many of the certification requirements that are either needed or preferred can be found here. This can help a service member determine what he or she needs to achieve to be more competitive for employment upon transition. Nowadays, in the competitive work environment, just having military service and a military specialty is not sufficient. Service members need to go above and beyond their transition preparation in order to gain employment quickly. The best bet is to be recruited for a civilian position prior to transitioning off active duty, not after separation from the service, but that is a separate conversation.

COOL can also help service members find and obtain the "resources available to fill gaps between military training and civilian credentialing requirements" based upon civilian-sector requirements.[24] COOL also outlines the requirements for credentialing in each field. If you are in the Army or Marine Corps, always check under the MOS of Manager (Army) and Leader (United States Marine Corps [USMC]). These are other areas in which you may qualify.

"What's covered?" you ask. The test. So, for each of the certifications listed, there is information regarding who is eligible to pursue each credential and how to get the service branch to pay for the test and, potentially, the maintenance fees. Study materials for the tests are not covered; however, the Department of Defense has partnered with Safari Books Online (http://techbus.safaribooksonline.com/) to offer some study materials. Not all of the study materials will be on this site. Some of the tests have free resources, so check each certification carefully before paying for outside material, and don't forget military and community libraries as potential sources for study materials. Also, there are limited openings for service members to access this site. If the site denies you entrance, wait a few days and try again (as advised by the analysts who run the sites).

Here are the COOL branch websites:

- Marine Corps: https://www.cool.navy.mil/usmc/
- Navy: https://www.cool.navy.mil/
- Army: https://www.cool.army.mil/
- Air Force: https://afvec.langley.af.mil/afvec/Public/COOL/

The US Department of Labor CareerOneStop Credentials Center (https://www.careeronestop.org/Credentials/Toolkit/find-certifications -help.aspx#ansi) is a go-to site for those interested in obtaining the civilian-sector credentials they need to get noticed, demonstrate their hands-on knowledge, or advance their careers. The site is not difficult to use, and it allows users to search using broad or specific terms. A key at the bottom of the page gives the meaning of the icons next to the credentials. There is even an icon that denotes a relationship with military skills through the COOL programs. Spend time getting acquainted with this site as it will help you match your military occupation to specific credentials available to pursue in the civilian sector. Pay special attention to those marked with the hot pepper as they are considered to be in demand within the industry.

Let's discuss some of the civilian-sector certificates that may help you round out your résumé and demonstrate that you paid special attention to the demands of employers in the field. Remember, you should tailor each résumé you submit to the employer receiving it, so pay special attention to the job description and other information in the announcement.

Civilian-Sector Certificates

First covered will be professional certificates offered through university extension programs, then some popular credentials and certifications offered by professional associations. Most universities have an extension program, or extended-studies department. Extension programs offered by some universities allow you to earn a professional certificate from a reputable institution. Every university is different and diverse in its assortment of certificate programs. They are designed in conjunction with workforce-training needs and industry associations to meet basic criteria for skills training. Many of the certificates offered are highly valuable and widely recognized by employers.

Extension certificates are for specialized training that helps you build immediate skills, competencies, and the vocabulary you need to enter a career field; they can offer you a quality addition to an already-earned bachelor's degree to sharpen your skills and prepare you for a career path. Extension certificates are offered across the broad fields of business, law, technology, engineering, education, environment, arts and entertainment, life sciences, and more. These programs usually cost between $3,500 and

$6,000 each, are offered online over nine to twelve months, and are taught by instructors who work in jobs related to the professional certificate's subject matter. Usually the fees are levied by course, not by program, so you can essentially pay as you go. Hence, these certificate programs can offer students preparing for a professional career a high quality, inexpensive, and quick course(s), taught by industry experts, that results in immediately marketable skills, skills that employers seek. Consider that major universities such as the University of California, Irvine (https://ce.uci.edu/), and Notre Dame University (https://www.notredameonline.com/) have robust extension programs. UC–Irvine, in particular, collaborates deeply with its regional employment community to determine which certifications offer the training needed for the local economy. UC–Irvine has secured reciprocity agreements with other universities where transfer credit from extension coursework will work toward a degree. Here is how they present that information to prospective extension students:

> UCI Division of Continuing Education partners with a number of universities to provide you a "next step" on your educational pathway. We have articulation agreements with the universities listed. These schools accept coursework from select UCI Division of Continuing Education certificate programs as credit toward specific degree programs.[25]

These programs span the workforce and may include traditional or emerging fields. The following subject areas/programs relate to the realm of business.

- Cybersecurity
- Data Science
- Human Resources
- Organizational Communication and Leadership
- Supply Chain Management
- Digital Marketing
- Meeting and Event Management
- Facilities Management
- Emergency and Disaster Management
- Applied Accounting and the Registered Tax Preparer's Certificate
- Personal Financial Planning
- Health Care Analytics

- Lean Healthcare Specialization
- Public Policy and Planning
- Regulatory Affairs and Compliance

Adding certificates to your résumé can definitely broaden your appeal to potential employers.

Consider researching universities near your hometown or target geographic locations to learn about local extension programs. Again, usually these programs are online, so if there is a university you'd like to have on your résumé, you can typically enroll to attend online, but verify with the institution first. Usually, the programs do not require a college degree as a prerequisite to attendance, but they are designed with degree holders in mind. Additionally, you do not have to enroll in the university nor go through their admissions department since the programs are meant to augment, not eliminate, a college degree. To attend, typically you simply enroll online, pay the fee, and start the classes at the beginning of the semester for which you enrolled. Always speak with an advisor before paying, as many of these programs offer discounts toward the tuition for active-duty personnel and veterans.

University programs are carefully designed in partnerships with regional employers and professional associations and hit the mark for delivering quality training at a reasonable price and time commitment. Be sure to investigate the programs available in your area as you research developing and transferring marketable skills into new occupational pathways.

There are specific credentials worth noting that are highly regarded, popular, and earned directly through professional organizations to consider as alternatives to university extension certificates. Two of these highly regarded credentials are in human resources (HR); the Professional in Human Resources (PHR) and the Society for Human Resource Management Certified Professional (SHRM-CP). The PHR is offered through the HR Certification Institute (https://www.hrci.org/), and the SHRM-CP is offered through the Society for Human Resource Management (https://www.shrm.org/certification/pages/default.aspx). These agencies oversee the credentialing process and grant the credentials to those who qualify. Both credentials help employees working within HR distinguish themselves from others.

The PHR is a credential for those who have some experience in HR and are in the early stages of establishing themselves. According to the HR Certification Institute:

The PHR demonstrates your mastery of the technical and operational aspects of HR management, including U.S. laws and regulations. The PHR is for the HR professional who has experience with program implementation, has a tactical/logistical orientation, is accountable to another HR professional within the organization, and has responsibilities that focus on the HR department rather than the whole organization.[26]

The Society for Human Resource Management (SHRM) offers the certified professional (CP) and the senior certified professional (SCP) credentials. The CP is the starting point, as the SCP requires advanced experience. According to the SHRM, "More than 5,000 employers are seeking SHRM credential-holders every month. The SHRM-CP and SHRM-SCP credentials are based on the current HR landscape, focusing on the competencies and knowledge HR professionals need to lead in today's business community."[27]

In some cases, the SHRM and PHR may be more valued than a degree. According to Catherine Blue, HR business partner with IKEA,

HR credentials, such as the ones obtained through HRCI or SHRM, validate a candidate's practical and ongoing knowledge and experience. In order to recertify your credentials, you must be up to date with current practices and laws. A degree demonstrates education in the field. You can get a degree in Human Resources without having any experience, but it is imperative to have experience in order to receive professional HR credentials. This difference is why many value credentials over a degree. However, having both would make you most attractive to an employer.[28]

Both demonstrate active experience and working knowledge in the field of HR. Determining which credential is best for you might require more in-depth research. These credentials let employers know that you are up to date with the current laws and have placed emphasis on demonstrating your ability to stay current with the trends. That does not mean that I would forgo pursuing a relevant degree. Think about how you can make yourself as competitive as possible. For most, this means achieving an applicable degree and the certification. If you are still on active duty or recently transitioned, check out the Syracuse University IVMF program for preparation and test funding for the PHR and other credentials offered through the Professional in Human Resources organization (https://onward2opportunity-vctp.org/course-offerings/).

Many service members find that their military experience translates into the supply chain management sector. The Navy rating of Logistics Specialist (LS) and the Marine Corps MOS 3043 Supply Chain and Material Management Specialist are two examples. For those of you who want to stay in this sector upon transition from the service, check out the following three certifications: Certified Supply Chain Professional (CSCP) through the Association for Operations Management (APICS); the SCPro through the Council of Supply Chain Management Professionals (CSCMP); the Certified Professional in Supply Management (CPSM) through the Institute for Supply Management (ISM).

The CSCP demonstrates mastery of best practices in the field, common terminology, and available resources. The certification has three modules that encompass supply chain design, planning and execution, and improvements and best practices. The CSCP is a solid credential for those looking into a broad spectrum of supply chain functions; think global supply chain management. The requirements for eligibility to take the exam are steep. APICS requires that applicants have five or more years of experience or a bachelor's degree and two years of experience. If you do not meet these parameters, you may consider another credential that APICS awards, the Certification in Production and Inventory Management (CPIM). The CPIM is designed for those who work in inventory management. The CPIM requires a high school diploma and two or more years of experience in the field. Earning the CPIM also qualifies you to take the CSCP. So, if you do not have a bachelor's degree yet, this is another route you can take to earning the CSCP credential. Many military jobs relate to this credential. For example, the Marine Corps COOL site lists fifteen MOSs that qualify for the CPIM.

Now, if you are thinking about taking these exams, you will learn that they are not cheap. The CSCP exam is $915 and the CPIM is $645. If you are still on active duty, check the COOL site for your occupational specialty and see if you can get it covered through the program. If not, check to see (on the COOL site) if the GI Bill can fund it, but be careful with this option as it will pull down on your GI Bill benefits.

The SCPro through the Council of Supply Chain Management Professionals (CSCMP) is another highly valued supply chain management credential. There are three levels to this credential the CSCMP SCPro Level One happens to fall under the MOSs of 92Y Unit Supply Specialist and 92A Automated Logistical Specialist on the Army COOL site. Army COOL describes the credential as "an entry-level credential for supply chain professionals."[29] According to the CSCMP (2017), the SCPro credentialing process "validates an individual's ability to strategically assess business challenges and effectively implement supply chain improvements through the analysis of real-world case studies and developing a comprehensive project plan to achieve results such as a positive ROI."[30] To be eligible for the multiple-choice exam, a candidate must have at minimum a bachelor's degree or possess four years relevant experience. Relevant experience includes "procurement, planning and scheduling, manufacturing and service operations, logistics, inventory, warehousing, and supply chain management."[31] The CPSM credential is listed by the U.S. Department of Labor CareerOneStop Credentials Center (https://www.career onestop.org/Credentials/Toolkit/find-certifications-help.aspx#ansi) as in-demand. This means that "the certification is frequently mentioned in online job postings."[32] In fact, a quick search on Indeed.com at the time of writing returned five pages of jobs available in California that listed this credential as desired or preferred.

According to the Navy COOL site, the CPSM "is for supply chain and procurement professionals with skills in areas such as finance, supplier relationship management, organizational global strategy, and risk compliance."[33] Heavy emphasis is placed on procurement. This credential requires applicants to pass three tests: Foundation of Supply Management, Effective Supply Management Performance, and Leadership in Supply Management. Candidates must have "three years of full-time supply management experience (nonclerical, nonsupport) and a regionally accredited bachelor's degree, or five years of full-time supply management experience (nonclerical, nonsupport)."[34] Take special note that the organization requires degrees to be from regionally accredited schools. This means that attending schools with national accreditation will not enable you to sit for the test. For more information on this topic, see the chapter on school and program accreditation.

Many of you have probably already heard about the Lean and the Six Sigma certificates. Both are highly valued in the civilian workforce and can help you be more competitive. While originally designed for manufacturing, these two tactics have moved beyond strictly being used in this discipline. Customer support, management, and delivery are just a sample of the areas in which these two methods can be used. Both aim for the same goal, eliminate waste, and create more efficient practices/production, but they go about achieving that goal in different manners.

Six Sigma focuses on identifying and removing the waste, and Lean focuses on process improvement. Purdue University defines the process of Six Sigma as "monitoring the supply chain for defects, identifying issues, and solving them as effectively as possible" and the Lean process as being "focused on eliminating waste, providing maximum value to customers with the lowest possible amount of investment."[35] So Six Sigma works to improve the existing process, and Lean increases productivity by minimizing waste. The authors have sent many service members to complete the Lean and the Lean Six Sigma credentials, and all have said they were satisfied with the results. It should also be pointed out that all have stated that the processes used are similar to the processes used by the military branches, but attending the courses helped them gain the civilian-sector language they needed to demonstrate this knowledge on résumés and during interviews.

Plug either credential into Indeed.com and you will find a wealth of positions that prefer applicants to have knowledge of these principles. But, which one should you pick? Ultimately, conducting research into your chosen field first. If one credential is more prevalent than the other, this would offer some indication. A search on Indeed.com demonstrated that both credentials were in demand. The CareerOneStop Credentials Center also lists the Six Sigma Green Belt as an in-demand certification, but call the HR departments of the companies you are interested in working for and ask if the company has a preference. Here's a crazy thought, why not get both? At the very least, you should try to complete whichever one is free to you if you are still on active duty. A quick search on the Marine Corps and Navy COOL sites brought up the Six Sigma Green Belt under the MOS/rating of Leader. So, if you have six months or more left on contract, and are eligible for the test, you may want to give it a shot. Call the local base education center to get more information on the COOL program. If you are within six months of separating from the service, have recently separated from the service, or are a military spouse, the Syracuse University's Institute for Veterans and Military Families (IVMF, https:// ivmf.syracuse.edu/) may potentially help you prepare (online classes) and pay for (one certificate test for free) the Six Sigma Green Belt (https:// ivmf.syracuse.edu/our-programs/).

Since we are discussing the IVMF program, the Project Management Professional (PMP) credential is also an option. The PMP exam can potentially be paid for through the military (COOL) program or through IVMF. The trick with IVMF is that only one certificate exam can be funded, but all the classes can be utilized for training. IVMF may also offer you another chance to retest for free if you are not successful in passing while using the COOL program.

The PMP credential is highly valuable in the civilian sector. Need more proof? Conduct an Indeed.com search. A quick search at the time this chapter was written produced ten pages of jobs located in and around Dallas (just pick a point to search) that listed the PMP as preferred or required in the announcement. There are two different eligibility pathways for approval to sit for the exam:

1. Option 1

   - Secondary degree (high school diploma, associate degree or the global equivalent)
   - 7,500 hours leading and directing projects
   - Thirty-five hours of project management education

2. Option 2

   - Four-year degree
   - 4,500 hours leading and directing projects
   - Thirty-five hours of project management education[36]

Notice that there is a required amount of project management education that must be completed for eligibility to sit for the exam. The online or classroom exam preparation training offered by Project Management

Training Institute (https://www.4pmti.com/) will suffice to meet the requirement, so will the online training offered through the IVMF program. The training courses offered through PMTI are expensive, plus they are not covered by the active-duty Tuition Assistance (TA) program. If you do not want to wait until you are within six months of separating from the service, or a veteran, many large universities also offer the training in an online format; however, most of the school programs award continuing education units which means they are not covered by TA. The cheapest program offered by a school that the authors could find was through California State Polytechnic University, Pomona, at around $1,500 (https://www.cpp.edu/~ceu/professional-development/courses-and-certificates/project-managment/project-management-professional-certificate.shtml). For more information on programs that offer qualifying contact hours, check the PMI website (https://www.pmi.org/).

The PMP is globally recognized. This may appeal to those of you who are thinking about a career that offers you more mobility or intend to study abroad (see chapter 4). In other words, if you want to work and travel abroad, the PMP might offer you a gateway to this goal. PMI's Project Management Salary Survey (July 2017) documented that, based on the organization's research, the median salary of PMP certified professionals in the United States was approximately $112,000.[37] PMP certification can benefit veterans who plan to work in many different career fields, such as IT, business, construction, finance, and research.

Retired Naval Submarine Officer, and current professor of computer studies and information technology (CSIT) at MiraCosta College, Rick Cassoni, states:

The PMP Certification was in demand when I first achieved the certification ten years ago. I am excited to see that demand is even higher today. Why, well, because projects are hard and the PMP provides proven methodologies. As this book says those of us with military backgrounds have been following project lifecycles our entire time in the military. The PMP training and certification process was great for honing and improving the knowledge and experience I gained in the Navy allowing me to transfer this skillset to industry as well. As an IBM Federal Senior Cloud Computing Architect, we always sought to save customers costs and/or solve hard datacenter problems. Many times, this evolved around visibility, control, and automation. One must first know all of the assets in their datacenters down to every last physical computer, virtual machine, cloud resource, and container (such as Docker) image. Once this was achieved, we strived to get control of resources including patching, determining if something was wrong with a workload, and optimizing computing loads for peak performance. Our ultimate goal was to automate these processes to save costs and being more efficient to better serve the end users. Throughout this visibility, control, and automation process, I always leaned on my project lifecycle knowledge experience and formal PMI/PMP training to better and more effectively serve my customers. The project lifecycle, especially when taking into account up and coming methodologies such as Agile Scrum, are being implemented in datacenters and any other project such as construction for efficient lifecycles. PMP is a great certification that will open many doors for those entering the workforce or shifting careers.[38]

The information that professor Cassoni wrote about demonstrates how diverse the PMP credential can be within different industries, including the IT industry. Some of you may be considering IT management as a likely option after completion of your service, but all of you considering management positions should spend more time researching credentials that will round out your résumé, give you an edge over others competing for the same positions, and support your quest for more knowledge.

Let's return to the discussion regarding the PMP. The focus of the credential is on a project life cycle and its Process Groups. There are five groups:

1. Initiating
2. Planning
3. Executing
4. Monitoring
5. Closing

These terms sound familiar to many service members the authors counsel regarding this credential. The process is very similar in nature to the manner in which the military operates, especially within some of the officer training programs such as the Marine Corps' Expeditionary Warfare and Command and Staff College programs, as a heavy emphasis is placed on organizational leadership.

If you do not meet the eligibility parameters for the PMP, consider the Certified Associate in Project Management (CAPM). The CAPM requires less hours of project experience than the PMP, just 1,500 hours, and a high school diploma or an associate degree. The other option for gaining eligibility to sit for the CAPM is to acquire twenty-three hours of project management education by exam time. The CAPM is also less expensive than the PMP at $300 and can be taken online on your computer while your proctor is offsite, but it is also newer than the PMP and holds less weight.

If you intend to pursue construction management or a small-business or franchise ownership, take a look at training in the field of occupational safety. The Occupational Safety and Health Administration (OSHA) offers many different kinds of training, with the OSHA ten-hour general safety course being the starting point. The training may help you run a business better and maintain a better environment for your workers as it seeks to help employers provide a safer worksite by preventing injuries and illness.

According to the OSHA website, "Safety is good business. An effective safety and health program can save $4 to $6 for every $1 invested. It's the right thing to do, and doing it right pays off in lower costs, increased productivity, and higher employee morale."[39] And, "Protecting workers also makes good business sense. Accidents and injuries are more expensive than many realize. Costs mount up quickly. But substantial savings in workers' compensation and lost workdays are possible when injuries and illnesses decline."[40]

The OSHA ten-hour general safety course card can be completed online or face-to-face. The price varies. Online courses can run around $100. Some community colleges offer the class in a face-to-face format as well, such as Chabot-Las Positas Community College District in California, but the classes are usually fairly expensive. Remember, as mentioned earlier in this chapter, if you are stationed, visit, or live in the Southern California area, you can get the OSHA ten-hour general safety course for free through the Veterans Transition Support nonprofit located aboard Camp Pendleton.

Don't have time to complete a full master's degree in business administration (MBA)? Consider the mini-MBA. Mini-MBAs are offered online or face-to-face. They can take a few months or up to a year to complete, and cost varies greatly. Schools such as Pepperdine, Harvard, Rutgers, Kennesaw State, Missouri State, and Loyola Universities all offer mini-MBAs. These programs allow for flexibility in business-based learning. Those who do not have an undergraduate background in business but hold business-related positions, or those looking to move into the field, can test the waters for significantly less time and financial input than for a full MBA. Plus, a mini-MBA certificate program may help align skills to a new career. Courses often consist of topics such as accounting, marketing, law, finance, economics, strategy, and project management. These programs do not typically award transferable college credit, although some do, so TA is not always an option. This means that available payment is typically going to be out of pocket, but some of the programs are built so that the credit is transferable into a full MBA program. Oftentimes, in these cases, credit may be converted into semester or quarter hours. In this case, they may be approved for TA. Check with the closest base education center for help. Some may also be approved for GI Bill benefits. If paying out of pocket, consider the cost-to-payoff ratio before applying.

Remember that certifications in the world of business usually do not take the place of experience and education. Consider them as items to demonstrate the depth of your knowledge and your commitment to learning and staying abreast of trends in the field. They are supplementary in nature in most cases, but not all, and may help you round out your résumé. In other fields, such as health care and IT, they may be mandatory. For those of you just completing your business-related education, certificates may give you a way to help your résumé stand out against other applicants'. You may even want to consider certificates that are broader in nature, such as Microsoft courses and certificates. They can often be completed online and at proctor centers relatively inexpensively. The COOL systems have some Microsoft certifications available. Be careful if you take this route, especially if your military branch restricts the number of COOL certifications it will fund. Check the local community college to see if it offers preparatory courses to help pass exams. And, remember that demonstration of computer-based skills is just one extra way to round out your résumé. Other options such as internships and volunteering may be helpful as well.

SYRACUSE UNIVERSITY INSTITUTE FOR VETERANS AND MILITARY FAMILIES (IVMF)

Syracuse University, in partner with JPMorgan Chase & Co., has several programs available through the IVMF (https://ivmf.syracuse.edu/) to assist transitioning Post-9/11 service members with future career plans depending upon their interests and pursuits. Many of the programs consist of free on-line courses that users can access from any location at any time to promote veteran preparedness and understanding of the civilian sector. Other courses are offered in a face-to-face format that lasts roughly two weeks, and they are now available in several different locations. IVMF offers courses for veterans, active duty, active-duty spouses, and disabled veterans.

The programs currently offered by IVMF include:

- EBV: Entrepreneurship Bootcamp for Veterans with Disabilities
- EBV-Accelerate: Entrepreneurship Bootcamp for Veterans with Disabilities that is focused on growth
- EBV-F: Entrepreneurship Bootcamp for Veterans' Families (caregivers and family members)
- V-WISE: Veteran Women Igniting the Spirit of Entrepreneurship for veteran women, female active duty, and female family members
- E&G: Operation Endure & Grow for guard and reserve members and family
- B2B: Operation Boots to Business: From Service to Startup for transitioning service members
- Onward to Opportunity (O2O): Available to transitioning service members and spouses

Entrepreneurship Bootcamp for Veterans with Disabilities (EBV)

http://ebv.vets.syr.edu/

"The aim of the program is to open the door to economic opportunity for our veterans by developing their competencies in the steps and activities associated with creating and sustaining an entrepreneurial venture" (http://ebv.vets.syr.edu/veterans/). Syracuse University, Texas A&M, Purdue University, UCLA, University of Connecticut, Louisiana State University, Florida State University, Saint Joseph's University, and Cornell University currently participate in EBV. EBV promotes long-term success for qualified veterans by teaching them how to create and sustain their entrepreneurial ventures (http://whitman.syr.edu/ebv/). All costs associated with EBV are covered by the program, including travel and lodging.

Entrepreneurship Bootcamp for Veterans with Disabilities-Accelerate (EBV-Accelerate)

http://ebv.vets.syr.edu/about/ebv-accelerate/

Focused on growth, the three-phase program tackles "topics such as the financial, management, marketing and strategic planning challenges established businesses face."[41] The program is meant to "propel their business to the next phase: sustainable growth." Program topics include the following:

- Acquiring growth funding
- Rebranding for expansion
- Determining a sustainable growth rate
- Establishing partnerships, managing cash flow

Attendees participate in a two-week online course and a three-day residency. Not all costs associated with this course are free. EBV-Accelerate is open to veteran business owners who:

- Have been in business for three years or more
- Employee five or more people
- Served on active-duty and received an honorable discharge

Entrepreneurship Bootcamp for Veterans' Families (EBV-F)

https://ivmf.syracuse.edu/veteran-and-family-resources/starting-growing
-a-business/ebvf/

Entrepreneurship Bootcamp for Veterans' Families is offered at Florida State University College of Business. The cost-free (including travel and lodging) four-week online and four-day face-to-face program assists family members in their pursuit to launch and maintain small businesses. Participants learn about "cutting-edge, experiential training in entrepreneurship and small business management," while integrating "training in entrepreneurship with caregiver and family issues, positioning participants to launch and grow a small business in a way that is complementary to other family responsibilities."[42] Eligible spouses include first-degree family members and the surviving spouse or adult child (of a service member who served in the military post-9/11).

Veteran Women Igniting the Spirit of Entrepreneurship (V-WISE)

http://whitman.syr.edu/vwise/

V-WISE is a joint venture with the U.S. SBA. The program helps female veterans along the entrepreneurship and small business pathway by arming them with savvy business skills that enable them to turn business ideas into growing ventures. Business planning, marketing, accounting, operations, and human resources are covered. The three-phase approach consists of a fifteen-day online course teaching the basic skills pertaining to being an entrepreneur, a three-day conference with two tracks (for startups or those already in business), and delivery of a comprehensive listing packet that details the community-level resources available to participants.

Eligible participants are honorably separated female veterans from any branch of the military from any time. Female spouses or partners of veteran business owners are eligible as well. Hotel rooms and taxes are covered, but other fees apply, such as travel.

Operation Endure & Grow

http://vets.syr.edu/education/endure-grow/

Operation Endure & Grow is a free online training program open to National Guard, reservists, and their family members. The program has two tracks, one for startups and the other for those who have been in business for more than three years. The tracks are designed to assist participants in creating a new business and all related fundamentals, or to help an operating business stimulate growth.

Operation Boots to Business (B2B)

https://ivmf.syracuse.edu/veteran-and-family-resources/starting-growing
-a-business/boots-to-business/

B2B is part of the Transition Readiness Program. The program is a one-week process that you complete prior to separation from the service. B2B is one of the additional two-day courses that you can select to complete, along with the Accessing Higher Education and the Career Exploration and Planning Track. B2B was developed by the SBA and the Syracuse University Institute for Veterans and Military Families, and they partner on instruction. Attendees learn about topics such as business ownership, tactics, feasibility of concepts, available start-up financing, and available technical assistance. There is an online, follow-up, eight-week course available upon completion of the two-day track that delves deeper into the process, assists in creating a business plan, and connects attendees to business mentors.

Onward to Opportunity (O2O)

http://onward2opportunity-vctp.org/course-offerings/

This program exists in a face-to-face and online format. It is open to active duty who are within six months of separation from the service, veterans who served at least 180 days and received an honorable discharge, and spouses of active-duty personnel, veterans (including the National Guard), or active member of the National Guard. O2O offers numerous classes for career training and preparation. Many of the courses lead to high-demand industry-level certifications. Participants also become Syracuse University students and receive non-credit-awarding certificates upon completion. Certificates include proficiency in subject areas such as business management, with courses offered in project management, to include the Project Management Professional (PMP) certification and the Certified Associate in Project Management (CAPM), and the Six Sigma Green Belt. Other areas of interest include human resources and the Professional in Human Resources (PHR) or the Senior Professional in Human Resources (SPHR). There are also many IT sector options, such as the Comp TIA (Server+, Network+, and A+), Oracle Database 11G, CCNA with CCENT certification, that might be interesting for those of you who are considering IT management as a career field.

Chapter Four

International Business Degrees and Study Abroad

Some of you have been stationed abroad or traveled extensively while in the service, which may have given you insight into different cultures. Ever consider harnessing this knowledge for a career in international business? If you are considering it, I would also recommend that you consider studying business abroad. This may be done by attending a university in the United States that offers a study-abroad program or by attending a foreign university. Both pathways are possible under the Post-9/11 GI Bill. This chapter demonstrates some of the available opportunities.

The following topics will be covered in this chapter:

- U.S. Colleges and Universities with Study Abroad Programs
- Foreign Colleges and Universities with Programs Taught in English
- WEAMS Institution Search

INTRODUCTION

International business is an intriguing field of study and also sometimes overlooked as an opportunity. Many Americans do not travel. In fact, only 42 percent of Americans hold U.S. passports, a figure that has increased in recent years due to changes in the law requiring passports or passport cards for travel to Mexico and Canada.[1] The number of college students enrolled in foreign-language courses has been declining; a study conducted in 2015 found that only 7 percent of U.S. college students were enrolled in foreign language courses.[2] According to the

Modern Language Institute, "foreign language enrollments dropped 9.2 percent from fall 2013 to fall 2016."[3] So, many Americans do not travel, nor do they learn foreign languages, and completion of high school foreign-language courses, which was once required for admission to most colleges, is now the exception rather than the rule.

Now, as service members, many of you have traveled abroad, sometimes multiple times. Some of you were stationed abroad on military bases or working at U.S. embassies or consulates. Many of you speak a foreign language, had foreign-language training, and were offered the opportunity to enroll in introductory language courses in host countries; some of you even spent many months at the Defense Language Institute. This means that you have an advantage in this area as foreign-language skills, and foreign-immersion experiences can be an asset for many companies and organizations operating in the business community.

Many military personnel and military spouses have an advantage in foreign language skills, often merely by circumstances of origin. Many active-duty personnel and veterans are from immigrant families and grew up speaking their parents' languages at home. The National Immigration Forum states that 511,000 veterans were foreign born as of 2016. This figure includes citizens and noncitizens, which works out to about 3 percent of the nearly nineteen million veterans nationwide.[4] The number increases if you add in the foreign-born military spouses and those who grew up in immigrant families.

For those of you who skipped foreign language classes, many foreign colleges offer language immersion programs, especially during the summer. The Study Abroad organization lists some schools offering such programs on its website: https://www.studyabroad.com/intensive -language-worldwide. There are also many small, private schools located in foreign countries that teach the language. In fact, one of the authors of this book attended one of these schools while she lived abroad in Istanbul, Turkey. It was inexpensive and also a great way to learn the basic building blocks of the language. The rest came with practice and full immersion.

If you are planning to attend college to earn a degree, many community colleges and state and private universities offer study abroad programs. The following is a small sample.

University of California, San Diego (UCSD)

https://studyabroad.ucsd.edu/

UCSD's website has information on six study abroad programs, five of which are specific to either UCSD or the University of California (UC) system as a whole. Some of the programs require students to attend foreign schools, where they are taught by foreign professors; other programs are taught and led by UCSD professors. You earn credit, either UC-based or transfer credit, during most of the programs. Programs are offered in Africa and the Middle East, the Americas, Europe, and Asia and Oceania. Consider studying in countries like Ghana, Morocco, Argentina, Brazil, Australia, China, Sweden, or Ireland. Yes, study abroad can even include English-speaking countries! UCSD majors that have study abroad options include, but are not limited to, business administration, economics, global and international studies, public and global health, and linguistics. The website is very thorough, offering detailed information on the different programs, estimating cost of attending, outlining financial aid and scholarship opportunities, and even giving information on how to prepare for the Peace Corps. UCSD has also developed internships in thirty countries and in fifty majors. This means that if you are interested in UCSD, you may have the opportunity to study, live, and/or work abroad, all during your pursuit of a degree.

State University of New York (SUNY)

https://www.suny.edu/studyabroad/; https://www.suny.edu/attend/academics/study-abroad/

The SUNY consortium offers study abroad, exchange, and SUNY-faculty-led programs. Some of the programs are also open to students attending other institutions. The programs typically require participating students to have a minimum GPA of 2.5. Academic references are also required during the application process. The SUNY consortium offers programs in over sixty countries.

University of Alabama (UA)

http://international.ua.edu/educationabroad/

This is a well-developed site offering information on the programs, financial aid and scholarships, and visa research as well as information from past participants. The school also hosts events that teach students about studying abroad and helps them decipher course equivalencies and determine visa requirements for specific programs. There are several different types of programs available, including faculty-led exchange programs, UA-affiliate and direct-enroll programs, and non-UA affiliated programs. Faculty-led programs are taught by UA faculty; students receive credit from the hosting department, travel as a group, and must have a minimum 2.2 GPA to be eligible. These programs take place in the summer. The UA exchange programs are considered immersion programs, as participating students spend one to two semesters studying at partnership foreign schools. Language requirements may vary based on the programs, and students must have a minimum 3.0 GPA to be eligible. UA-affiliate and direct-enroll programs are provided through third parties. Students pay tuition and fees to the host provider in this program, not to UA, but are awarded credit in a pass/fail manner at UA when they return. Non-UA affiliated programs are provided through third parties. These are not UA-vetted programs; hence, other areas of concern may arise, such as scholarship money and awarding of credit. Programs take place in countries such as South Korea, Germany, France, Taiwan, Australia, England, Scotland, Italy, Belgium, Denmark, the Netherlands, and Japan.

Washington Community College Consortium for Study Abroad (WCCCSA)

http://wcccsa.com/

Sixteen Washington State community colleges banded together to create the WCCCSA program. Faculty from these colleges facilitate the programs, but language and culture in the host nation are taught by local instructors. Credits and grades are posted by the students' home institution. Programs occur during the fall, summer, spring, and winter. Students must have a minimum 2.5 GPA, have completed a minimum of twelve credits at their home school, have a valid passport, be at least eighteen years old, and submit an essay and two letters of recommendation. To find out more about the program, review the website and meet with the WCCCSA campus coordinator at the community college you are attending. Upcoming program groups are traveling to Costa Rica, Morocco, the Netherlands, Scotland, Spain, and Germany.

There are some advantages of studying at foreign colleges or participating in internships in foreign countries. Foreign study can stand out on a résumé as an experience that can make the job seeker stand out among job candidates. There are also opportunities for networking with citizens and corporations of foreign countries. For those who would like to go into franchising with the idea of expanding into foreign countries, international study can help a business owner become familiar with local laws and customs. For example, some countries require American or other foreign businesses to partner with a citizen in that country or a company headquartered in the country.

Foreign study can demonstrate to students where potential problems with translation of ideas and language may occur. Stories abound of translation blunders; for example, when KFC expanded to China, there was a blunder in the translation of "finger-licking good." Initially the phrase was translated into Chinese as "eat your fingers off."[5] When Coors beer expanded to Spain, the company used the tagline "Turn It Loose." When the company attempted to translate the phrase into Spanish, the result was "suffering from diarrhea."[6]

Studying abroad can also help familiarize students with local customs and culture. For example, the now famous blunder that the Disney Corporation made with its Euro Disney Park in France. Initially, no alcohol was served with meals, which was unconscionable in a country where wine is routinely served with meals. No one had studied French dining habits. In the United States, tourists visiting Disney parks do not eat their meals at set hours. That was not the case in France. Disney found that the French customarily eat their meals at set hours during the day and also found its restaurants overwhelmed during customary meal hours. Someone who studied international business in France could have helped the Disney Corporation avoid some major problems well in advance and save the company significant amounts of money required to fix the errors.

There are so many details people learn just by spending time in a foreign country. How about facial expressions and hand gestures? One of the authors of this book lived in the Philippines for four years during his time in the military. He stated that once, in a bar, he was asked if he wanted to buy a round of beer for his fifteen Filipino friends who had just arrived. He raised his eyebrows in surprise, and the bartender wandered off before he could answer. He found out, after buying fifteen people beers, that raising eyebrows in the Philippines is a way to answer yes. It was an expensive lesson in nonverbal communication for him! Another such experience was during a visit to the Arab nation of Bahrain. He was nearly arrested for giving the thumbs-up to a police officer who was gesturing to him to leave a sensitive area. In Arab countries, the thumbs-up is considered to be a rude and insulting gesture. Just think of the problems in communication that could result for someone unfamiliar with local customs, especially when pursuing a business proposal in a country like Saudi Arabia!

There are many subjects you can study while attending school abroad. A good source of top international business degrees is the annual listing from *U.S. News* (https://www.usnews.com/best-colleges/rankings/business -international). Included in the list are both public and private universities. One such school is San Diego State University, a public university listed as twelfth in recent rankings. There are three major components to its baccalaureate degree program in international business: academics, study abroad, and internships (http://ib.sdsu.edu/index.html):

- Academics: Students complete two emphases, one in foreign language and one in regional/cultural studies.
- Study Abroad: All students spend a semester abroad in their region and language of emphasis, as well as business specialization. A list of available universities for the semester abroad includes schools located in Europe, Asia (including China and Vietnam), the Middle East (United Arab Emirates only), Latin America (including Mexico, Central America, and South America), the Caribbean (including Cuba), Africa, Canada, Australia, and New Zealand.[7]
- Internships: Internships are available locally, across the United States, and internationally, which is especially beneficial for those who want complete foreign-language immersion as part of the internship.

Another example is Florida International University, a state-supported school that was listed seventh in the rankings from *U.S. News*.[8] The school has short-term faculty-led study abroad programs. It also has study abroad options through universities located overseas. Like some other schools, Florida International University requires completion of foreign language courses to graduate. Any student who is a native Spanish speaker who wants to use Spanish to satisfy the language requirement must enroll in special classes for bilingual speakers without formal Spanish training.

There are many college and universities in foreign countries with business-degree programs, including U.S.-based colleges with satellite campuses overseas. Study in a foreign nation can be a way to learn a great deal about international culture and business. The GI Bill, both Montgomery and Post-9/11, can be used at overseas colleges. The full tuition is not always covered, so veterans should contact the colleges for more information. In 2019, the maximum GI Bill tuition payment to a foreign school was $24,476.79 per year. The Post-9/11 GI Bill also provides a housing allowance based on the payment rate for a military E-5 with dependents and is based on the U.S. zip code for the fifty states, District of Columbia, and U.S. territories of Puerto Rico, the U.S. Virgin Islands, Guam, and American Samoa. The housing allowance for all countries that are not U.S. territories is not equivalent to the E-5 housing allowance for foreign countries. Instead, it is an average of the housing allowance for the forty-eight contiguous states. In 2019, the foreign housing allowance rate under the Post-9/11 GI Bill was $1,789.00 per month, which may not be enough to pay the rent in many countries. Also bear in mind that the housing allowance is not paid over any school break in the country where you are attending school. Many countries do not have school breaks that coincide with summer and other holiday breaks in the United States. An example is the University of Southern Australia, which has two major breaks. Typically, there is a mid-year break of over two weeks in July and an end-of-year break from December through February.[9] Of course, the Australian summer is December through February since it is in the Southern Hemisphere where the seasons are reversed. At University College Utrecht in the Netherlands, the longest break is the two months coinciding with the Christmas season. In any event, even those with the GI Bill should plan to have some other means to pay expenses. Prospective students should check with the foreign schools to see if there are any special programs available to help foreign students pay expenses, including authorized work programs. Yes, in many countries you may be allowed to work a certain number of hours per week. If you are studying international business of any sort, you would be wise to take advantage of this option. But, remember, anyone truly serious about pursuing degrees in foreign lands would be well advised to accumulate some savings beforehand.

Going to college in an English-speaking country certainly avoids the need to learn another language in order to make it through degree programs. There are many fine colleges and universities in Canada, the United Kingdom (England, Scotland, Wales, and Northern Ireland), Ireland, Australia, and New Zealand that accept the GI Bill.

The British Council is the United Kingdom's international organization for cultural relations and educational opportunities. Its Study-UK website has extensive information on college and university programs of study in England, Scotland, Wales, and Northern Ireland: https://study-uk.british council.org/. On the website, you can search for different colleges and universities and programs of study. Useful information is posted on visa requirements, cost of education, and budgeting recommendations.

The government of Australia encourages students from around the world to study at Australian colleges and universities and provides useful information on the website Study in Australia: https://www.studyinaustralia .gov.au/english/home. Despite having a population of only twenty-three million, Australia has the third highest number of international students, behind only the United States and the United Kingdom.[10] The government of Australia even budgets 200 million Australian dollars (156 million U.S. dollars) annually for scholarships intended for foreign students attending college in Australia. Information is provided on visa requirements and accommodations. There is even an inexpensive option called "homestay," which gives the students the opportunity to stay with a family in their home. Students on a visa are actually allowed to work up to forty hours every two weeks while courses are in session and for unlimited hours during school breaks.

The New Zealand government has its own Study in New Zealand website: https://www.studyinnewzealand.govt.nz/. It includes information on choosing what to study, entrance requirements, planning a budget, tuition, applying for a student visa, and scholarships available for overseas students. New Zealand allows students to work up to twenty hours a week while courses are in session and full time during holidays. More information can be found here: https://www.studyinnewzealand.govt.nz/live-work/.

Enterprise Ireland is the Irish state agency responsible for promotion of Irish higher education institutions overseas; it maintains an informational website on study in Ireland: http://www.educationinireland.com/en/. Ireland is another nation that allows foreign students to work: up to twenty hours a week during class terms and forty hours a week during school breaks.

Canada, of course, is a bilingual nation of English and French. Most Canadians who speak French as their primary language live in the province of Quebec. English is the primary language of most of the other Canadian provinces and territories. The Canadian government provides information on higher education in Canada at: http://www.cic.gc.ca/ ENGLISH/study/index.asp. Canada is another nation that allows foreign students to work while attending school and during school breaks. Canadian institutions of higher learning also offer cooperative work-study programs and internships as well as the opportunity for a temporary work permit after graduation.

The English-speaking island nations of the Caribbean have the University of the West Indies with campuses in Jamaica, Barbados, Trinidad, and Tobago. While formal English is spoken in the classroom, each island nation has its own version of an English creole or patois. The everyday language of the streets is different from formal English.

A number of U.S.-style colleges and universities operate overseas as independent campuses and satellite campuses of U.S.-based schools. Instruction is in English, though some have requirements to study the languages of the host countries. Here are some examples:

- Webster University of Missouri is a private, nonprofit university with campuses located in Austria, China, Ghana, Greece, the Netherlands, Switzerland, and Thailand. Visit http://www.webster.edu/locations/.
- The University of Armenia was established in 1991 and has U.S. regional accreditation. Armenia is an independent nation that was once part of the former Soviet Union. Visit http://aua.am/.
- American University of Bulgaria was established in 1991 and is the first American-style liberal arts college established in Eastern Europe. Students are required to live on campus. The expenses for tuition and room and board are very reasonable. The school has U.S. regional accreditation. Visit https://www.aubg.edu/.
- The University of Hong Kong is in the Hong Kong Special Administrative Region of the People's Republic of China and opened its doors in 1912. Hong Kong was a crown colony of Great Britain from 1842 to 1997 and has a long tradition of English as a widely spoken second language. Visit https://www.hku.hk/.
- Anglo American University is in the Czech Republic, in the ancient city of Prague, and has U.S. regional accreditation. Education is personalized with classes averaging only fifteen students. Bachelor's degrees can be completed in three years. Located in Central Europe, the Czech

Republic borders Germany, Austria, Poland, and Slovakia. Visit https://www.aauni.edu/.

- American University in Dubai (United Arab Emirates) has degree programs that include engineering, business, and international studies. It also has U.S. regional accreditation. Visit http://www.aud.edu/.
- Finland has colleges and universities offering 450 degree programs in English. The government of Finland has a website with information about degree programs offered in English. Visit: http://www.studyinfinland.fi/home. There is also a downloadable brochure with a complete listing of degree programs in English. Visit http://www.studyinfinland.fi/instancedata/prime_product_julkaisu/cimo/embeds/studyinfinland wwwstructure/100601_Higher_Education_Finland_2016_2017.pdf.[11]
- The American University of Paris was founded in 1962 to provide an American-style education and today enrolls students from around the globe. While instruction is in English, students must develop a certain level of proficiency in French in order to graduate.
- In Germany there are reportedly nine hundred college degree programs with instruction in English. The Federal Republic of Germany administers a website with complete information. Visit https://www.daad.de/deutschland/studienangebote/international-programmes/en/.
- Triatma Mulya Stenden in Indonesia offers an international business bachelor's degree involving two years of study at the campus in Bali and one year of study in the Netherlands. Visit http://www.triatmamulya-stenden.ac.id/international-business-administration/ for details.
- Tel Aviv International University in Israel has bachelor's and master's degree programs in English and has U.S. regional accreditation. Visit https://international.tau.ac.il/about_tau.
- John Cabot University is a small American-style liberal arts university in Rome. The school has U.S. regional accreditation. Visit http://www.johncabot.edu/.
- Sophia University is a Jesuit-run university in Japan with English-track degree programs. There are also options for different levels of Japanese language training. Visit https://www.sophia.ac.jp/eng/index.html.
- Temple University is a state-supported school in Pennsylvania and has a satellite campus in Japan. The Japan campus is also U.S. regionally accredited. Visit https://www.tuj.ac.jp/.
- American University of Madaba was established in 2005 and is in the Hashemite Kingdom of Jordan. Visit http://aum.edu.jo/en/.

- Sacred Heart University's Jack Welch College of Business in Luxembourg offers a master's of business administration. The program has U.S. regional accreditation. Visit http://www.shu.lu/.
- The University of Malta offers university degree programs with instruction in English through its national university. Malta is a small island nation in the Mediterranean Sea, and English is one of its two official languages. Visit https://www.um.edu.mt/.
- The College of the Marshall Islands is located in the Republic of the Marshall Islands. It has U.S. regional accreditation, but only offers associate degrees. Visit http://www.cmi.edu/.
- Maastricht University in the Netherlands offers half of its degree programs in English. It is part of the university system of the Netherlands. Visit https://www.maastrichtuniversity.nl/.
- Norway has many degree programs with instruction in English. Visit https://www.studyinnorway.no/study-in-norway.
- Florida State University has a satellite campus in the Republic of Panama. It shares U.S. regional accreditation with its main campus. Visit http://panama.fsu.edu/.
- Many major universities in the Republic of the Philippines offer instruction in English, but check with the individual university for information on the language of instruction. English is widely spoken due to a long association with the United States. Because of the Spanish American War, the Philippines, a former Spanish colony, was under American rule from 1898 to 1946. Here are some major universities in the Philippines with instruction in English:

  ◦ University of the Philippines: http://www.up.edu.ph/admissions
  ◦ De La Salle University: http://www.dlsu.edu.ph
  ◦ Ateneo De Manila University: http://www.ateneo.edu.ph
  ◦ University of Santo Tomas: http://www/ust.edu.ph/

- Romanian-American University offers many degree programs. Romania, sometimes called the "crossroads of southeastern Europe," borders the Black Sea, Bulgaria, Ukraine, Hungary, Servia, and Moldova. Visit http://www.ro-am.ro/index.php.
- The National University of Singapore offers degree programs with instruction in English. Singapore is a modern city-state, a city that is an independent country. It is on the Strait of Malacca, a narrow strait between the Pacific and Indian Oceans. Three countries can be viewed

at once from the strait: Singapore, Malaysia, and Indonesia. Visit http://nus.edu.sg/.

- Slovenia is an independent nation that was part of the former Yugoslavia. The Republic of Slovenia borders Italy, Austria, Hungary, Croatia, and the Adriatic Sea. Numerous degree programs are offered with instruction in English. Visit http://studyinslovenia.si/study/programmes-in-english/.
- The University of Cape Town (founded in 1829) in the Republic of South Africa is the oldest university in that nation. The university has nearly 30,000 students from South Africa and around the world. In 2016 there were 5,278 students enrolled from 112 countries, including 39 African nations. Visit http://www.students.uct.ac.za/.
- Sweden offers over nine hundred degree programs in English. The nation of Sweden maintains a helpful website for more information. Visit https://studyinsweden.se/universities/.

This is not an all-inclusive list of foreign college degree programs taught in English. Explore on your own to find even more. Study Portals is one resource for finding programs. Check out Study Portals at https://www.studyportals.com/about-us/our-mission-and-core-values/. Another resource is the Top Universities website at https://www.topuniversities.com/student-info/studying-abroad/where-can-you-study-abroad-english.

The *Washington Post* and the *New York Times* have both published informative stories on opportunities for studying in English overseas. We highly recommend reading the following:

- A *Washington Post* story from October 29, 2014, "7 Countries Where Americans Can Study, in English, for Free (or Nearly Free)." https://www.washingtonpost.com/news/worldviews/wp/2014/10/29/7-countries-where-americans-can-study-at-universities-in-english-for-free-or-almost-free/?utm_term=.6c5b10f63598.
- From the *New York Times*: "A Guide to Getting a Bachelor's Abroad." https://www.nytimes.com/2016/11/06/education/edlife/a-guide-to-getting-a-bachelors-abroad.html.

For more information about GI Bill-benefit coverage, visit these two websites:

- WEAMS Institution Search: https://inquiry.vba.va.gov/weamspub/buildSearchInstitutionCriteria.do (or google VA WEAMS Institution Search).
- GI Bill Comparison Tool: https://www.vets.gov/gi-bill-comparison-tool.

The WEAMS Institution Search and the GI Bill Comparison Tool will assist you in making a determination about attending a foreign school. The GI Bill Comparison Tool can tell you how many students are using GI Bill benefits at a school, including many foreign colleges and universities that are in the GI Bill database. GI Bill Comparison Tool also estimates benefits that can be paid to the school. If a foreign school has students using the GI Bill, the school has already been approved by the Department of Veterans Affairs as GI Bill eligible.

The WEAMS Institution Search can provide more information and has a search feature for looking up a school by country. For example, a search of the University of Western Australia provides helpful information including the DoD housing rate versus the GI Bill housing allowance. If the school has already designated officials to certify GI Bill enrollment, they will be listed as well (https://inquiry.vba.va.gov/weamspub/buildViewOrg.do). If the school does not currently have GI Bill students attending, it is still possible that it can be approved. Check with the Department of Veterans Affairs and the school's admissions department. If the school has never had a GI Bill student attend, it can apply for approval using VA Form 22-0976, Application for Approval of a Program in a Foreign Country. The form and information can be found here: https://benefits.va.gov/gibill/foreign_program_approval_information_for_schools.asp.

For those who are fluent in languages other than English, even more opportunities are available for study in foreign lands. Spanish, for example, is the second most widely spoken language in the United States. There are also twenty nations in the world where Spanish is the official language. For more information, visit https://www.babbel.com/en/magazine/how-many-people-speak-spanish-and-where-is-it-spoken. Other language skills can be useful for degree programs that do not offer instruction in English. Adding fluency in a foreign language to your résumé will always set you apart from others applying for the same position, especially if the language you speak is relevant to the company you are applying.

Chapter Five

Preparation and Resources
for Career Planning

I often hear from transitioning active-duty personnel that they don't know where to look for the information they need on state- and job-specific criteria for employment planning and support. The purpose of this chapter is to give you reputable resource tools that are reliable, valid, and useful in your employment-search planning, even if you are still in school. In fact, if you are still in school, these resources can augment the resources that should be available through your school's career center. That means double the support. Career planning takes quite a bit of time. Starting long before you separate from the service will give you your best shot. Plus, there are internship programs that may be viable, depending on the time left on your contract and the base where you are stationed. For educational resources, see chapter 3.

The following topics will be covered in this chapter:

- Online and Face-to-Face Resources

  - Bureau of Labor Statistics Occupational Outlook Handbook
  - O*NET OnLine
  - CareerOneStop
  - CareerScope
  - My Next Move for Veterans
  - Indeed, Glassdoor, and Payscale
  - LinkedIn
  - Service-Disabled Veteran-Owned Small-Businesses Program (SD-VOSB)
  - Department of Veterans Affairs First Contracting Program

- ◦ National Veteran Small-Business Coalition
- ◦ State-Based Sites
- ◦ Small Business Administration
- ◦ SCORE
- ◦ Small Business Development Centers
- ◦ Chambers of Commerce
- ◦ State Sites

- Base Transition Departments
- Military-Based Workshops
- Recruiters
- Résumés
- Cover Letters
- Informational Interviewing
- Interviewing
- Networking
- Internships

INTRODUCTION

Before you decide on a specific school to attend or a specific career pathway, you need to complete an in-depth search of your available options. Using the free research tools outlined in this section will help you to find a school that will meet your academic and career needs. This chapter also offers useful career-based information that will help you better prepare during your quest for employment. These sites are not foolproof but are a good start. Each tool offers invaluable information on the different levels involved in planning your future, whether a long-term career goal that requires you to attend college first or employment immediately after separation from the service. Using all of these sites and cross-referencing the information will benefit the overall organization of your career research and academic preparation. If possible, always check with an academic specialist on the base where you are stationed for information relevant to your needs—for example, if you are using GI Bill benefits, you will need to determine whether the institution you have selected is approved for the GI Bill, how the benefit works, and how to activate it.

ONLINE RESOURCES

Bureau of Labor Statistics Occupational Outlook Handbook

After taking vocational assessments and determining that business is the right sector for you, you must conduct career reconnaissance to determine which career field within business is the best fit. The Bureau of Labor Statistics Occupational Outlook Handbook (BLS OOH) (http://www.bls.gov/ooh/) is a resourceful tool to use to begin this process and is one of the easiest tools to use. I will detail this site more extensively than some of the others as it holds the most thorough and accessible information. Remember that earlier we discussed the proper way to determine your future career path: find a career, match a degree/training, then pick a school. Keeping this method in mind will assist you in making more knowledgeable decisions regarding your education. It is time to get out a notebook to keep track of the pros and cons of each career and to note information that may be relevant and important to have as you progress through your research.

The BLS OOH should be used early on in the decision-making process. It is a broad-based tool that will help you narrow your choices down into a list that is manageable. On this site, you can search career fields by pay levels, educational requirements, training requirements, projected job openings, and projected job-growth rates. You can research various career sectors or find the current fastest growing job fields.

You can also search specific occupations. For example, if I want to find out the level of education required to be an accountant and how much money they make, I click on the "Business and Financial" tab and scroll down (the options are in alphabetical order). Here I can view a short job summary and see that the field requires a minimum of a bachelor's degree. Clicking on the link takes me to more in-depth information regarding the field. For example, I can see on this page that accounting is expected to have a faster than average growth rate (10 percent) in the decade from 2016 to 2026, and that the pay rate in 2016 was around $69,000. Also listed: "Required Work Experience in a Related Occupation," "On-the-job Training," "Number of Jobs," and "Employment Change 2016–2026," which means the number of jobs expected to be added over the course of the decade.

Table 5.1. Quick Facts: Accountants and Auditors

2017 Median Pay	$69,350 per year
	$33.34 per hour
Typical Entry-Level Education	Bachelor's degree
Work Experience in a Related Occupation	None
On-the-job Training	None
Number of Jobs, 2016	1,397,700
Job Outlook, 2016–2026	10% (Faster than average)
Employment Change, 2016–2026	139,900

Source: https://www.bls.gov/ooh/business-and-financial/accountants-and-auditors.htm

Now, if I want to delve deeper, I will follow the links forward for more information. Notice that the links across the top of the page (from left to right) correlate with the links listed on the left-hand side of the page (from top to bottom). The best way to process through these links is to read each page then click on the blue tab at the bottom right-hand side of each page that directs the reader on to the next one. This way you will see each page, which will give you solid information to begin your search and, if you need to conduct specific career reconnaissance at a later date, allow you to directly target the information you need.

Let's review the information listed within each section of figure 5.1.

Summary

The Summary page gives readers a snapshot of the material that will be outlined for each job. A quick review often helps service members get a better understanding of the career and whether they want to dig further. Don't forget to keep notes as you read through this data and watch the video!

What They Do

This page highlights the main duties in the career field. Readers can begin to develop a better understanding of the daily responsibilities that people in this position are assigned and expected to perform. Also listed are areas of specialization and the different sectors in this career field. Career fields that have many sectors offer a variety of outlets for employment. Notice that figure 5.2 states that people in this profession will be expected

Summary

Quick Facts: Accountants and Auditors	
2017 Median Pay 🛈	$69,350 per year $33.34 per hour
Typical Entry-Level Education 🛈	Bachelor's degree
Work Experience in a Related Occupation 🛈	None
On-the-job Training 🛈	None
Number of Jobs, 2016 🛈	1,397,700
Job Outlook, 2016-26 🛈	10% (Faster than average)
Employment Change, 2016-26 🛈	139,900

What Accountants and Auditors Do

Accountants and auditors prepare and examine financial records. They ensure that financial records are accurate and that taxes are paid properly and on time. Accountants and auditors assess financial operations and work to help ensure that organizations run efficiently.

Work Environment

Most accountants and auditors work full time. In 2016, about 1 in 5 worked more than 40 hours per week. Overtime hours are typical at certain times of the year, such as at the end of the budget year or during tax season.

How to Become an Accountant or Auditor

Most employers require a candidate to have a bachelor's degree in accounting or a related field. Certification within a specific field of accounting improves job prospects. For example, many accountants become Certified Public Accountants (CPAs).

Pay

The median annual wage for accountants and auditors was $69,350 in May 2017.

Job Outlook

Employment of accountants and auditors is projected to grow 10 percent from 2016 to 2026, faster than the average for all occupations. In general, employment growth of accountants and auditors is expected to be closely tied to the health of the overall economy. As the economy grows, more workers should be needed to prepare and examine financial records.

State & Area Data

Explore resources for employment and wages by state and area for accountants and auditors.

Similar Occupations

Compare the job duties, education, job growth, and pay of accountants and auditors with similar occupations.

More Information, Including Links to O*NET

Learn more about accountants and auditors by visiting additional resources, including O*NET, a source on key characteristics of workers and occupations.

Figure 5.1. Accountants and Auditors Summary

What Accountants and Auditors Do

About this section 🛈

Accountants and auditors prepare and examine financial records. They ensure that financial records are accurate and that taxes are paid properly and on time. Accountants and auditors assess financial operations and work to help ensure that organizations run efficiently.

Duties

Accountants and auditors typically do the following:

- Examine financial statements to ensure that they are accurate and comply with laws and regulations
- Compute taxes owed, prepare tax returns, and ensure that taxes are paid properly and on time
- Inspect account books and accounting systems for efficiency and use of accepted accounting procedures
- Organize and maintain financial records
- Assess financial operations and make best-practices recommendations to management
- Suggest ways to reduce costs, enhance revenues, and improve profits

Accountants and auditors examine financial statements for accuracy and conformance with laws

In addition to examining and preparing financial documentation, accountants and auditors must explain their findings. This includes preparing written reports and meeting face-to-face with organization managers and individual clients.

Figure 5.2. What Accountants and Auditors Do

https://www.bls.gov/ooh/business-and-financial/accountants-and-auditors.htm#tab-2

to examine financial statements, compute taxes, maintain records, assess financial operations, and suggest ways to reduce costs. If you took the Dantes.kuder.com assessments and tested high in the social, artistic, and entrepreneurial sectors, you may not be drawn to this type of a career. This profession would be more attractive to service members who score high in the conventional and enterprising interest areas.

Work Environment

This section is important. Consider that if you prefer to work outdoors and be on the move, and if you are sociable and like to interact with others, the accounting field may not align to your preferences. See figure 5.3, which states that most people in this profession work in offices and often complete their work alone. If you took the career assessments on Dantes. kuder.com, and you know that you are social and prefer activities that require creativity, this may not be the best fit for your needs. If you tested high in the areas of conventional and enterprising your personality may align better with this career.

Accountants and Auditors

Summary	What They Do	Work Environment	How to Become One	Pay	Job Outlook

Work Environment

Accountants and auditors held about 1.4 million jobs in 2016. The largest employers of accountants and auditors were as follows:

Accounting, tax preparation, bookkeeping, and payroll services	25%
Government	8
Finance and insurance	8
Management of companies and enterprises	7
Self-employed workers	7

Most accountants and auditors work in offices, but some work from home. Although they complete much of their work alone, they sometimes work in teams with other accountants and auditors. Accountants and auditors may travel to their clients' places of business.

Figure 5.3.   Work Enviornment
https://www.bls.gov/ooh/business-and-financial/accountants-and-auditors.htm#tab-3

How to Become One

Many service members I counsel already know the career field they want to work in upon separation from the service, but don't know how to attain the job. That is, they are unsure of the education level they will need or which subjects to study. The BLS OOH is the first, and easiest, place to look for that information. This page breaks down the information to explain the following important information: type of degree (subject), level of degree (associate, bachelor's or master's degree), certifications required in the field (some of these may take more than a year to achieve!), and required apprenticeships and internships. Understand that it may still require preparatory work, such as an internship, to get hired fulltime, even if this site does not list it. Some career fields are very difficult to break into and require internships or job shadowing for the applicant to gain practical experience and/or to interact with hiring managers in order to build rapport with those doing the hiring. However necessary, this is a burden because this is mostly unpaid work. In some fields the internship will be built into the degree. For example, engineering students, who often have practical-application experiences during their bachelor's degree and construction management majors, usually have a full semester of internship to complete. Note that construction management usually falls within the realm of business or engineering and computer science departments of a college and requires a bachelor's degree. The field is currently experiencing high levels of growth nationwide as shown by the 10 percent growth rate listed on the BLS OOH. Did I mention that the pay is good, too? Take a look at the data from the BLS OOH (table 5.2).

Table 5.2.   Quick Facts: Construction Managers

2017 Median Pay	$91,370 per year
	$43.93 per hour
Typical Entry-Level Education	Bachelor's degree
Work Experience in a Related Occupation	None
On-the-job Training	Moderate-term on-the-job training
Number of Jobs, 2016	403,800
Job Outlook, 2016–2026	11% (Faster than average)
Employment Change, 2016–2026	44,800

Source: https://www.bls.gov/ooh/management/construction-managers.htm

Remember that you still need to check growth and income levels in the area of the country you want to live in. For those of you currently on active duty or married to a service member and who require the flexibility of online learning, construction management is becoming a more attainable degree. Some reputable schools, such as Indiana State University and National University, which are both approved for tuition assistance (check this information on the Department of Defense website of approved schools: dodmou.com), now offer online options. For more information on the programs offered through Indiana State and National Universities, check the following websites:

- Indiana State University: https://www.indstate.edu/academics/online/undergraduate/construction-management
- National University: https://www.nu.edu/OurPrograms/SchoolOf EngineeringAndTechnology/AppliedEngineering/Programs/BS ConstructionManagement.html

For more information regarding construction management, check with the American Council for Construction Education: http://www.acce-hq.org/.

All right, back on track. Figure 5.4 shows information from the BLS OOH that explains the educational level required to work in the accounting field.

How to Become an Accountant or Auditor

Most accountants and auditors need at least a bachelor's degree in accounting or a related field. Certification, including the Certified Public Accountant (CPA) credential, can improve job prospects.

Education

Most accountant and auditor positions require at least a bachelor's degree in accounting or a related field. Some employers prefer to hire applicants who have a master's degree, either in accounting or in business administration with a concentration in accounting.

A few universities and colleges offer specialized programs, such as a bachelor's degree in internal auditing. In some cases, those with associate's degrees, as well as bookkeepers and accounting clerks who meet the education and experience requirements set by their employers, get junior accounting positions and advance to accountant positions by showing their accounting skills on the job.

Many colleges help students gain practical experience through summer or part-time internships with public accounting or business firms.

Figure 5.4.   How to Become an Acountant or Auditor

https://www.bls.gov/ooh/business-and-financial/accountants-and-auditors.htm#tab-4

The site also lists the required or optional certification for accountants (see figure 5.5).

In this case, it is the certified public accountant (CPA). CPA requirements are state based; you must be approved to work in the field based on the requirements in the state in which you want to practice. According to the National Association of State Boards of Accountancy (NASBA):

> A CPA is a certified public accountant who is licensed by a state board of accountancy. To earn the prestige associated with the CPA license, you are required to demonstrate knowledge and competence by meeting high educational standards, passing the CPA exam and completing a specific amount of general accounting experience. The two most important aspects of becoming a CPA are passing the Uniform CPA Exam and meeting licensing requirements in the state where you want to practice.[1]

This means that you need to research two topics if you want to pursue work in this field: the CPA exam and state-based requirements. Many states also require applicants to have passed an ethics exam, have graduated from a specific type of academic program that holds specific accreditation, and have accumulated a specific amount of experience in the field.

Licenses, Certifications, and Registrations

Every accountant filing a report with the Securities and Exchange Commission (SEC) is required by law to be a Certified Public Accountant (CPA). Many other accountants choose to become a CPA to enhance their job prospects or to gain clients. Many employers will pay the costs associated with the CPA exam.

CPAs are licensed by their state's Board of Accountancy. Becoming a CPA requires passing a national exam and meeting other state requirements. Almost all states require CPA candidates to complete 150 semester hours of college coursework to be licensed, which is 30 hours more than the usual 4-year bachelor's degree. Many schools offer a 5-year combined bachelor's and master's degree to meet the 150-hour requirement, but a master's degree is not required.

A few states allow a number of years of public accounting experience to substitute for a college degree.

All states use the four-part Uniform CPA Examination from the American Institute of Certified Public Accountants (AICPA). Candidates do not have to pass all four parts at once, but most states require that candidates pass all four parts within 18 months of passing their first part.

Almost all states require CPAs to take continuing education to keep their license.

Certification provides an advantage in the job market because it shows professional competence in a specialized field of accounting and auditing. Accountants and auditors seek certifications from a variety of professional societies. Some of the most common certifications are listed below:

The Institute of Management Accountants offers the Certified Management Accountant (CMA) to applicants who complete a bachelor's degree. Applicants must have worked at least 2 years in management accounting, pass a two-part exam, agree to meet continuing education requirements, and comply with standards of professional conduct. The exam covers areas such as financial statement analysis, working-capital policy, capital structure, valuation issues, and risk management.

The Institute of Internal Auditors (IIA) offers the Certified Internal Auditor (CIA) to graduates from accredited colleges and universities who have worked for 2 years as internal auditors and have passed a four-part exam. The IIA also offers the Certified in Control Self-Assessment (CCSA), Certified Government Auditing Professional (CGAP), Certified Financial Services Auditor (CFSA), and Certification in Risk Management Assurance (CRMA) to those who pass the exams and meet educational and experience requirements.

ISACA offers the Certified Information Systems Auditor (CISA) to candidates who pass an exam and have 5 years of experience auditing information systems. Information systems experience, financial or operational auditing experience, or related college credit hours can be substituted for up to 3 years of experience in information systems auditing, control, or security.

For accountants with a CPA, the AICPA offers the option to receive any or all of the Accredited in Business Valuation (ABV), Certified Information Technology Professional (CITP), or Personal Financial Specialist (PFS) certifications. The ABV requires passing a written exam, completion of at least six business valuation projects, and 75 hours of continuing education. The CITP requires 1,000 hours of business technology experience and 75 hours of continuing education. Candidates for the PFS also must complete a certain amount of work experience and continuing education, and pass a written exam.

Figure 5.5.   Licenses, Certifications, and Registrations

Information on the Uniform CPA Examination can be found on the Association of International Certified Professional Accountants' website: https://www.thiswaytocpa.com/segmented-landing/exam-101/. This is not an easy exam, and it often takes people multiple tries to succeed. Make note of the exam information and hyperlink embedded on the website. Clicking on this link gives you instant access to the information regarding the exam and certification by the premier agency, the American Institute of Certified Public Accountants (AICPA).

State-based requirements will require some digging. This is typical of professions that states have jurisdiction over: nursing, law, most health care, and trades (e.g., plumbers and electricians). So, if you would like to work in Illinois as a CPA, start your search with "Illinois State CPA Requirements." The top link leads me to the Illinois Board of Examiners website: https://www.ilboe.org/. Notice that it is a dot-org website. It is important to make sure that you are on the state site and not a dot-com website operating outside of the state credentialing authority, as this might lead you to inaccurate information. This site has the official state seal of Illinois. Here you'll find the exact requirements, based on the different routes available, that you need to fulfill. A bit lower in the same section, you can research options for advancement within the field and the important qualities demonstrated by people who already work in the field.

Pay

Now we are at the meat and potatoes of this professions, the pay! This page (figure 5.6) is a quick rundown of the national median wages of the career. Pay levels are important to recon before making any final decisions about the career field. You want to see high wages and room for growth the longer you stay in the career. Stagnant wages are not good for long-term growth and personal career satisfaction. Figure 5.6 breaks down the pay ranges for accountants working in the different sectors.

Job Outlook

The job outlook page (figure 5.7) shows the growth rates for the different sectors of this field. A good place to start is with the national employment growth rates, but you'll need state-specific information to get a better idea of employment levels for your location.

Figure 5.6.   Job Outlook

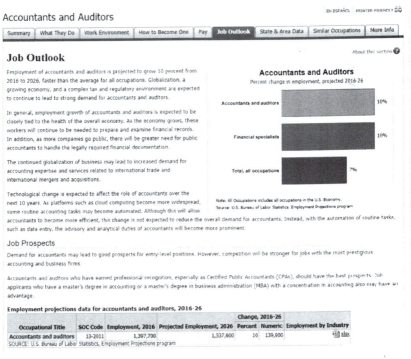

Figure 5.7.   Job Outlook

https://www.bls.gov/ooh/business-and-financial/accountants-and-auditors.htm#tab-6

You can download the spreadsheet from the link at the bottom of the page. The spreadsheet is confusing but offers good insight into the growth rates of the different sectors. You do not want to see negative numbers here.

State and Area Data

This page (figure 5.8) is extremely helpful, as national statistics are a good starting point, but ultimately you need to know the state statistics for your chosen profession. Many professions are tied to specific states and areas. For example, if you want to live in a rural environment, and you want to work in the field of finance, how many opportunities will be available? You need this data, because some states/local areas have declining growth in certain professions. If location is the most important factor for you, you may need to consider a different career choice.

Everything on this page is important! This is where you will get your best state-based data. The first section, "Occupational Employment Statistics," has a link to:

- Industries with the highest levels of employment
- Industries with the highest concentration of employment
- Top-paying industries

Also included are the geographic profiles for this occupation. Hover over the areas to see the income levels:

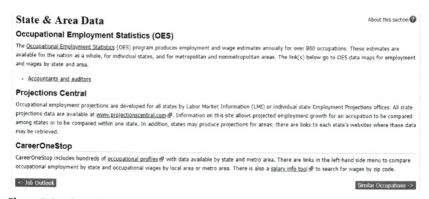

Figure 5.8.   State & Area Data

https://www.bls.gov/ooh/business-and-financial/accountants-and-auditors.htm#tab-7

- States with the highest employment levels
- States with the highest concentration of jobs
- Top-paying states
- Metropolitan areas with the highest employment levels
- Metropolitan areas with the highest concentration of jobs
- Top-paying metropolitan areas

Next, use the "Projections Central" and "Salary Information Tool" links for further exploration. Projections Central allows users to search growth rates in career sectors by states. On the landing page, make sure to check long-term projections, as this will give you a better understanding of the strength of the career field in the future. Next, scroll down to select the state and career field.

On the "Salary Information Tool" page, select the career name from the drop-down menu, then the city or zip code. Not all cities and zip codes are listed. For example, a search on the site recently showed that salary information was not listed for the Orange County, California area, and the search had to be expanded to the Los Angeles area. Now, income levels between Los Angeles and Orange County may not differ much, but levels may differ noticeably between cities and surrounding rural areas. This may help you decide where to live. For example, maybe it is more financially prudent to work in the urban area and live in the rural area. Checking travel times and available public transportation may help with this decision.

Scroll down to the bottom of the page, where you will see the link "Learn more about this occupation." Click on it to see the "CareerOneStop Occupation Profile," a side-by-side comparison of a specific state versus the national data. Also listed is a career video (to give you a visual reference), job outlook, description of the career field, the education level of the percentage of people polled who work in the field, required education and experience for people getting started in the field, and any certifications, licenses, or apprenticeship programs required.

Similar Occupations

The two links to "Projections Central" and the "Salary Information Tool" should have opened in another tab in your browser. At this point, you need to return to the BLS OOH website, which should still be open to the "State and Area Data" page. Click on "Similar Occupations," in the lower right-hand corner. This page (figure 5.9) lists occupations with job duties similar to the position you initially searched. This page is important to use to conduct research, as it may demonstrate significant differences between fields that are similar in nature. Maybe you thought you could make more money as an accountant and are not satisfied with the national and/or state salary level. In this instance, you would see that there are several other similar in nature career fields that pay a higher wage. For example, the financial managers' median income level is listed at $125,080 and the financial analysts' at $84,300. Median is similar to average but is calculated differently. Now you have the links to begin searching the fields that most interest you.

Similar Occupations

About this section 🛈

This table shows a list of occupations with job duties that are similar to those of accountants and auditors.

OCCUPATION	JOB DUTIES	ENTRY-LEVEL EDUCATION	2017 MEDIAN PAY
Bookkeeping, Accounting, and Auditing Clerks	Bookkeeping, accounting, and auditing clerks produce financial records for organizations. They record financial transactions, update statements, and check financial records for accuracy.	Some college, no degree	$39,240
Budget Analysts	Budget analysts help public and private institutions organize their finances. They prepare budget reports and monitor institutional spending.	Bachelor's degree	$75,240
Cost Estimators	Cost estimators collect and analyze data in order to estimate the time, money, materials, and labor required to manufacture a product, construct a building, or provide a service. They generally specialize in a particular product or industry.	Bachelor's degree	$63,110
Financial Analysts	Financial analysts provide guidance to businesses and individuals making investment decisions. They assess the performance of stocks, bonds, and other types of investments.	Bachelor's degree	$84,300
Financial Managers	Financial managers are responsible for the financial health of an organization. They produce financial reports, direct investment activities, and develop strategies and plans for the long-term financial goals of their organization.	Bachelor's degree	$125,080
Management Analysts	Management analysts, often called *management consultants*, propose ways to improve an organization's efficiency. They advise managers on how to make organizations more profitable through reduced costs and increased revenues.	Bachelor's degree	$82,450
Personal Financial Advisors	Personal financial advisors provide advice on investments, insurance, mortgages, college savings, estate planning, taxes, and retirement to help individuals manage their finances.	Bachelor's degree	$90,640
Postsecondary Teachers	Postsecondary teachers instruct students in a wide variety of academic and technical subjects beyond the high school level. They may also conduct research and publish scholarly papers and books.	See How to Become One	$76,000
Tax Examiners and Collectors, and Revenue Agents	Tax examiners and collectors, and revenue agents determine how much is owed in taxes and collect tax from individuals and businesses on behalf of federal, state, and local governments. They review tax returns, conduct audits, identify taxes owed, and collect overdue tax payments.	Bachelor's degree	$53,130
Top Executives	Top executives devise strategies and policies to ensure that an organization meets its goals. They plan, direct, and coordinate operational activities of companies and organizations.	Bachelor's degree	$104,700

Figure 5.9.   Similar Occupations

https://www.bls.gov/ooh/business-and-financial/accountants-and-auditors.htm#tab-8

Contacts for More Information

For more information about accredited accounting programs, visit

AACSB International—The Association to Advance Collegiate Schools of Business

For more information about the Certified Public Accountant (CPA) designation, visit

American Institute of Certified Public Accountants (AICPA)

For more information about management accounting and the Certified Management Accountant (CMA) designation, visit

Institute of Management Accountants

For more information about internal auditing and the Certified Internal Auditor (CIA) designation, visit

The Institute of Internal Auditors

For more information about information systems auditing and the Certified Information Systems Auditor (CISA) designation, visit

ISACA

For more information about certifications in accounting, visit

Global Academy of Finance and Management

O*NET

Accountants

Accountants and Auditors

Auditors

<- Similar Occupations

Figure 5.10.   Contacts for More Information

https://www.bls.gov/ooh/business-and-financial/accountants-and-auditors.htm#tab-9

More Information

Finally, the "More Information" tab is the last link to click on. It is also located in the bottom right-hand corner of the page. Once on the "More Information" page (figure 5.10), you can use the links to conduct a more detailed investigation of the profession(s): to find the accrediting bodies for the profession, school programs, licensing agencies, and any relevant international agencies. At the bottom, you will see links to O*NET, which will be reviewed in the next section.

O*NET ONLINE

Occupational Information Network (O*Net Online) is a Department of Labor (DoL)–sponsored career/occupation website (http://www.onet online.org/) that enables users to complete detailed research on professions they are interested in (see figure 5.11). It replaced the *Dictionary of Occu-pational Titles*, which was a massive paper manual that listed over twelve thousand occupations and occupational profiles. Thankfully, they finally created a digital version!

Those of you who have already attended the mandatory transition seminar prior to separating from the service learned that O*NET can be used for résumé development and job research. However, the information the career advisors gave you about the site is just a fraction of the site's benefits. Mostly they showed you how to conduct quick career reconnais-sance (occupational exploration) and how to use the site for résumé de-velopment, but it can do so much more. For example, on O*NET you can search for careers that use your specific skills; find occupations related to

Figure 5.11.   O-NET OnLine
https://www.onetonline.org/

the one you are researching (which will help you diversify your research); use the crosswalks to find corresponding occupations that fall under other classification systems (military to the civilian sector); research links that go to other career resources find apprenticeship programs; search occupational information by state; and find occupational outlook data, such as growth or decline within the sectors. The site also hosts interest assessments; see them if you are unsure which pathway to take and need some direction.

O*NET can be used to directly research a potential occupation as well. On the main page, enter the name of the occupation in the upper right-hand corner under the "Occupation Quick Search" tab. For example, I entered *advertising*. Upon clicking the link, I was taken to a page that listed civil advertisers and promotion managers along with numerous other possibilities that are similar in nature: marketing managers, advertising sales agents, business teachers, and marketing strategist. This option enables users to research a broader base of potential career pathways prior to settling on one.

Occupations listed as "Bright Outlook" have growth rates that are faster than average in that field and are projected to have a large number of job openings during the 2016–2026 decade. These fields are also considered to be new and emerging, meaning that they will see changes in areas such as technology over the upcoming years. Offering several different occupations under one search, the site enables users to broaden their horizons and complete numerous searches that are similar in nature.

Clicking on one particular career pathway will allow you to find the national and state-based median wages for the chosen occupation—for example, a search under *civil engineer* listed the national median wages at $41.65 hourly, or $86,640 annually (scroll to the bottom of the page for this information). The projected annual growth rate is between 10 and 14 percent (which is higher than average), with 25,900 openings between 2016 and 2026. Also listed are the majority of industries where job seekers are finding employment—in this case, professional, scientific, and technical services in government.

Last, schools that offer the proper education pathways can be searched by state. Unfortunately, the school search cannot be narrowed down further by location, type of institution, or other details. For more detailed searches, use College Navigator.

Now, let's walk through a few of the other uses of the site so that you can learn how to conduct your own research. Notice that the links running from left to right at the top of the main page are also listed as search options at the bottom of the page. Let's start under "Find Occupations." In the drop-down menu, There are seven search options: "Bright Outlook," "Career Cluster," "Green Economy Sector," "Industry," "Job Family," "Job Zone," and "STEM" (science, technology, engineering, and mathematics).

Find Occupations

Bright Outlook

The Bright Outlook tab takes you to a new page with a new drop-down menu. From this menu, you can search by: *occupations with rapid growth*, *numerous job openings*, or *all bright outlook occupations*. See figure 5.12 for information from O*NET regarding "Bright Outlook" occupations.

Browse Bright Outlook Occupations

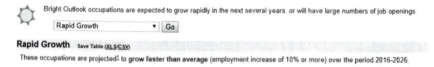

Bright Outlook occupations are expected to grow rapidly in the next several years, or will have large numbers of job openings

Rapid Growth ▾   Go

Rapid Growth Save Table (XLS/CSV)

These occupations are projected[1] to **grow faster than average** (employment increase of 10% or more) over the period 2016-2026.

Figure 5.12.   Browse Bright Outlook Occupations
https://www.onetonline.org/find/bright?b=1&g=Go

This page (figure 5.13) presents an alphabetical list of jobs currently experiencing and expected to experience higher levels of growth over the decade 2016–2026. Always check back periodically as the site gets updated approximately every two years; you want to see long-term growth. Why is this important to you? Higher numbers mean that the occupation is experiencing economic growth and a strengthening job market. Translation: high job growth means more opportunity for you. If you click on an occupation (such as *financial analyst*) and scroll down to the bottom of the next page, the projected national growth rates are listed.

Wages & Employment Trends

Median wages (2017)	$40.53 hourly, $84,300 annual
State wages	Local Salary Info
Employment (2016)	296,000 employees
Projected growth (2016-2026)	Faster than average (10% to 14%)
Projected job openings (2016-2026)	29,000
State trends	Employment Trends
Top industries (2016)	Finance and Insurance Professional, Scientific, and Technical Services

Figure 5.13.   Wages & Employment Trends
https://www.onetonline.org/link/summary/13-2051.00

For this particular occupation, the listed growth rate is 10 to 14 percent. So, who is predicting these numbers? Economists at the Bureau of Labor Statistics (BLS). Predications are shown within the following ranges:

- Increases of 14 percent or greater, much faster than average
- Increases between 9 and 13 percent, faster than average
- Increases between 5 and 8 percent, as fast as average
- Increases between 2 and 4 percent, more slowly than average
- A decrease or increase of less than 1 percent, little or no change
- A decrease of 2 percent or more, in decline

Numerous Job Openings   Return to the search menu under "Bright Outlook Occupations." Clicking on the second link from the drop-down gives you occupations expected to have one hundred thousand (or more) openings in the current decade (figure 5.14).

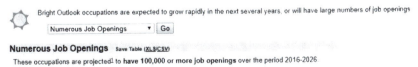

Browse Bright Outlook Occupations

Bright Outlook occupations are expected to grow rapidly in the next several years, or will have large numbers of job openings

Numerous Job Openings ▼ | Go

Numerous Job Openings Save Table (XLS/CSV)
These occupations are projected¹ to have **100,000 or more job openings** over the period 2016-2026

Figure 5.14.   Browse Bright Outlook Occupations
https://www.onetonline.org/find/bright

So, can an occupation have average growth and a high number of job openings? It is possible, and, according to the BLS,

A fast rate of employment growth does not always translate into many new jobs. For example, employment of occupation "A" is 2,000 and is projected to grow 20 percent. Because of the occupation's relatively small size, this percent growth accounts for only 400 new jobs over the 10-year projection period. In contrast, employment of occupation "B" is one million and projected to grow 5 percent. The large size of occupation "B" will still result in 50,000 new jobs over 10 years despite the lower growth rate.[2]

All Bright Outlook Occupations   What's better than finding out that the occupation you are interested in pursuing is experiencing rapid growth or will have over one hundred thousand openings in the next decade? Those that have both! The third option from the drop-down menu will give you this information (figure 5.15).

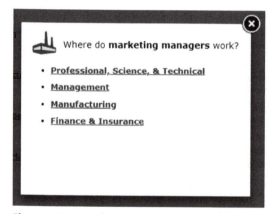

Figure 5.15.   Marketing Managers
https://www.mynextmove.org/vets/find/browse?c=55

Career Clusters

Return to the main drop-down menu, under "Find Occupations." Click on the second link, "Career Clusters." This search option contains occupations that are in "the same field of work that require similar skills."[3]

There are several sections that represent business and business-related occupational fields:

- Business management and administration
- Finance
- Marketing

The last search link, "Transportation, Distribution & Logistics," also has managers, a business-related occupation, within its realm. This is a logical pathway for those of you who worked within the logistics and supply field while on active duty. The knowledge you gained from the military can be combined with a management- or project-management-based degree on your résumé. This way you can use your applicable military training to help you secure employment. Another training option you may want to pursue for a career in logistics is "Lean" or "Lean Six Sigma," which focus on process improvement. There are some programs available for free if you are still on active duty or have recently separated.

The purpose to researching the business-related occupations under the "Career Clusters" tab is to learn about other, closely related occupations that you may be qualified for or interested in and, at the same time, see if the occupations have a bright outlook.

At this point, you should be getting the hang of this particular search section. The last review will be under the "Find Occupations" tab, "Job Family."

Job Family

The "Job Family" link allows you to search by sectors. There are two sectors specifically related to business, "Business and Financial Operations" and "Management." Now, some of you will still need to conduct research in other sectors, especially if you are going to be a small-business owner. Many of the service members that the authors have worked with come from families who own small businesses, and they intend to return home after they obtain a business or business-related education and run the family business. In this case, you may need to conduct research on the type of employee you need to help you run the business. This site enables this type of research.

CAREERONESTOP

CareerOneStop (http://www.careeronestop.org/) is one of the most thorough go-to sites for career exploration and is the first site to visit if you are interested in apprenticeship programs. The site holds valuable information regarding topics other than apprenticeships as well. It is a comprehensive career exploration site. CareerOneStop has six main sections for exploration:

- Explore Careers—learn about career fields, explore different industries, take self-assessments, and research different job skills
- Salary and Benefits—get information on relocating, wages and salaries, benefits, unemployment insurance, and paying for education or training
- Education and Training—get information on traditional education and apprenticeship programs, conduct a search for community colleges, find credentials, and research employment trends
- Job Search—learn how to network, interview, and negotiate and find special tips on veterans' reemployment
- Résumés and Interviews—view samples and formats, create a cover letter and thank-you note, and find out how to get ready for an interview
- People and Places to Help—see workforce services in different locations

If you are searching for information regarding apprenticeships programs, click on the "Education and Training" tab, then under the "Find" section, click "Apprenticeship." This page hosts links that cover the following:

- Apprenticeship videos
- A state-based search site
- Information from the Department of Labor (DoL)
- American Job Center information

Use the state-based search option to find a program in the state and county of your choosing. For example, Staff Sergeant Bowen is from Maryland. He would like to participate in an electrician registered apprenticeship program. He clicks on the "Find registered apprenticeship programs" tab, then selects his state. At this point, each state will have designed their own websites, so the directions will vary, but you need to find the link to apprenticeship programs. Sergeant Bowen clicks on "Find an Apprenticeship" at the top of the page, then "View Links to Program Websites." On this page, he can search for the appropriate link to an electrical program and its contact information. He can also click the "Veterans ReEmployment" link at the very top of the main page to enter his particular MOS and find occupations he may be qualified, or nearly qualified, for based on the specific military training he received in the Air Force.

CareerOneStop also has links to the American Job Centers located across the country. These sites provide a vast array of services. Topics range from filing an unemployment claim to youth employment permits. Many of these sites have veterans' representatives available for appointments to help you with your employment needs. They also often have computers, printers, copiers, internet access, and rooms available for interviews, and some have child care or can help with training and assessing your interest areas and skill levels.

CAREERSCOPE

CareerScope (https://www.benefits.va.gov/gibill/careerscope.asp) hosts an interest and aptitude assessment tool similar to DANTES Kuder's. CareerScope is hosted by the VA on the main GI Bill webpage. The free site assists service members transitioning from active duty to higher education in finding and planning the best pathways to pursue. Assessments are conducted directly through the site, and a corresponding report-interpretation document explains how to interpret assessment results. The easy-to-understand site is a valuable research tool both for those who have already identified the career pathway they want to take and those who are still undecided.

MY NEXT MOVE FOR VETERANS

My Next Move (http://www.mynextmove.org/vets/) pulls its information from O*NET, so it is organized in a similar fashion. There are three different options to search by, but we are going to focus on the option "Browse Careers by Industry" (see figure 5.16) since we are focused on business or a business-related sector for the purposes of this book.

Figure 5.16. My Next Move

https://www.mynextmove.org/vets/find/browse?c=52

The two most encompassing selections will be "Finance and Insurance" and "Management." Click on "Management." The resulting pages will divide the sectors into those that some people marketing work in.

Click on the first symbol next to "Marketing Managers" and a new window will pop up (see figure 5.17).

Now you can click on each sector to learn more about it.

The second symbol next to "Marketing Managers" is a bright sun. The bright sun means there will be rapid growth in this sector in the coming decade (figure 5.18).

Figure 5.17.   My Next Move

https://www.mynextmove.org/vets/find/browse?c=55

 Marketing Managers

Figure 5.18.   symbols

Now, click on the "Learn More" link, or click on the occupational title on the main page. Now you are on a page that presents the occupation as a snapshot (see figure 5.19).

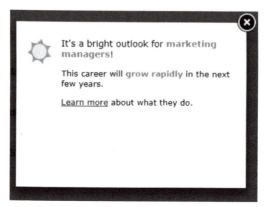

Figure 5.19.   Browse Bright Outlook Occupations
https://www.mynextmove.org/vets/find/browse?c=55

There's so much on this page. Where should you start? At the very top and work your way down methodically. Notice that at the top of the page, there is a selection of alternate titles that describe marketing managers. Directly under this is the tab "In the military." On this link, you can see the jobs in the military that relate to the civilian career sector you are researching.

Review the next five sections to get a better idea of the occupational requirements. At the bottom of the page you will see "Education," "Job Outlook," and "Explore More." These are the three tabs most often used on this page. Be careful using the "Find Training" tab, as it does not filter out less-than-reputable schools. For school searches, use College Navigator. Spend time on each of the links. You will notice that some of the links take you to the BLS OOH site that we reviewed earlier in this chapter.

INDEED, GLASSDOOR, AND PAYSCALE

When conducting career reconnaissance, Indeed (https://www.indeed .com/), Glassdoor (https://www.glassdoor.com/), and Payscale (https:// www.payscale.com/) are three sites that you should use intermittently. The sites help you round out your career research with practical knowledge. For example:

- What are employers in a particular area looking for in a candidate?
- What level of pay are they offering?
- Which companies are hiring?

These are important questions to answer, as they help you get an idea of where to look for a job and what you need on your résumé. When looking at entry-level positions, you can also find out if experience is necessary. *Why is this important for you to know if you are just starting your college journey?* Because you have time to prepare. If employers are looking for some experience, then you need to find an internship while attending college or look for job shadowing ideas. *Where can you find this information?* Try the career-services office at your college/university first. Next, give the local Chamber of Commerce a call. Finally, research employers in the area, check their websites for possible opportunities, then call their HR office. Always consider any personal connections you may already have and reach out to them as well. While they may not be in a position to give you an internship, they may know someone who is.

Indeed

Indeed.com is an easy-to-use website for quick research. It can be used to check the current postings in a specific area. For example, last week an officer interested in project management in the Austin, Texas, area came into the office. A search on Indeed for project management jobs in Austin resulted in approximately ten pages of jobs ranging in pay from $55,000 to $130,000. Not very interesting in itself; however, many of the employers prefer that potential employees have Microsoft Office skills. Microsoft offers certification exams in many subject areas. These exams may help you demonstrate validated, higher level skills. This particular service member decided to seek certification for the Microsoft Office Specialist. Now, since he was an officer, TA was the only option for him, if he intended to stay in the military for another two years upon completion of the project-management program. Otherwise, costs would need to be out of pocket. However, enlisted personnel may have funding through the COOL program. A quick search on the Marine Corps COOL site under "Leader" (see section on the COOL program for more information) proved fruitful, as both the Microsoft Office Specialist 2013 and 2016 are approved for funding.

Indeed does offer advanced filtering options, which you will need because the site takes free listings. That means there will usually be a long list of results from your search. So try to narrow your search as much as possible. You can use search terms such as *part time, full time, contract, salary range,* and *experience level.* Always check under specific keywords and titles.

Now, when you are ready to apply, you may want to consider going directly to the hiring company's website. You can also go to LinkedIn to see if you can connect with a hiring manager. With the number of applications coming through Indeed for the specific announcement, you are bound to get lost in the sauce. Try to find a way to connect in a more direct and personal fashion, as an in-person referral is more likely to get you through the door.

Glassdoor

Glassdoor offers users the opportunity to dig for information about companies before applying. You can research employers, read authentic reviews from people who currently or previously worked for the company, research salaries and benefits, look for job opportunities, and read interview questions. I always use the site for checking salaries, determining what an acceptable salary is, and reading employee feedback. When you are first starting out in an occupation, it is difficult to know what a reasonable salary offer should be. Researching salaries on this site can offer insight on this topic. And, if you look up a specific company on Glassdoor, and the reviews are all bad, you might consider this a warning and move on to the next company on your list. Since it is sometimes difficult to narrow down search parameters, these two areas offer a place to start. This is a tool to help you decide where you might want to work. Think of the site as offering insider knowledge on companies you may be interested in working for.

Payscale

Payscale does a lot more than its title implies. Yes, you can use the site to search for salary information, but you can also use it to determine your worth in today's market. It hosts information regarding salary negotiations, career research, and career advice. It can be used for researching companies and job openings where the salary is not listed. When researching employment data for service members, it can be used to conduct quick searches on companies and job announcements that don't list salaries.

LINKEDIN

A LinkedIn (https://www.linkedin.com/) profile is a critical resource allowing you to showcase your experience and be findable to hiring managers and recruiters. LinkedIn uses an algorithm based on the search criteria another user enters to find you, so be sure that the words you use in your profile match words in the job descriptions of the jobs you are seeking. You do not need to be a mathematician or understand the intricacies of an algorithm to have an effective LinkedIn profile. You just need to match some of the general phrasing and keywords to your occupational target.

LinkedIn has multiple sections you need to fill out (or upload your photo to) to complete your profile. The most important ones are *Picture*, *Headline*, *Summary*, *Work Experience*, *Education*, *Skills*, and *Jobs*. Each of these factors into the algorithm significantly; and they are the primary categories that hiring managers view to learn more about you. Be sure to write your profile not just for the algorithm, but for the human reader, too.

In general, your profile should tell a little more than what the hiring manager would find in your résumé. Maybe add some volunteer experience, personal interests, or more details about the responsibilities you've had in your work or military experience to show the reader a wider picture of you as a candidate. Use the Headline and Summary sections to tell them what you're looking for and to give yourself a voice in representing your goals and enthusiasm.

LinkedIn is a live, dynamic application that is run by a highly dedicated team of professionals, and they are always looking to add new features that bring people together on the platform to look for jobs and to find candidates. Do not be surprised if one day you log on to update your profile and find that the application has new fields or is arranged differently than the last time you looked at it. The company is constantly trying to attract both new companies and candidates to the platform, and to eagerly and aggressively augment the interface to improve their users' experience.

The core of LinkedIn will not change much, just the look and feel. So don't get confused or frustrated. It's technology. Just roll with it and keep your profile updated by taking your time to adjust to any of the frequent changes they make.

Profile Edits

To edit your profile, click on your picture on the far-right side of the horizontal navigation bar at the top of the page. If you haven't put a picture up yet, click on the blank avatar titled "Me." From there, click "View Profile," and your profile will appear with a little blue pencil icon to the right of each section. To edit a section, just click on the pencil.

Picture

Do you need a picture? Yes! Yes! Yes! This is a key to the algorithm working for you. LinkedIn will make available profiles with pictures before those without them. When a hiring manager does a candidate search, you'll have a better chance of appearing in their results. Use a professional-style picture, not something from a wedding with you in a tuxedo, or out enjoying a day on the lake with your family. It should be a picture of you alone.

If you have a military picture you like, you can use it. Or, if you are headed to corporate America, you can have a professional headshot taken. It's not important to spend a lot of money on a headshot for LinkedIn. Just wear a pressed shirt with a collar, comb your hair, and stand tall against a wall with a neutral background. A friend or family member can take the shot, and then you can upload it directly to your profile. The picture will appear as a thumbnail, so this is not a close-up.

Headline

Your Headline is the first thing that appears with your picture, so it is very important to customize it; otherwise LinkedIn will default to posting the most recent job title from your Work Experience section. If you are a veteran, be sure *veteran* is in your Headline. Your Headline should consist of four to six words and can be a combination of *veteran* and a job title you are targeting, for example, TRANSITIONING MILITARY VETERAN | LOGISTICS AND SUPPLY CHAIN SUMMARY.

Your Summary section should be about a paragraph long; here you can list some key skills. This paragraph should give the reader an idea of your military background, responsibilities, and level of authority, along with why that background is meaningful and valuable to hiring managers. Be sure to do your research to understand how to position yourself to companies in this statement.

A brief overview will suffice. Resist the temptation to write too much or use military language. It's important to "civilianize" your Summary, much as you would in your résumé, so the reader can see the business value of your military experience.

Work Experience

The Work Experience sections should be filled out carefully and completely. Write your job title and add your military branch of service into the Company field. LinkedIn will provide a drop-down menu of choices, and after typing in just a few letters of your organization, you should be able to scroll down and select the appropriate option. Fill in your dates accurately, and begin writing a brief summary of your responsibilities. If you have already adapted your military experience to the business audience on your résumé, simply copy and paste from your résumé. If you have not, or if you want to expand upon it, you can do that on LinkedIn.

It is also important to put your geographic location into LinkedIn. If you are job searching in a location different from your last (or current) military station, you will be able to add your target location in the Jobs section. For Work Experience, match your work location to the most appropriate option on the LinkedIn drop-down box.

In a short paragraph with a few bullet points, describe your major responsibilities and scope of duties by describing your main work activities, the number of people you managed, and any dollar amounts that could quantify the scope of your responsibilities. You want your reader to understand just how much impact your role had, so they can consider you for the appropriate level within their organization.

Education

Fill in the Education section with the name of your degree(s) such as Bachelor of Arts, Bachelor of Science, Master of Arts, and so on. Then add the name of the university, and list your major in the Field of Study area. If you were involved in clubs or took coursework relevant to your target line of work, you can add the details in the Description or Activities sections.

Skills

The Skills section is important because this is where you put the top fifty keywords a hiring manager can use to search for you. These keywords should be a list of your soft and hard skills. If you need ideas for these, print out a job description that represents the type of work you are pursuing, and highlight the keywords on it. Those are most likely the keywords that will both describe your value and be searchable by hiring managers.

Jobs

Now that you have completed your profile, it's time to make LinkedIn work for you. The Jobs tab will do that and is the portal where you can customize how you want LinkedIn's algorithm to search and find jobs for you.

Click on the Jobs tab and locate the Career Interests link. At the time of this writing, the link is small and near the top of the page. Find the Career Interests tab and click on it. This will lead you to your Jobs profile; it is very important to fill this out completely.

At the top of the page, turn on the Let Recruiters Know You're Open feature by clicking the button to the color blue. You are given three hundred characters to briefly describe yourself and your job target to a recruiter, should one land on your page. For example: "Transitioning military leader with 20 years of experience guiding teams, managing operations and reporting directly to executive leadership. Currently seeking a Supply Chain leadership position in a Fortune 500 company or highly matrixed organization where stability and efficiency are key."

That was about 290 characters, with spaces, which is about all the space LinkedIn gives you to make a quick hello to a recruiter. Don't be afraid to summarize! Overcome your shyness about how you may fit in, and build the confidence to just deliver the value in a few short sentences. After you have populated the section for recruiters, go through each of the other sections, and set them up according to your preferences.

Making Connections

LinkedIn is a powerful tool to help you build a defensive online job-search strategy. Take the time to fill out your profile completely and with high-quality content, and you will find that companies will likely land on your profile. Be sure to check your messages on the LinkedIn intranet, their internal peer-to-peer communication platform. This is where any messages from recruiters or connections will arrive. Recruiters are not hard to find and usually want to hear from you, so even typing the keyword "recruiter" in the LinkedIn search box may help you make a connection with a recruiter.

You should be continually expanding your network by connecting with the profiles of friends, managers, subordinates, colleagues, and anyone else you know or have known. The power of LinkedIn is not in your connections, but in the total connections of all the people in your network. With just one hundred connections on LinkedIn, a search can easily yield thousands of potential results since the algorithm pulls from both your network and the networks of each of your connections. If you query LinkedIn, and the result is a friend of one of your connections, you may choose to ask your friend to introduce you or reach out to that person directly. As the popularity of LinkedIn has grown and become a trusted resource, it is now more appropriate than ever to connect and interact directly with these second-degree connections.

Finding Companies

Search for each of the companies on your target list by typing them in the search bar and clicking the Follow button. Following companies is smart and provides another piece of data for the algorithm. You are more likely to show up in searches by workers of that company, and you will see the company's news and posts feeding through your home page. If a company receives your application and looks on LinkedIn to view your profile, you will strengthen their impression of you if you are following their company.

Outreach to Companies

Many companies have recruiting programs just for veterans. Visit their website to confirm this; if they do, you can follow their application instructions or use LinkedIn to search for their veterans' program recruiters. The same method works for finding anyone on LinkedIn. If you want to work in a department of a company, search for it, and reach out to introduce yourself.

LinkedIn is a key resource to presenting your employment brand to hiring managers, your peers, and friends who may only know you socially. The words you use to populate your LinkedIn profile will help recruiters and hiring managers find you. The companies you follow on LinkedIn will populate your news feed with rich information and press releases that may not be published in newspapers, so be on the lookout for information you can use to start a conversation. The network you develop on LinkedIn can lead you to thousands of people who can lend a hand, give advice, or make an introduction. Most importantly, your online professional reputation is your LinkedIn profile, so make it count.

SERVICE-DISABLED VETERAN-OWNED SMALL BUSINESSES PROGRAM (SDVOSB)

Becoming an SDVOSB (https://www.sba.gov/federal-contracting/contracting-assistance-programs/service-disabled-veteran-owned-small-businesses-program) allows your company to compete for government set-aside contracts. The government set-aside program provides opportunities for a small business to gain contracts that large companies would typically dominate. The program helps small businesses be more competitive in the federal marketplace. Your business must be a registered SDVOSB in order to be eligible to compete for the set-asides. For more information about registering your company as an SDVOSB, visit https://www.sba.gov/federal-contracting/contracting-guide/basic-requirements. This program is separate from the VA's Veterans First Contracting Program.

DEPARTMENT OF VETERANS AFFAIRS FIRST CONTRACTING PROGRAM

The Department of Veterans Affairs uses their Veterans First Contracting Program (https://www.va.gov/osdbu/verification/) to award VA set-aside contracts to businesses owned by veterans and/or service-connected disabled-veteran-owned companies. The Center for Verification and Evaluation (CVE) certifies/verifies SDVOSBs/VOSBs. To apply, visit https://www.vip.vetbiz.va.gov/. For more information on government contracting programs, visit https://www.sba.gov/federal-contracting/contracting-assistance-programs.

NATIONAL VETERAN SMALL BUSINESS COALITION

The National Veteran Small Business Coalition (NVSBC) (https://www nvsbc.org/) is a resource partner of the federal SBA. Through this coalition, veteran entrepreneurs promote opportunities for veteran business owners to compete in the federal marketplace. NVSBC offers three programs to eligible participants:

- Coaching Program (https://www.nvsbc.org/coaching-program-2/): Senior-level business owners share information and knowledge earned with those who have new entities.
- Govmates (https://govmates.com/): This platform helps small government contractors connect with government agencies or large businesses in need of small partners.
- GoVets (https://www.nvsbc.org/govets/): In partnership with Veratics (an SDVOSB), GoVets developed an electronic ordering marketplace that allows government agencies and commercial enterprises to purchase products and services from SDVOSBs.

STATE-BASED SITES

The federal government offers resources to assist people in becoming business owners, and many states, such as California, Illinois, and New

Hampshire, have websites for high school students, college students, and workers that holds job information specific to the state. Most states also have well-developed brick-and-mortar sites for employment assistance. These sites are important for the state-specific information and resources they offer. Information on employment statistics and trends is referred to as "labor market" information; this information can assist you in planning for your future career in a business-related realm. Remember that business is a broad field, and labor market information in one area of business, such as accounting, may have vastly different opportunities from another area, such as marketing. Getting this information up front is an important step in your ability to plan for your future, mainly by helping you plan a pathway to gaining employment.

The following sites are just a sample of what may be available to you. Always check the state's DoL website for more information.

State-Based Information

California Career Zone

https://www.cacareerzone.org/

While the California Career Zone is obviously geared for California, it can be a useful tool for research regardless of which state you are looking to settle in. And, if you are planning on attending college in California, this site will be a valuable tool in planning your academic and career pursuits. The site hosts four different self-assessment tests that allow users to test based upon their current needs. The assessments are:

- Quick Assessment: users match their personality type to potential career fields.
- Interest Profiler: users explore occupations based upon their interests.
- Skills Profiler: users determine what skills they already have and explore occupations that align with those skills.
- Work Interest Profiler: users determine which career fields reflect their values.

California Career Zone hosts a wealth of information regarding different types of job families including videos for each field. Students can use the site to determine topics such as calculating their college costs, finding schools or training programs, determining the level of education required for the different career fields, creating résumés, building references, and creating budgets.

Illinois workNet

https://www.illinoisworknet.com/

This website is peppered with helpful information to help you prepare for a career in Illinois; however, at first glance it may seem a bit overwhelming. Start by watching the tutorials. To access them, scroll down to the bottom of the main page and click on "Quick Start Guide."

Next, apply for an account. You need to confirm registration for the account through an email link the site will send you. Then you can access your dashboard. This is your starting point. Scroll down the page to see the sections available for you to use to conduct research or begin the career-search process. The ease of using the "Resume Builder" section is appealing, and strategic résumés can be built quickly.

The site can also lead you to face-to-face assistance based upon your location in the state. To find it, click on the logo at the top, center of the page (see figure 5.20).

Figure 5.20.   Illinois Work Net
https://www.illinoisworknet.com/

Then click on "Find Services and Locations." Then import the information accordingly.

For Illinois-based labor information, click on "Menu" at the top left-hand side of the page, then choose "Explore Careers." You can see that there is a wealth of information to research. Remember that data will help you drive employment. Scroll down to "Careers, Wages, and Trends." Click on the "Explore Career Pathways" link. Then find your appropriate sector. Once you are on the appropriate career page, make sure to review the information listed below the three main tabs: Jobs Facts and Wages,

Skills and Training, and Find Jobs and Information. Also remember that the information is specific to the state of Illinois.

New Hampshire Works

http://www.nhworks.org/

Similar in nature to the Illinois state site, New Hampshire Works also helps users find labor market information, create résumés and cover letters, find education and training, and locate New Hampshire Works centers. These centers "also hold workshops for technical assistance on preparing resumes and cover letters, job search workshops, employment counseling, aptitude and skills testing, and career exploration tools."[4]

To find your state employment site, use this link from CareerOneStop: https://www.careeronestop.org/JobSearch/FindJobs/state-job-banks.aspx. The links on this page will take you to state-specific employment information on topics such as job banks, unemployment, veterans' services, apprenticeships, training, disability resources, and job searches. These services are often offered in person as well, and these locations can be found on each site.

California Employment Development Department

https://www.edd.ca.gov/

The California Employment Development Department (EDD) helps Californians find jobs and file unemployment claims and helps employers manage their tax account and connect to resources. Data is specific to California; EDD offers information on industries, occupations, employment, and wages through the EDD's Data Library. This type of information can help employers make more informed decisions that impact their companies and can help employees make decisions on the type of work they are pursuing. The EDD also provides workshops tailored to a range of interests. Included are subjects such as understanding and finding veterans services, finding employment by using the internet, and résumé writing.

Texas Career Check

https://texascareercheck.com/

Like the California EDD, this site offers users the ability to explore career and school information. Information such as occupational employment data, as well as an interest profiler and a school comparison tool are included. The information on this site is specific to Texas.

Nationwide Options

Small Business Administration

The SBA is a federal organization that offers support for those who want to plan for, launch, manage, and grow their businesses. According to the website: "The SBA was created in 1953 as an independent agency of the federal government to aid, counsel, assist and protect the interests of small business concerns, to preserve free competitive enterprise and to maintain and strengthen the overall economy of our nation."[5]

The SBA provides support to small businesses/entrepreneurs by offering the following services:

- Free business counseling assistance (mentoring) at this site: https://www.sba.gov/local-assistance/find/.
- SBA guaranteed business loans: Access information from various lenders through the SBA Lender Match system (https://catran.sba.gov/lendermatch/form/contact.cfm). While the SBA does not lend money directly to entrepreneurs, the organization does set guidelines for partner lenders and helps to reduce risk for lenders, which in turn makes it easier for small-business owners to access them. They do this by offering competitive loan terms, ongoing support to lenders, and lower down payments, sometimes with no collateral.
- Disaster assistance: The SBA can provide low-interest loans meant to help businesses, renters, and homeowners recover from declared disasters. The assistance is meant to help with physical damage and economic injury.
- Guidance for those interested in pursuing government contracts: The SBA offers programs that can assist entrepreneurs/small-business owners in competing for government contracts.

The SBA offers local assistance through its partner organizations at https://www.sba.gov/local-assistance/find/. Other organizations, such as SCORE, the Women's Business Centers, and the Small Business

Development Centers (SBDC), offer free business-consulting services (mentors!) and low-cost training programs. There are some special programs just for military veterans and an overview is available at https://www.sba.gov/business-guide/grow-your-business/veteran-owned -businesses. Author Jillian Ventrone often recommends the workshops offered by the SBDCs as the offices are often located nearby, and workshops are free and usually only about two hours long (quick and easy!). They cover topics such as writing a business plan, sales prospecting, financial projections, social media marketing, and payroll taxes.

Another service offered through the SBA is the Office for Veterans Business Development (OVBD). The OVBD's purpose is to use these programs to promote entrepreneurship in veterans, service-connected disabled veterans, active-duty personnel, those in the Reserves, and those transitioning off of active-duty service as well as their dependents or survivors. Services offered through this program include workshops to help you write a business plan, concept assessments, training, and building networking connections.

OVBD centers are located across the country, some at local community colleges, such as MiraCosta College just south of the Camp Pendleton Marine Corps Base. When you visit or contact one, ask about the SBA Veterans Advantage program, which offers loan guarantees to businesses that are at least 51 percent veteran owned. More information can be found here: https://www.sba.gov/business-guide/grow-your-business/veteran -owned-businesses#section-header-0. There is another program, the Military Reservist Economic Injury Disaster Loan Program (MREIDL), which "provides loans of up to $2 million to cover operating costs that cannot be met due to the loss of an essential employee called to active duty in the Reserves or National Guard."[6]

The VA's Office of Small and Disadvantaged Business Utilization (OSDBU) houses the Veteran Entrepreneur Portal (VEP), which is designed to help veterans streamline the process of becoming an entrepreneur and also maintain their businesses, as well as to hand users off to the appropriate resources, including linking information from the SBA. Information is available on the program's goals; the verification process to participate in the Vets First Contracting Program; resources for veteran-owned businesses; marketing and networking opportunities; acquisition and contracting support; and resources for procurement readiness.[7]

The USA.gov website (https://www.usa.gov/start-business?source= busa) also has helpful information on starting a business, including information on:

- ten steps from the SBA for starting a business;
- funding options;
- tax requirements;
- business insurance;
- hiring;
- consumer-protection law;
- help for military veterans and minority business owners;
- self-employment and working from home; and
- home office deductions.[8]

Chambers of Commerce

US-Chamber of Commerce: https://www.uschamber.com/

The U.S. Chamber of Commerce advocates for small and large businesses across many sectors. The organization offers support by pushing for policies that promote jobs and grow the economy. It also offers resources and information on best business practices. Hiring Our Heroes (https://www.hiringourheroes.org/), which many of you are familiar with through the organization's visits to military bases, is a U.S. Chamber of Commerce–driven program. More information on the program can be found later in this chapter. Local-area Chambers of Commerce often house SBDC programs (discussed in the earlier section on the SBA), such as the monthly workshops. They can also typically provide mentoring to those who seek out the Chamber for support in starting a business. Usually, for support, the local Chamber will try to connect you with a member in the community who has opened a similar business. Local Chambers also host monthly networking groups.

The mother of one of the authors had her own law firm for many years. She had two other lawyers working for her and an office in a Chicago suburb. She regularly attended the local Chamber of Commerce meetings to promote her business and drum up new clientele. So she practiced law but as a small business owner, she had to bring in new clients to keep her business profitable. When she attended the meetings, she made sure to spend time chatting with as many people as she could. She passed her business cards out. Then, when one of the attendees or one of the attendee's business partners, friends, or family members needed the services of a divorce lawyer, she was the first person they contacted because she had spent time getting to know these people. She stated that her attendance at these events created quite a bit of business for her over the years. This process went both ways. She also referred many clients and people she knew to the small businesses of the people she met at the Chamber meetings. The local-area Chamber of Commerce was a great resource for her in opening her business as well. She didn't know which permits she needed nor which paperwork needed to be completed. Phone calls to the local Chamber helped with all of these details. So, if you were considering law school as a graduate school option, you can still be a small, or maybe even a big, business owner.

There are a few other options that offer assistance or programs to those in the military and military-affiliated population interested in starting a business. Some of the options are open to those across the country but do require participants to be able to go to specific sites. The following are a few innovative options.

Dog Tag, Inc. (DTI)

https://www.dogtaginc.org/our-mission

A DC-area program open to service-connected disabled veterans, caregivers, and military spouses. It is a five-month-long fellowship program that takes a multifaceted approach to teaching veterans about business ownership. The program components include an academic foundation in which students earn a certificate in business administration from Georgetown University, gain firsthand experience in managing a small business and attend lectures by seasoned entrepreneurs; all of this is tied together with a holistic, wellness-based approach. The program offers a monthly stipend to help with expenses, and students are not expected to use their GI Bills.

National Veterans Entrepreneurship Program

https://business.okstate.edu/riata/veterans/

Oklahoma State University (OSU) (with new programs starting at the University of Tennessee at Chattanooga and the University of Florida).

Part online and part face-to-face, this free program (travel, courses, books, food, etc.) offers entrepreneurship and small-business-management training to service members who are disabled due to their military service. Students learn from experienced faculty members and entrepreneurs as they progress through training modules and hands-on learning experiences.

National Center for Veteran Institute for Procurement
https://nationalvip.org/Home/Home

A program that specifically addresses federal procurement, it is offered with funding from the Montgomery County Chamber Community Foundation and grants from Lockheed Martin and the state of Maryland. Three different programs are offered—Grow, Start, and International—based on the needs of participants. Qualified participants from SDVOSBs and VOSBs nationwide attend a twenty-seven-hour, three-day comprehensive certification program, which is free once attendees get to the course, located in Washington, DC.

Bunker Labs
https://bunkerlabs.org/our-impact/

A nonprofit designed to help veterans, military spouses, and family members begin, grow, and maintain a business. The organization has a nationwide network of entrepreneurs that provide support through three different programs:

- Launch Lab: An online class where participants learn about entrepreneurship at their own pace. This class is also open to active-duty personnel. It helps attendees learn about themselves and their customers, review their product, and gain market information.
- WeWork: Veterans have access to free workspace, networking, and special events for six months.
- CEO Circle: Designed for those from companies that have demonstrated higher-level growth, it holds monthly meeting of CEOs, who are veterans or military spouses, from validated, stable companies.

Vet to CEO
https://www.vettoceo.org/

A free, seven-week program for active-duty personnel, veterans, Guard and Reserve members. Designed in part by a former Navy SEAL, the program is meant for those exploring entrepreneurship and who are already involved in the process. Learning modules include information on:

- Marketing
- Mission and purpose
- Legal and organizational issues
- Financial planning and forecasting
- Funding resources
- Networking

The Vet to CEO blog offers interesting informational tidbits: https://www .vettoceo.org/blog.

BASE TRANSITION DEPARTMENTS

If you are still on active duty, you may have access to career services at the base where you are stationed; otherwise, contact the transition department at the last base where you served and request assistance. Many of these departments are well staffed with individuals who can help you with a variety of tasks, such as résumé and cover-letter development for civilian and federal jobs, interview preparation, and job searching. Some bases host career fairs that bring in employers interested in recruiting military talents. Some of the hiring fairs are even targeted to specific MOSs and ratings. A few bases also have nonprofit groups that operate on or around them that offer helpful career services. For example, the Camp Pendleton Marine Corps Base has a nonprofit organization (https:// www.veteranstransitionsupport.org/) that operates around and sometimes on it. Russell Levy, who runs the nonprofit, puts on free classes that help service members gain employment upon transition off active service. As often as possible, he has Marines and sailors who are eligible teach these classes. Classes consist of subjects in OSHA and Lean theories. Russell is also available for résumé writing and cover-letter assistance. He also organizes meet-and-greet events with local employers to help create personal connections that may produce employment opportunities.

MILITARY-BASED TRANSITION WORKSHOPS

The military Transition Readiness Seminar program offers two-day classes in three subject areas: accessing higher education, career exploration and planning track, and the entrepreneur rack. These programs seek to expand upon a service member's knowledge base to better prepare him or her for the transition into employment, education or training, or entrepreneurship. To attend, contact your local transition department. The two-day tracks are not mandatory, unlike the week of TRS.

Accessing Higher Education

The higher education track teaches how identify the education required to support your goals, such as which subject to study, what level of education to have, important factors to consider when choosing an institution of higher education, how to fund your education, and how to prepare for transition into school. Attendees research institutions to learn about the different departments such as veterans' resources, the registrar, the bursar, disability resources, and student services. Students also compare institutions to determine which institution would be the best fit for their personal, academic, and career goals.

Career Exploration and Planning Track

The focus of the career track is to help you with career exploration and development. Labor market data shows you factors such as expected job growth of an occupation, wages, unemployment statistics and which industries people are employed in. Attendees learn how to conduct career exploration through:

- vocational assessments;
- learning about their skills and interests;
- labor market conditions;
- salary ranges; and
- career preparation programs (licensing or certification programs, technical schools, community colleges, apprenticeships, internships, etc.).[9]

This course will benefit service members who have not determined their future career goals, who need assistance in determining the viability of their current plan, or who need further career exploration.

Entrepreneur Track

The entrepreneur track is for those interested in pursuing self-employment. The curriculum for this track was developed by the SBA, and once completed, service members can enroll in a follow-on eight-week course (through the SBA) that provides them with a mentor to assist in the startup process. This course is also designed to support those interested in opening nonprofits. Attendees learn about some of the benefits and challenges of being an entrepreneur. Topics include market analysis, strategies, legal business structures, and financing options.

RECRUITERS

Job seekers are too quick to cling to the idea that an outside recruiter can find them a job. The most important thing to know about any recruiter is this: They don't work for you. They work for a company and answer to the company; all of the reciprocal client service you may expect from them is service they owe not to you, but to their paying clients.

Don't be too quick to hope that a recruiter will do your job search for you. Remember, they don't work for you! A well-orchestrated job search will be sufficient to yield the interviews you are looking for, and that search includes a clear direction, a quality résumé, and lots of applications.

Basically, there are two kinds of recruiters. Outside recruiters, also known as "headhunters," are hired by a company to perform a search on the company's behalf. They are essentially a short-term HR vendor hired to fill a specific job. Companies will hire a headhunter for a number of reasons: they have more job openings than they can handle; they are looking for a candidate with specialized qualifications; or they simply don't have the manpower or time to research, identify, and screen candidates in their regular business model. Some companies use headhunters because they are not big enough to have a dedicated HR professional or staff.

Headhunters are usually happy to hear from well-qualified candidates like you, but they can receive up to hundreds of résumés weekly and you, unfortunately, are just a number to them. Unless you fit a specific job description for a search they are performing, you will most likely not hear from them. If you do, however, you can expect a call or email from them. Always assume a headhunter is performing a search for a number of client companies and may have several openings to fill simultaneously. If you can get a conversation started with them, there is a chance they will screen you for one of the openings.

Headhunters usually work with clients at the more senior hiring levels because they are paid on commission based on the first year's salary. Therefore, it is in their best interest to concentrate on placing someone with a $100,000 base salary rather than someone with a $50,000 base salary. The best way to approach a headhunter is to reach out directly to them via email or phone; introduce yourself and keep at it until you get either their interest or a polite "thank you but we are not interested at this time."

Recruiters are easily found online through web and LinkedIn searches. If you fit their profile of a mid-to-senior level professional, they actually want to hear from you. Don't hesitate to reach out to them via email, phone, or LinkedIn and see if you can get on their radar. Remember, you may have to contact them a few times, and if they do not have any openings at the time for your qualifications, they may not show interest in you or call you back.

As for a company's internal recruiter, they are employees of the target company whose job it is to be continually searching for qualified candidates. They may also be part of the team that selects, manages, and works directly with the headhunters on hard-to-fill positions, but they also have their own caseload of jobs to fill.

If a company is big enough to have internal recruiters, the strategy is the same. Definitely try to reach out to them directly, and don't take no for an answer. You are not pestering them until they say, "We are not interested." In job hunting, the squeaky wheel gets the grease.

When a company has a job posting online and you want to reach out to the internal recruiter, it's best to apply to the position first so that your résumé is in their database. That way, they can easily search for your information when you call or email them. Many recruiters will direct you to apply online first and then contact them after you are in the database. The reason for this could be simply tracking metrics. Every large company measures its hiring process to continually improve its recruiting metrics (time to hire, candidate experience, etc.) so you are helping them by getting "in their system" first so they can track every email, conversation, and interview they schedule with you.

It is important to remember that not every company hires in the same way. If working with a headhunter or a recruiter is part of your job-search strategy, always remember to be persistent and polite, and assume they want to hear from you. If you hear from them that you are not a match, do not take it as a rejection as a candidate at large. It simply means there is not a fit for you in that company at this time or within that headhunter's current list of job requisitions. If you don't get anywhere with a recruiter, move back to the original strategy of reaching out to managers, networking with friends, and trying to open new doors at new companies—possibly by interacting with new recruiters. Assume they are good people with a highly developed ability to match skills to jobs. They are busy, not rude, and if they are not returning calls, keep trying.

Working with outside recruiters or "headhunters" can definitely open some doors for you, especially if you are a senior-level employee who matches a specific job requisition they are trying to fill. Working with inside recruiters or "corporate recruiters" is a straight line into the company, and these individuals have a clear and defined idea of the skills, qualities, and personality style they are looking for in a candidate. With any recruiter, be polite, helpful, available, and quick to return emails and phone calls. And if you get no response, keep trying until you do.

RÉSUMÉS

A well-written résumé is not just a long listing of your experience, nor is it a document that should be written and tailored for hundreds of jobs. A well-written résumé accomplishes two goals:

1. It articulates a career focus.
2. It substantiates a career focus with related skills and career experiences.

Résumés are not legal documents; rather, they function as sales documents. Information listed must be precise. Stick to facts; include dates, job titles, experience, and education and training. Now, experience and job titles must be translated before the service member can expect the civilian reader to make a connection. Veterans must pay special attention to the fact that the responsibility for making these connections is theirs as, in many cases, civilian hiring managers must sift through numerous résumés and will be looking for reasons to eliminate as many as possible to narrow the field of candidates.

One of the authors of this book, a career counselor, refers to adjusting the language in a service member's résumé from military-speak to corporate-speak as "civilianizing the résumé." Essentially, in the military, a service member's role is often to target the enemy. In business, it is the customer who must be targeted. Competition must be researched (not enemies), and, as in the military, operations must be organized, and technology must be leveraged for success. If too much military-speak is on the résumé, the reader will be left wondering if the applicant can do anything valuable in their setting. Never leave the reader wondering, as you will be left wondering why you did not get a call to interview for the job.

Job titles must also be translated to be functional so that your role is evident to the reader. Imagine a civilian seeing your Marine Corps position on your résumé as:

- Company Gunnery Sergeant, Bravo Company, Infantry Training Battalion, School of Infantry West, Camp Pendleton, CA.

instead of as:

- Chief Instructor, Infantry Training Battalion, Camp Pendleton, CA.

The first title leaves a civilian reader dazed and confused. The second one leaves the reader with the impression that the service member operated as a teacher, facilitator, or instructor, which the reader will understand. This makes your role in the military position more evident to the reader. Remember, the point of a résumé is to get the document into the pile that makes it through the HR department to the hiring manager. This means that your résumé must adhere to the following three principles while also targeting the job announcement criteria for each position:

- It must be focused.
- It must be substantiated.
- It must be aesthetically pleasing (format).

Focus

Having a career path in mind before writing a résumé will assist in your ability to target a specific career field. Since résumés must be aligned to the career field in which you intend to work, determining this prior to putting pencil to paper will give you guidance in developing the format and subject matter of the résumé. Without these details, the reader will not understand:

- the type of work you want to perform;
- your work experience; and
- how you qualify to fulfill their needs.

If you are unsure of the type of work you are interested in performing, try taking an assessment (see chapter 1), make an appointment with a career counselor, take a look at translating your military occupational specialty (see section on translating military skills) or, on your own, start to conduct some reconnaissance regarding career fields you may be interested in (see section on career research).

Next, begin to consider which parts of your background will transfer easily. For example, several different career pathways in the military provide significant experience in the field of safety.

Consider the infantry occupations, especially if you have spent time on a rifle range or as a combat instructor, and the Navy Seabees, or the Marine Corps Combat Engineers. Safety is paramount to success in these fields. The civilian sector has safety experts as well. They are usually qualified at varying levels in the field of Occupational Safety and Health Administration (OSHA) and/or with the Board of Certified Safety professionals (BCSP). More information on these two organizations can be found here:

- OSHA: https://www.osha.gov/
- BCSP: https://www.bcsp.org/

Consider whether you are missing formal experience or classroom training in your intended career direction, then acquire either a professional certification in the field or the education the career field requires. Most universities have an extended-studies or professional-education department where you may be able to obtain the credentials needed to reflect current content and applied skills for a number of growing fields. Speak with a specialist at the base education center for help with this task. They can help you find the required credential or schooling and determine means to pay for it. And remember that the education center can help you even if you have already transitioned into the civilian sector. Additionally, community colleges offer one- to two-year certificate programs in a number of disciplines that can help you shape your training toward a new field. We recommend this type of advanced formal training, even at a certificate level, that results in valuable, skills-based certificates designed collaboratively between the school and industry partners, and reflects the skills that companies are currently trying to acquire in their employees.

Once you have a career goal in focus, select two to three job titles that reflect this focus and put them at the top of your résumé as the headline. This shows the reader exactly what you are looking for, and also what they should be looking for within the body of your résumé. This approach makes for a focused, effective résumé.

Substantiate

Use your résumé to construct a profile of your capabilities and potential, given the roles you are pursuing, not to list everything you have ever done. The document should be precise in its wording to target the job so it does not dilute the focus or confuse the reader. Also, be sure to only include pertinent information that substantiates the career direction you want to take and to show the reader that you are the best person for the job.

After identifying your chosen career pathway, visit O*NET (https://www.onetonline.org/), and review the "Tasks" section. This section provides a comprehensive overview of the work activities you will find in many of the roles within that career trajectory. Begin to compare your work history and education with the bullet points in the section to ascertain how your experience transfers, and learn how the industry articulates the vocabulary in that career field. That is, use this section as a reference point in targeting verbiage for knowledge learned and experience for your résumé. For example, if there are fifteen tasks in your target occupation and your experience matches six of them, then rewrite your experience to use these six items in your résumé. This will produce a substantiation of your experience for the reader.

Format

Résumés should be simple, aesthetically pleasing, and easy to read so that the hiring manager can gather information on you quickly. They can be up to three pages long, depending on your stage of career. Try to stick to one page for zero to ten years of experience, two pages for ten to twenty years of experience, or three pages for twenty-plus years of experience. However, some types of résumés (e.g., curriculum vitae or federal résumé) and career fields may make résumés longer than three pages necessary.

While there are no specific requirements to keep to a minimum number of pages, one page should be sufficient for a junior résumé (zero to ten years of experience). You may need to pare down some of the information you want to list, such as volunteer experience. So, instead of listing experiences separately, try grouping them. For example, if you have coordinated events for two different nonprofit organizations, list them under *Volunteer Work* or *Community Service* as "Event Coordinator—Nonprofit A and Nonprofit B." In a junior résumé, the top half of the page can reflect your career focus, and the bottom half can describe the two to three positions you have already held that reflect the current career choice. Follow the jobs section with an education section.

Two-page résumés are effective for a mid-level professional, who is moving up in seniority, in reflecting the extent of promotions and responsibilities in their experience. Employers need to see behind the job title to gain better insight into the individual's accomplishments, types of projects worked on, and the level and size of these projects in order to evaluate the potential candidate. In a career that spans ten to twenty years, the résumé writer most likely has substantial evidence of her developing professional skill sets. And at this stage, she will need more space to expand upon career accomplishments to demonstrate her upward career trajectory.

Aesthetics

Résumés should be aesthetically pleasing to invite and motivate the reader to pick it up. Such a résumé is not dense, does not have wide margins or a tiny font, and has well-organized information that is easy to find and read. Review the following elements and incorporate them into your résumé to stimulate interest in your reader. Remember, if the document looks overwhelming to the reader, he or she may not ever pick it up. That means that the battle is lost before it ever began.

- Bullet points: These are the key to drawing the reader's attention to a specific qualification. They should be strategically used to display key competencies for the role and to substantiate experience listed for each position. You will see in the following examples how to edit the bullet points to adjust the résumé focus.
- White space: Regular, one-inch margins help the writing appear properly spaced, not dense, while drawing the reader's eye to the areas where information stops and new information begins. This promotes greater gathering of data by the reader.
- Font and size: A sans serif font, such as Arial, makes reading easier on the eye as script is less ornate than serif fonts such as Times New Roman. Remember, your résumé's initial contact will be with an individual reading it or with a computer program scanning it. Oftentimes, the résumé-scanning software programs can have difficulty interpreting the text of serif fonts. Jason Hanold, a recruiting expert, in an interview published by CNBC Make It stated, "A poorly selected font can indeed derail one's chances for an interview, especially if other factors aren't as strong," and "fonts set a subconscious tone for the reader."[10]
- Keywords: If you have substantiated your résumé, then all the keywords you need to get noticed will be present, but just to be sure, research the descriptions of the jobs you are applying for, and incorporate any missing keywords or language that references the skills and qualifications required by the job. Your experience is unique and should reflect this, but you should also use vocabulary that is common within the industry you are pursuing to limit any miscommunications.

Case Examples

Two résumé examples (textboxes 5.1 and 5.2) are presented showing changes that are explained next. The résumé writer has experience as a logistics manager from prior military experience.

If you are a logistics manager in the military and intend to remain in the same career as a civilian, then much of the experience you gained while in the military will transfer. Your career goal would be *logistics manager*, and the headline on your résumé would read "Logistics Manager / Operations / Security Management." Remember, use two to three job titles to articulate your career focus to the reader.

If you were a logistics manager in the military, enjoyed managing people but not the field of logistics, and you want to move into a field focused on HR, then you would obtain the required education for the career change and focus your résumé by including substantiating evidence of managing, coordinating, delegating, hiring, onboarding, training, and reviewing staff, rather than the logistics and operations aspect of your experience. Your career goal would be *human resources manager* or *organizational development specialist*, and the headline of your résumé would be "Human Resources." In the textbox 5.2 example, we expanded the focus to include senior leadership and organizational development positions, so this individual's headline is "Human Resources Leader / Organizational Development Specialist."

Résumé Examples

The résumé examples in textboxes 5.1 and 5.2 show one individual's résumé written two ways. This individual's logistics experience (textbox 5.1) has been adapted for a human resources/organizational development role (textbox 5.2). Review each example to see how the use of white space, bullet points, keywords and substantiating evidence create an effective and easy-to-read résumé. Read the logistics manager résumé first, as it is the original. Then, read the HR version; it is the adapted version. Each change has been noted by a strikethrough or an underline for you to easily find. A strikethrough indicates the content from the original logistics manager role that has been deleted. Underlined content is new content that has been added.

Your Name

12345 Street Address, City, ST ZIP
(999) 999-9999   youremail@gmail.com

LOGISTICS MANAGER / OPERATIONS / SECURITY MANAGEMENT

Proven Operations and Logistics professional with over 10 years of senior leadership management and extensive project management experience. Particular expertise designing and implementing highly effective security, logistics and operations plans, developing policies and procedures, and training and managing staff to perform above expectations in decentralized organizations. Personable and professional with a mentoring nature and the ability to build and manage high performing teams in growing, changing and developing organizations.

KEY COMPETENCIES

- Operations Management
- Logistics Management
- Resource Planning / Project Management
- Operations Policies and Procedures
- Metrics / Measurement / Goals
- Staff / Department Leadership
- Complex Problem Solving
- Reorganization / Consolidation

PROFESSIONAL EXPERIENCE

United States Marine Corps   **2/1986–2/2016**

Operations Manager (2012–present)

Acted as advisor to senior executives, managing $200M in assets and allocating appropriate resources to ensure deadlines were met and goals achieved.

Responsible for developing, coordinating, and executing training plans for 6 geographically separated companies.

- Led a team of 30 in the planning and implementation of 3 highly successful training events for 1,200 personnel
- Senior member of project team that evaluated and restructured enterprise-wide training metrics and output standards
- Supervised the preparation activities for 5 policy and procedure inspections, resulting in an average of 97% percent rate of adherence

Operations Manager (2008–2012)

Responsible for conceptualizing and developing innovative solutions to solve complex operational problems, coordinating with multinational team leaders, and assembling and developing operational teams to manage a global workforce. Primary duties included designing and establishing a complex $500K Operations Center, and developing, planning and implementing training for thousands of personnel in preparation for two international deployments.

- Significantly improved the operational capabilities for global partners, as member of a multinational team that led and directed 2 major operations with global partners
- Reorganized the operations center creating a reduction of on shift personnel of 25% with a savings of 48 man-hours daily and consolidating all team members in the same building
- Received multiple recommendations from executives for a broader role with greater responsibilities within the organization

Operations Manager (2005–2008)

Responsible for developing and implementing logistical plans which supported and synchronized with another key department in a major operation. Primarily responsible for developing, planning and executing training for thousands of personnel for two global operations, and establishing a Ground Operations Centers to support operational commitments in a highly complex environment.

- Project manager for a team that redesigned an antiquated perimeter security system which yielded an increase in observation capability of 20%
- Developed a support request system that enabled a processing time reduction of 50% from request to support action completion

PRIOR LEADERSHIP EXPERIENCE

Mid-Level Manager (2002–2005)

Chief Instructor and Curriculum Developer (1999–2002)

Team Leader (1996–1999)

Recruiter (1993–1996)

Instructor and Curriculum Developer (1990–1993)

Team Member (1986–1990)

EDUCATION

Associate of Arts–Coffeeville Community College, Coffeeville, KS

Additional Qualifications–Experienced Operations Manager, Crisis Manager, Instructor Certified, Curriculum Developer Certified, Professional Selling Skills (PSS) Certified

TRAINING, AWARDS, AFFILIATIONS AND CLEARANCE

Professional Development—Senior Advisor Seminar, Advanced Leadership Academy, Career Leadership Academy

Honors and Awards—6 US Military personal decorations for superior achievement and leadership, Twice Distinguished Graduate from Leadership Academy Courses

Personal Affiliations—Marine Corps Association, Marine Executive Association, American Legion

Security Clearance: Active Secret

Your Name

12345 Street Address, City, ST ZIP
(999) 999-9999   youremail@gmail.com

HUMAN RESOURCES LEADER / ORGANIZATIONAL DEVELOPMENT SPECIALIST

<u>Proven Organizational Leadership professional with over 10 years of senior management experience training, coordinating and managing staff. Particular expertise designing and implementing highly effective staffing and performance plans with a focus on developing policies and procedures, and training and managing staff to perform above expectations in decentralized organizations.</u> Personable and professional with a mentoring nature and the ability to build and manage high performing teams in growing, changing and developing organizations.

KEY COMPETENCIES

- Organizational Leadership / Development
- Enterprise-wide Training / Staff Performance
- Human Resource Allocation / Planning
- Staff Policies and Procedures
- Department Reorganization / Consolidation
- Metrics / Measurement / Staff Goals
- Complex Problem Solving / Communication
- Cross Functional Collaboration

PROFESSIONAL EXPERIENCE

United States Marine Corps   **2/1986–2/2016**

Operations Manager (2012–present)

~~Acted as advisor to senior executives, managing $200M in assets and allocating appropriate resources to ensure deadlines were met and goals achieved.~~ Responsible for developing, coordinating, and executing training plans for 6 geographically separated companies, <u>and collaborating with senior executives regarding the appropriate allocation of over $200M in assets</u>.

- <u>Provided organizational leadership to</u> ~~Led~~ a team of 30 in the planning and implementation of 3 highly successful training events for 1,200 personnel
- Senior member of project team that evaluated and restructured enterprise-wide training metrics and output standards
- <u>Continually monitored and improved staff productivity levels by supervising</u> ~~Supervised~~ the preparation activities for 5 policy and procedure inspections, resulting in an average of 97% percent rate of adherence

Operations Manager (2008–2012)

Responsible for <u>collaborating and</u> ~~conceptualizing and developing innovative solutions to solve complex operational problems,~~ coordinating with multinational team leaders, and assembling and developing operational teams to manage a global workforce. Primary duties included ~~designing and establishing a complex $500K Operations Center, and~~ developing, planning and implementing training for thousands of personnel in preparation for two international deployments.

- Significantly improved the operational capabilities for global partners, as member of a multinational team that led and directed 2 major operations with global partners
- Reorganized the operations center creating a reduction of on shift personnel of 25% with a savings of 48 man-hours daily and consolidating all team members in the same building
- Received multiple recommendations from executives for a broader role with greater responsibilities within the organization

Operations Manager (2005–2008)

~~Responsible for developing and implementing logistical plans which supported and synchronized with another key department in a major operation.~~ Primarily responsible for developing, planning and executing training for thousands of personnel for two global operations, and establishing a Ground Operations Centers to support operational commitments in a highly complex environment.

- ~~Project manager for~~ Staffed, managed and delegated a team that redesigned an antiquated perimeter security system which yielded an increase in observation capability of 20%

- Streamlined communications across the organization by developing ~~Developed~~ a support request system that enabled a processing time reduction of 50% from request to support action completion

PRIOR ~~LEADERSHIP~~ HUMAN RESOURCES EXPERIENCE

Mid-Level Manager (2002–2005)

Chief Instructor and Curriculum Developer (1999–2002)

Team Leader (1996–1999)

Recruiter (1993–1996)

Instructor and Curriculum Developer (1990–1993)

Team Member (1986–1990)

EDUCATION

Certificate in Human Resources—University of California, Irvine Extension Program (in progress)

Associate of Arts—Coffeeville Community College, Coffeeville, KS

Additional Qualifications—Experienced Operations Manager, Crisis Manager, Instructor Certified, Curriculum Developer Certified, Professional Selling Skills (PSS) Certified

TRAINING, AWARDS, AFFILIATIONS AND CLEARANCE

Professional Development—Senior Advisor Seminar, Advanced Leadership Academy, Career Leadership Academy

Honors and Awards—6 US Military personal decorations for superior achievement and leadership, Twice Distinguished Graduate from Leadership Academy Courses

Personal Affiliations—Marine Corps Association, Marine Executive Association, American Legion

Security Clearance: Active Secret

INFORMATIONAL INTERVIEWING

So far, we have reviewed many resourceful websites and educational resources that can guide you in your quest for career information, but we have missed one major resource: people who already work in the occupation. Information from hands-on sources is the best you can get. It is real-time information, which means it is current and relevant to your career research, it may arm you with information to use during future job interviews, and it will expend your professional network. When you meet with these people you will need to conduct an informational interview. Informational interviews are not solicitations for jobs. According to the University of North Carolina's Career Center, "It is a conversation with an objective to learn."[11]

The interviews, which should be roughly thirty minutes in length, help you get a glimpse into a position from someone who currently holds or previously held it. The interviews help you practice your professional communication skills and begin to develop a vocabulary specific to your chosen industry. This will help you during the oral portion of the job application process. One consistent concern for all transitioning service members is the inability to rid themselves of military-speak. Think of the number of acronyms you use daily and the strange names for things (civilians don't call pens "ink sticks"!). Now think about wiping all of it out of your vocabulary overnight. It isn't possible. Practicing informational interviewing will help you along this journey. Pay attention to the vocabulary your interviewee uses. If he uses unfamiliar words or terms, ask him to explain them to you. Make notes and review them before you interview for positions you applied to. Try to bring some of the new vocabulary into your daily speech to familiarize yourself with it and gain fluidity.

To get started on your informational interviewing, create a list of questions you would like to ask. Make them open-ended questions that call for more detailed answers than a simple yes or no. Questions should relate to the specific career field. Topics covered should include the following:

• Information about the industry:

  ◦ Is the industry experiencing growth?
  ◦ What changes do you think will occur in the industry in the next few years?

- ◦ Why do people leave this occupation?
- ◦ Are there work-from-home opportunities?
- ◦ Are there opportunities for self-employment?
- ◦ Are there any major developments occurring?

- Information about the work:

  - ◦ Typical day in the job
  - ◦ Skills required on a day-to-day basis
  - ◦ Best part of the job
  - ◦ Hours worked on a weekly basis
  - ◦ Challenges
  - ◦ Daily likes and dislikes about the company

- Pay and advancement:

  - ◦ Reasonable salary and long-term potential
  - ◦ Opportunities for advancement and pathways to achieve it
  - ◦ Length of time it takes to become a manager, or to go from entry-level to vice president

- Skills and experience required:

  - ◦ Best educational pathway to attain employment
  - ◦ Qualifications the company wants to see for entry-level positions or new hires
  - ◦ Best gateway into the profession
  - ◦ Ask the person to review the skills and experience you have already attained, what they may qualify you for, and if you have any gaps that need to be addressed
  - ◦ Target companies to research

- Culture of the company/industry:

  - ◦ Does the occupation require travel or late hours?
  - ◦ What qualities are essential to achieve success?
  - ◦ How does the environment compare to other companies?
  - ◦ How can I explore more about the company's culture?

- Career preparation:

  - ◦ Are there specific courses that may help me better prepare or make me a more valuable asset?

- ◦ Are there any resources or organizations I should join?
- ◦ Does the company offer internships?
- ◦ Ask if the person might review your résumé and offer feedback.
- ◦ What are the best options for networking in this field?

Now you need to find someone to interview. The University of California, Berkeley, Career Center lists the following information on its website:

- Pursue your own contacts, including those in different career fields, as it may lead you to people you do not know but who work in your desired sector.
- Reach out to your current or previous professors and teaching assistants to see if they have recommendations.
- Identify alumni from your institution who may be able to help.
- Ask people you meet—this technique has led me to many excellent leads.[12]

So, now you are prepared with questions and an interviewee. But you need to prepare to introduce yourself. Spend time creating a brief introduction that tells the interviewee a bit about your background and what you hope to gain from the meeting. You may consider including information on your military experience, your educational experience or goals, job shadowing you have done or internships planned, and the interests you have in the interviewee's career field. Keep it brief. No one needs a listing of every rank you held during your time in the military. You can say something like "I am a recently separated sergeant in the United States Marine Corps where I spent five years working in logistics" or "I separated from the Army, where I worked in public affairs, and am now actively seeking information about the field of marketing." It's quick and concise, letting the interviewee know that you have military experience, but not overwhelming them with information they may not understand. And, you never know, maybe your interviewee also served in the military. This will give you a commonality, which may help the interview process proceed more smoothly.

Also, take a minute to explain how you found the individual, that you are looking for information but not soliciting a job, and ask if the person has time to assist you and if they prefer contact through email or by phone. You should have your information already prepared. What if the person has time right at that moment?

After you conduct the informational interview, make sure to send a follow-up email or call to thank the person for taking the time to help you. Keep notes on the information you learned and what you would still like to learn about the career. Consider keeping in touch with the interviewee; ask if this would be okay. This person may become a part of your business network. Make sure you tell them that you followed up on their advice and how it helped you. Finally, make note of what your next steps should be. Maybe you need to find other people to interview, people in different positions or at different companies. Maybe you need further training or schooling. Maybe you need to reformat your résumé. Whatever the case, keeping detailed notes will help you track your progress.

For more information on informational interviewing visit at the following sites:

- University at Buffalo: http://mgt.buffalo.edu/career-resource-center/students/networking/mentorlink/40-questions-to-ask-in-an-informational-interview.html
- University of California, Berkeley: https://career.berkeley.edu/Info/Info Interview
- CareerOneStop: https://www.careeronestop.org/JobSearch/Network/informational-interviews.aspx
- Indeed: https://www.indeed.com/career-advice/interviewing/what-to-expect-in-informational-interview
- Penn State: https://studentaffairs.psu.edu/career/resources/networking/informational-interviewing
- Live Career: http://www.miracosta.edu/instruction/careerservices/for students-career-exploration-resources.html and https://www.livecareer.com/career/advice/interview/information-interview

INTERVIEWING

Interviewing can be either one of the most nerve-wracking experiences in securing employment or a time you're actually really proud of. Choose an approach that will result in the latter; the process will be more enjoyable, and it will also produce better results. This chapter is meant to guide you through the preparation and strategy planning for an interview. Remember, the focus of this book is on those who are interested in working in the realm of business. If you want to be a teacher, while many of these same tactics will work, the process may need to be altered to be relevant to that career field.

Before the Interview

Ask anyone what to do before an interview, and the answer will be the same: research the company. The goal of researching a company is to orient yourself to the company; the leadership team; the people who will be interviewing you; how your job target fits into the big picture of the company at this time in its growth; and the job itself. Do your research with the goal of figuring out the company's strategy and how you can help them in this role.

Spend time reading about the company on its website, not to memorize everything, but to familiarize yourself with the company history, product lines, major projects, and any current press releases or those from the last year. Reading the executive bios will give you an idea of the leadership team's background. Consider these questions as you read:

- Do they come from bigger companies?
- Did they start this company on their own?
- Do they have technical backgrounds?
- Are they more focused on the products or the business management?

It's important to get a feel for the culture; you can garner quite a bit of information from what you read. For example, if everyone on the leadership team has a PhD in engineering, you can safely assume there will be a technical culture. If most people on the leadership team have been put in place to manage the business, you can safely assume there will be a less technical culture. Perhaps the website describes the culture explicitly, and this is always good information to begin formulating an interview approach. Usually if a company has gone to the trouble to publish its mission or values, it actually tries to fulfill them. Not every company can do this, and there will be struggles within any company's culture, but understanding their cultural goals and approach to business will help you develop valuable questions about their teams, how they formed, how they treat their clients and most importantly, how they treat each other.

There's no question that a company's LinkedIn page is a treasure trove of information about a company. Read carefully how the company describes itself, and read the bios of several of its employees. Note how they write about the company. Do they write proudly about it? Have they been there long? What are their backgrounds?

As well as a place to read about the company and its employees, LinkedIn is where to get current company information. Not every press release hits the newswire, but often they are published on LinkedIn. Then read the company's other news. Usually companies will post exciting developments such as hiring an important key employee or executive, funding, acquisitions, new products, or major contracts. These are the important events that usually trigger a company to hire someone. Try to guess why the company is considering you, and see if you can tie their need to fill a position to a press release or company post of some kind. Knowledge is power! This will also help you formulate good questions in an interview about the event, transaction, contract, or person you are interviewing with. You will sound informed because you will be, and you will sound as though you did your homework— because you did!

It's surprising how much valuable company and industry information gets posted on Twitter. Twitter has become a robust conversation platform for people highly interested in what others are doing. It is a platform offering a broad and deep array of information to bring you closer to the heart of what's happening in an industry, a company, or even a specific product. It's really incredible how much you can find out just by following trails of information on Twitter. Twitter is especially helpful for finding interesting information about technology or engineering companies, or other highly innovative companies in medical-device, advanced-manufacturing, or emerging technologies of any kind. This is a fantastic resource for not only researching a company further, but finding out the trends in the industry! You will sound as though you have done your homework, and this type of research is valuable to help you understand how a company is positioning itself in its market.

Conduct a bit of research on the people who will interview you. It is absolutely acceptable to ask, prior to an interview, for the names of the people you'll be meeting with. Get their first and last names, the correct spelling, their job titles, and the format of the interview. In other words, will it be a brief meeting with one person, then a second, then a third? Or will it be a panel interview? Or is this just a screening meeting with one manager? Orient yourself well to the interview, who you will be meeting with, and even what to wear. You want to feel comfortable going in, and it's perfectly acceptable to ask the HR manager a lot of questions when scheduling the meeting.

Look up each person you'll be meeting with, and spend a full ten minutes or more reading up on them. Look for information such as:

- How long have they been with the company?
- What has been their career progression?
- What are their responsibilities at the firm?
- What is their educational background, and does it match their career trajectory?
- What has been their career trajectory according to LinkedIn, and is it a progressive build or do they seem to have entered this field by happenstance?

If this information is available, your goal is to estimate what their role would be in relation to the one you are interviewing with, and to find out what's important to them. Some managers value subject matter expertise and quality over completion or accuracy. Some managers value team players over individual performers. It can be difficult to guess the internal culture of a company, but if you look for clues as you read the bios of the management team, you can make some educated guesses that will help you build rapport in interviews and adjust quickly to interviewers' communication styles and expectations.

Interview Questions

There are three main questions to prepare for:

1. Tell me about yourself.
2. What are your strengths and weaknesses?
3. Why should we hire you?

Additionally, you will be asked the following types of questions:

1. Behavioral questions
2. Skills or job-specific questions

The following are a few questions that you should be prepared to answer at every interview. Proper preparation will establish a natural flow in the interview.

Questions Asked at Every Interview

Tell me about yourself.

This answer should be scripted, rehearsed, and delivered in about ninety seconds. Here is a formula to follow that should tell the story about your career arc and what you bring to the company today:

1. Born and raised in . . . .
2. Earned a degree in . . . From . . . .
3. Spent the bulk of my career doing . . . .
4. Where I learned these three things . . . .
5. At this time in my career, I'm making a transition because . . . .
6. And close with an enthusiasm statement, like: "I'm really excited to be here today to learn more about this company, all of you who work here, and how my background might help you achieve your goals.

Remember to write out your script, rehearse it, and condense it to about ninety seconds. That way when you sit down and they pitch you this question, you are ready to deliver.

What are your strengths and weaknesses?

Everyone has a few core strengths, and with every strength comes a weakness. The corollary is true: with every weakness comes a strength. For example, someone with a visual disability will develop exceptionally strong hearing skills. This is called a compensatory skill, and these skills are not just related to physical disabilities. Look for your weakness and related compensatory skill, or look for your greatest strength and how it may work against you. Here are some examples:

- Strong leadership skills, but not a technical specialist
- Strong technical specialization, but not as good at time management
- Strong with time management, tends to take on too many projects
- Eager to take on projects, not as good at prioritizing
- Strong at prioritizing, not as good at following up

You can see a few examples where a highly developed strength *could* work against someone. These core characteristics usually work together, so deliver them in a three-step sequence:

1. Strength
2. Weakness
3. How you've improved it

Here are a few examples:

- My strength is prioritizing and delegating projects, but I found earlier in my career that I wasn't as focused on following up. I have learned over the years to trust my team but always follow up, and I think this has really helped me become a great manager across an entire project.
- I believe my strength is in my leadership, and that includes working collaboratively with people, and providing guidance, structure and feedback so everyone is focused on the same goals. I've found that learning more about the subject matter has helped me become a better communicator and a better leader, so you can expect me to take extra time so I can relate and communicate stronger with my teams.
- I really enjoy learning, and with my positive attitude, it's hard to say no, so I'm definitely someone you can count on to take on those extra projects. Where this can work against me is that I can get a lot on my plate and, in the past, it was hard to prioritize, but I've learned to delegate and set boundaries so the important work is being completed, and the rest can be handled by someone else.

Why should we hire you?

Don't let this be a tough question. Use the power of contrast. Simply state how you are just like the other candidates (education, training, years of experience, etc.), and then state that one thing that makes you stand out. This should be one thing no one else will have, like a specific project you worked on that is useful to their goals. Perhaps it's subject matter expertise, or that you worked for their competitor, or know their key accounts well from working at another company. It could also simply be a personal characteristic like your temperament, your positivity, your flexibility, your responsiveness. Think broadly about what could make you stand out, and deliver that in a statement that shows some contrast to their field of applicants.

Behavioral Questions

Expect behavioral questions, which are simply open-ended questions about how you would or how you have behaved in a given situation. Behavioral questions usually begin with "Tell us about a time when. . . ." or "What would you do in a situation like . . . ?" These can be tricky because it feels as if there's no right answer. Remember your research when they ask you these questions. Hopefully you will have investigated what is important to the company and the people you're speaking with to understand what they are hoping to hear from you. With a clear focus, deliver your answer, such as "providing leadership," "asking someone else," "delegating," "following up," or "following through," or even "staying late." Be sure to answer in a way that feels natural to you because although they are looking for you to fit into their culture, you want to feel like you fit there, too. Answer as honestly and intelligently as possible, and if it's a good fit on both ends, you will both know it.

Skills or Job-Specific Questions

In preparing for an interview, reread the job description and anticipate questions they may ask for each of the bullet points. Then draft an answer based on this three-step process:

1. Affirm the skill
2. Tell them where you learned it
3. Tell them what this means to them (the value)

Here are a few examples:

- Manage program objectives, plans, schedules, upcoming events, risks, issues, changes and change-control, and current performance status.
- (Affirm the skill.) Yes, I can definitely manage your performance status, changes, and monitor risk.
- (Tell them where you learned it.) In the military I was responsible for managing, monitoring, and reporting on all distribution activities and this included project changes, coordinating schedules and plans, and making sure all distribution activities aligned with our objectives.
- (Tell them what this means to them.) What this means to you is that I can be trusted to manage these important project details with accuracy and efficiency with a focus on integrating the projects into the overarching strategy.

Do you have any questions for us?

With your research will come knowledge about the company, and that is a great place to look for intelligent questions about the position, the department, the company, or the industry. Refrain from asking about the salary or room for growth until a formal offer is being made. Instead, use this time to strengthen your relationship with the interviewer and your position as a qualified candidate.

If this is a newly created position, ask about it. It would be nice to know if the position is being created because of a new contract, a new client, a product launch, a consolidation between departments, the acquisition of a new company, or another reason. There is always a reason and knowing why they are hiring at this time will help you understand more about their priorities.

It is perfectly acceptable to ask specific questions about the role to get a clear understanding of reporting structure, job activities, and their highest priorities. Culture questions are also acceptable. Ask a few questions to investigate a little more about their culture and how you may fit in. Asking these questions also helps them see that you are making an effort to learn about how to fit in to their groups. Asking about additional training offered, the department goals, or general questions about how they service their clients is also acceptable.

The following are some examples:

- Is this a new position, or am I replacing someone?
- Is the department expanding?
- What is the first priority I would be expected to focus on?
- Who would I report to?
- What is the team like?
- Are there any major projects starting that I would be asked to help with?
- What's the most important characteristic or skill you are looking for?
- Can you tell me a little about your customers?
- How long have the managers been here? Are the employees long term?
- How does the company/department/manager define success?
- What do you enjoy most about working here?
- Where would the company/department like to be in five years?
- Will there be any training, formal or informal, available?
- Are there any classes or trainings I can take on SkillShare prior to starting, if offered the job?

Interviews can be tricky but with some guided research and planning, you can predict the questions they will ask, what they expect of you, and how you can present yourself to fit in to their culture and department needs. As a reminder, always show up on time, take notes, wait to be seated, use manners, listen and respond, and be yourself. The more you relax and enjoy their company, the more they will feel relaxed around you and enjoy yours, too.

NETWORKING

In the late 1990s, one of the authors of this book was planning to make a major career change after decades with one employer. He was a bit rusty on the basics of searching for career opportunities. In preparation, he attended many workshops about career changes and employment opportunities, and learned something very quickly—the importance of networking to seek out career opportunities.

What is networking? Why is it important in any job search? Networking is a way of interacting with others to exchange information and develop professional and social contacts. The Career and Workplace website (https://www.champlain.edu/online/blog/career-workplace) of Champlain College of Vermont points out some of the many benefits of networking, including finding out about open positions that are not advertised, cultivating important contacts in business, building relationships with people who have something in common with you, and finding professionals who can mentor you.[13]

The résumé service company TopResume believes networking is important because "the right employee referral can increase your chances tenfold of landing a job."[14]

An article in the *Harvard Business Review*, "Learn to Love Networking," states that many professionals say networking makes them feel uncomfortable, but is a necessity in today's world. One approach suggested is to focus on learning by approaching a social event with the idea that you may learn something interesting.[15]

In the article "The Networking Advice No One Tells You" appearing in *Forbes* magazine, the author suggests that people limit themselves in their networking by having the wrong mindset.[16]

CareerOneStop recommends having clear ideas about what you will say to others and what information you want to learn from them. Think about the kind of jobs you are looking for and the industry you want to target. Identify skills needed for particular jobs and your own skills. Think about whether you want to stay in your area or have particular locations in mind.[17]

Think about your elevator speech when networking. An elevator speech is a short sound bite or commercial about yourself. Monster.com calls it a fifteen- to thirty-second pitch that explains who you are and what you are seeking.[18] CareerOneStop recommends closing your elevator speech with "Do you have any advice for me?"[19]

Remember to put a personal spin on your elevator speech. Do not sound robotic. One recommendation is mentioning your hobby and how it relates to your job; you can find more information on this recommendation here: https://www.monster.com/career-advice/article/how-to-do-an-elevator-pitch. You may ask if the person to whom you are making the pitch would be willing to look over your résumé and offer advice. If that's the case, do not forget to ask for an email address.[20]

Always remember to keep a list of the contacts you make in your networking. Have some simple business cards made just for your networking opportunities. Keep track of the connections you make. Write them in a notebook, and make some small notes regarding the conversation you had and whether follow-up is required. CareerOneStop recommends: "When someone in your network refers you to an employer, make direct contact in-person, by phone, or by e-mail."[21] When making those contacts, be professional and do not use nicknames. Introduce yourself and keep messages short and to the point. If you do not receive a reply, email or leave a message. Texting is not recommended.

There are more ways to network than you may realize. Does your college have an alumni association? Better yet, does your college have a local chapter of the alumni association? Many of us have heard the stories about the Ivy League graduates with a list of contacts (or rolodex, back in the day). Reaching out to fellow alumni is not just an Ivy League tactic. Some colleges have career centers available to alumni, which can provide an opportunity for more alumni networking. The Career Centers can often put alumni in contact with other alumni employed in business, industry, and the public sector.

Military veterans have organizations to join, including the American Legion and the Veterans of Foreign Wars (VFW). Other organizations include:

- Navy League: https://www.navyleague.org/
- Marine for Life Network: https://www.usmc-mccs.org/services/career/marine-for-life-network/
- Association of the United States Army: https://www.ausa.org/
- Air Force Association: https://www.afa.org/
- Fleet Reserve Association for the Navy, Marine Corps and Coast Guard: https://www.fra.org/

People from all walks of life are members of veterans' organizations, including business owners, working professionals, and executives in major companies. These are all valuable contacts when you are looking to make that next career move.

Public service and volunteer organizations offer networking opportunities. Rotary International is a network of 1.2 million people who work toward growing local economies, support education, assist mothers and children, and conduct other projects to make the world a better place.[22] Rotarians volunteer on projects locally and even globally. They call themselves "people of action—where neighbors, friends, and problem solvers share ideas, join leaders, and take action to create lasting change."[23] The organization is global and promotes this on their website by stating, "Club activities, social events, and volunteer projects offer networking opportunities that build personal and professional connections. And Rotarians can extend those networks by visiting other clubs around the globe."[24]

Last, consider the Lion's Club International, Kiwanis International, Optimist International, and Moose International. All of these organizations mentioned have informative websites with information about their pursuits and causes and listings of their clubs and chapters. Find one that might fit your needs, and at the same time, take advantage of the networking opportunities available through your participation.

Job fairs offer many opportunities for networking. The job assistance site Undercover Recruiter (https://theundercoverrecruiter.com/5-tips-successful-career-fair-networking/) offers some good tips on networking at job and career fairs:

- Network, do not interview, at job fairs. Regard the recruiter or human resources manager as the first point of contact in the process of gaining an interview. Introduce yourself and tell a little about your background, then follow up with an email or phone call.
- Be prepared. Dress well and prepare well. Have plenty of copies of your résumé and be ready with a "quick pitch about who you are and what you do."[25]
- Do your research. Career fairs are good opportunities to find out about companies, but do your own research on companies that will be in attendance. Go to the company websites and find out which ones are hiring in your field and which ones are not.
- Stand out in some way. That can mean dressing sharper or highlighting awards and honors on résumés.[26]

Social media for job seekers is another way to network, and one of the best-known resources is LinkedIn. Currently it has over 610 million users in over 200 countries and claims to be the largest professional network on the internet.[27] Members of LinkedIn grow a network of fellow professionals based on common connections including profession, type of business, alumni, military background (active, reserve, and veterans), common industry, and similar job titles. Users can create a profile in résumé format. Want a good way to demonstrate your knowledge about your occupation? Remember that LinkedIn users can write and post their own articles.

There are résumé and portfolio online services that allow for creativity so you can network your own brand. One such service is PortfolioGen (https://www.portfoliogen.com), which allows people to build an online portfolio that can include the résumé itself, presentation videos, awards, certificates, college transcripts, listing of publications you have authored, and more. You are assigned a specific web address for your portfolio, and it can be linked to your LinkedIn profile. The link can be printed on your business card.

Creating your own blogs and Facebook pages is a creative way to network. A friend of ours, "Ms. J," works in education but has to change jobs every few years because she is a military spouse. Her spouse receives transfer orders every few years that require moving to other geographical areas. Ms. J and her spouse have found themselves moving from duty stations in Virginia and California to duty stations overseas, including Japan, Bahrain, and Indonesia. Ms. J has learned to be creative in her networking efforts. She has developed her own Facebook page and blog to discuss education programs for the military and their family members. Ms. J started out with a Facebook page on opportunities for military education, not just for service members but for their family members as well. She refers to her education Facebook page as a think tank for the free exchange of ideas. To build up her education Facebook page, and to expand her network, she combed through her Facebook friends and invited people with certain commonalities to join, such as active-duty members, spouses of active-duty members, military reservists, people working with college programs on military bases, and other college administrators and professionals. These people joined her Facebook page and, in turn, invited their fellow military members and education professionals to join.

Next Ms. J started a blog about her experiences as a military spouse and linked it on her military education Facebook page. This led to even more networking connections. Soon Ms. J. had connections across many military bases, colleges, base education centers, and spouse organizations across the United States and overseas. Whenever her spouse was up for orders and a military move was impending, Ms. J. would announce it on her Facebook page and blog. Sometimes she would have job offers, or at least offers of job-search assistance, before even moving to the new duty station. She also networked with military education professionals who had written books on military education. She communicated with these authors and received advice on writing her own books and on publishers to contact. Soon she had her own books published on military education and life as a military spouse.

While one of the authors of this book was working for the Navy's education program, he had an acquaintance who had worked as an admissions representative for a local college. Let's call him Mr. G. He wanted to start working with the military in education and had submitted many applications for civil service positions with military organizations. Mr. G did not have success. He had never even been invited for an interview after applying for civil service jobs. Mr. G approached the local director of the base Navy College Program and asked if he could work as an unpaid volunteer when his schedule permitted. The director was very surprised because no one had ever volunteered to do unpaid volunteer work for the Navy's education program. The director had to check with upper-level management to see if such a thing could even be permitted. No one could find any regulation saying it could not be done, so Mr. G was allowed to do unpaid volunteer work with the Navy College Program. He made many networking connections. Mr. G did not get an offer, but he did meet a college representative who was impressed with his cheerful can-do attitude. He ended up with a great job working with a community college program for the military; it was a well-paying position with a local college.

What did Ms. J and Mr. G have in common? They both became creative in their networking efforts and found new opportunities through their due diligence. You can be creative, too. There are other social media possibilities. How about YouTube videos on topics related to your profession? YouTube videos sometimes go viral. There are possibilities in Twitter. Use your imagination to create opportunities.

Eventbrite is a good resource to discover job and business networking events. Eventbrite is an event management website used to market and sign up people for many types of events. Start out by doing an Eventbrite search using the word *networking* and do it for specific cities. Recently, I gave it a try for several cities including "networking San Diego" and the cities of Cleveland, Boston, Atlanta, and Seattle. The following are some events that came up by city.

Eventbrite networking events in San Diego:

- Sola Business Opportunities
- Speed Networking for Business Professionals
- San Diego Startup Meetup
- San Diego Job Fair
- Indie Broker Network
- Veterans Employment Committee Job & Resource Fair

Eventbrite networking events in Cleveland:

- In the Company of Women—A Celebration of Female Entrepreneurs
- Cleveland Career Fair
- Black Professionals Foundation
- The Multi-Profession Diversity Job Fair
- Board Recruitment and Volunteer Fair
- Vision Board for Your Business

Eventbrite networking events in Boston:

- Social Innovator Showcase
- Boston Career Fair
- Massachusetts Bay Transportation Authority Union & Trades Career Fair
- American Marketing Association Boston's Marketing Mingle
- Customer Marketing Industry Meetup

Eventbrite networking events in Atlanta:

- Job Fair ATL
- Atlanta Professional Career Fair
- A Community Talk Event for Small Business
- Network under 40
- ATL Real Estate Industry Day

Eventbrite networking events in Seattle:

- Bellevue College Spring Networking & Job Fair
- Seattle Career Fair

- Women of Color in Tech
- Business Networking Night
- Pride after Five LGBTQ Business Networking Reception

Business networking is another way for business people, owners, and entrepreneurs interact for business opportunities. "The 5 Types of Business Networking Organizations" appearing in *Entrepreneur* magazine, suggests these as types of business networking: casual contact, strong contacts network, community service clubs, professional associations, and online media social networks.[28]

Casual contact groups are made up of overlapping professions. Members hold regular mixers with guest speakers. Chambers of Commerce across the United States are examples of casual contact groups. Strong contact groups are intended to help members exchange business referrals and provide opportunities for marketing. These groups are smaller and meet often, sometimes weekly.[29] An example of a strong contact group is Business Network International (BNI) the world's biggest business and referral organization with chapters in many communities. A large city will have multiple BNI chapters.[30]

Community service clubs are organizations like the Rotary, Lions, and Kiwanis Clubs. Such organizations are not set up with the purpose of business referrals. The primary motivation is community service. However, participation offers the opportunity to make important contacts in the business community.

Professional associations focus on specific industries like banking, accounting, health, retail, and others. The idea is to join groups that contain your target audience and customers. Many groups limit members to companies with specific credentials. To use these associations to the best benefit, ask your clients and customers which organizations they have memberships with.

Online social media networks have become almost mandatory for businesses and industries. In the early days of the internet, just having a website was a novelty. Now the public expects an interactive social media presence. Author Robert W. Blue Jr. knows of a colleague who was not getting any responses from her insurance company while trying to get the full benefit from her homeowner insurance policy. No one responded to phone calls or emails regarding the progress of damage claims. How did she finally get the insurance company to do the right thing? She posted her difficulties on the company's Facebook page. In less than twenty-four hours, a concerned insurance company representative got the claims process going smoothly.

Remember, every encounter is a potential networking opportunity. Always be friendly, professional, and courteous to everyone you meet. You never know who may provide you with an employment referral or business opportunity.

INTERNSHIPS

Some companies and organizations sponsor internships for veterans. Eligibility parameters vary greatly depending upon the program. Some require you to be enrolled in college, and others are only available for wounded warriors. Internships can give you a soft introduction into the civilian sector by offering you a position, sometimes paid and sometimes not; giving you material for your résumé; and introducing you to people who might employ you, open other doors to employment for you or, at the very least, supply you with letters of recommendation. Some of the following internships are offered through transition programs aboard certain military bases. Some are offered by well-known national and international companies. Others are offered through local communities. The following is just a sample.

American Corporate Partners (ACP)

http://www.acp-usa.org/

http://www.acp-advisornet.org

The husband of one of the authors is in the process of retiring from the military after twenty-six years. He is participating in the ACP program. His mentor works in corporate at Disney. He initially wondered how a civilian working there might mentor an infantry marine, but he kept his mind open to the potential outside assistance. Several months later, he found out that even though he wasn't interested in pursuing a similar career, his mentor was helping him expand his career search to areas that he previously was not aware of.

To get a better understanding of the purpose of ACP, we reached out to ACP and received a statement from the executive director, Colleen Deere.

American Corporate Partners is a nationwide nonprofit based in New York City dedicated to assisting returning veterans find meaningful careers post-their military service. Founded in 2008 by retired investment banker Sidney E. Goodfriend, ACP is modeled after Big Brothers Big Sisters and takes a high touch-customized approach to easing veterans' transitions to the private sector. ACP currently partners with more than 75 Fortune 500 companies who each engage their employees as mentors in the program.

Through one-on-one mentoring, networking and professional development sessions, veterans have the opportunity to make direct connections with America's top companies to explore industries and career paths, conduct mock interviews and receive resume advice. The program is tailored to each veteran's unique goals and long-term career plans.[31]

ACP has three available mentorship programs that include one for active-duty personnel and veterans, one for female veterans, and one for spouses of active-duty personal. The free program connects participants with mentors from major companies, who are matched based on the participants' career interests. The companies include, but are not limited to, Bloomberg, British Petroleum, Bank of America, John Deere, Deloitte, Unilever, UPS, GM, Home Depot, Raytheon, VISA, and USAA. A full list can be found here: https://www.acp-usa.org/about-us/partners. The yearlong mentorship is designed to help you create an action plan and track your goals. Mentors are there for career guidance including assistance with résumés, interview preparation, career exploration, networking, and leadership and small-business development.

Many veterans have found ACP to be integral in helping them prepare for a civilian career. Army veteran Jake Henne participated in the program in 2017 and had the following to say regarding his experience:

ACP has been a critical part of my transition and I am very thankful for the mentorship opportunities I have had. I first engaged ACP in September 2017 after returning home from Afghanistan and starting to contemplate transitioning. I had a world of emotions going on about what I wanted to do, as I had always planned on staying in for 20 years. I had an idea of what I wanted to do, mostly built around my project and program management skills from the Army, but it was not a developed plan. ACP linked me up with a great mentor who played a huge part in my transition in multiple ways. He helped guide me as I figured out what I wanted to do, he gave me insight in to the corporate world, he acted as a sounding board for the good times and the hard times, and was always there to lend support as I tried to navigate this major change in my life. Through ACP and some other transition programs I took part in, I discovered my true passion was in tech sales, which is what I do now. My ACP mentorship played a huge part in that discovery and due to some personal circumstances, they actually aligned me a new mentor a few months ago who is in sales and extended my mentorship. Both my first and now my current mentor are incredible people and I gain so much from every conversation from there. I cannot recommend ACP highly enough for their dedication and commitment to service members and their families. I will always have a deep appreciation for the entire team and the work that they do.[32]

Hiring Our Heroes Corporate Fellowship Program

https://www.hiringourheroes.org/fellowships/

The Hiring Our Heroes Corporate Fellowship Program immerses transitioning service members in a hands-on, civilian-sector work experience that is part of the Department of Defense SkillBridge Program. The program is designed to help smooth the transition process for participants. The program runs for twelve weeks, three times a year, but it is not currently available at every military base. Some of the programs are available for veterans and military spouses. Participants are matched with companies based upon their skill set and the needs of both parties.

To be eligible, service members must:

- Be on active duty and within a 180-day window of their end of active duty service date
- Have a bachelor's degree and a minimum of three years of leadership experience
- Have an associate degree and a minimum of five years of leadership experience

Here are the current locations and points of contact:

- Atlanta, GA: John Phillips, jphillips@uschamber.com
- Camp Pendleton, CA: Melinda Gomez, mgomez@uschamber.com
- Chicago, IL: Kris Urbauer, kurbauer@uschamber.com
- Fort Bliss, TX: Carla Miller, cmiller@uschamber.com
- Fort Campbell, KY/TN: Christina Comer, ccomer@uschamber.com

- Fort Carson, CO: Lindsay Teplesky, lteplesky@uschamber.com
- Fort Hood, TX: Stefanie Watson, swatson@uschamber.com
- Fort Leavenworth, KS: Ursla McCarthy, umccarthy@uschamber.com
- Joint Base San Antonio, TX: Carla Miller, cmiller@uschamber.com
- Mid-Atlantic Region, NJ/NYC/PA/DE: Karen Hrach, khrach@us chamber.com
- Remote Locations: Elizabeth Garcia, egarcia@uschamber.com
- St. Louis, MO: Bailey Rinella, brinella@uschamber.com

Once per week, participants gather for a classroom-based educational component. Training during this portion includes topics such as project management, strategic communications, digital marketing, cloud computing, and so on. Participating employers include such companies as Amazon, CarMax, Dell, Prudential, Schulz Family Foundation, IBM, Starbucks, UPS, and Lockheed Martin.

San Diego Airport Veterans Fellowship Program

https://sdcraa-careers.silkroad.com/Careers/Interns—Vets.html

The San Diego Airport Veterans Fellowship Program is a yearlong opportunity for transitioning service members to gain a gateway into the civilian sector. Veterans are placed based on the current needs of the airport and will be offered assistance in career development to gain exposure to corporate business practices.

Austin-Bergstrom International Airport

http://austintexas.gov/department/veteran-fellowship-program-austin -bergstrom-international-airport

Internships are available at the Austin, Texas, airport for honorably discharged veterans within twelve months of their EAS/EAOS date. An exception to the twelve months would be made if the veteran has not worked full time or has maintained full-time enrollment in school since discharge. The paid program lasts for one year and has opportunities in areas such as accounting, finance, construction management, safety, security, property management and airport operations. Potential applicants must provide letters of recommendation, documentation of an honorable discharge, a résumé, and a cover letter that details how the internship is applicable to their education and career plans.

Defense Intelligence Agency, Wounded Warriors Internship

http://www.dia.mil/Careers-and-Internships/Veterans/

This program is for those who are wounded, ill, or injured and assigned to a military treatment facility. The internship offers participants a way to begin building employment skills and to list federal government experience outside of their military service. The internship typically lasts approximately three to six months with a twenty-hour-per-week commitment. Veterans are not required to have experience in intelligence in order to participate.

Los Angeles County Veterans Internship Program

https://hr.lacounty.gov/veterans-internships/

This program is designed to help veterans gain experience and be more competitive for county positions. This is a paid internship that lasts between twelve and twenty-four months. Areas available include administrative support, information technology support and office and clerical support.

Internal Revenue Service (IRS)

https://www.jobs.irs.gov/resources/equal-opportunity/veteran-hiring

The IRS houses three internship programs for veterans in three different categories: those going directly into the workforce, student veterans, and wounded warriors. The internships are not paid and vary in length. Employment upon completion of the programs is not guaranteed, but support is given in areas such as résumé development, the federal hiring process, and searching for employment with the IRS.

- The wounded warrior internship program lasts four to six months. Candidates are still on active duty and must be categorized as wounded, ill, or, injured and currently undergoing medical treatment. They must also be in the process of transitioning back into the civilian sector.
- The Non-Paid Work Experience Program (NPWE) is for veterans who are currently enrolled in the VA Vocational Rehabilitation and Employment program. Participants receive a small subsistence allowance during their participation. Program participation is typically completed in ninety-day increments, but can sometimes be extended to a maximum of eighteen months. Participants must have a service-connected

disability rating of approximately 20 percent, and a discharge other than dishonorable, and they must apply for services through the VA Vocational Rehabilitation and Employment VetSuccess program.

• The Non-Paid Student Veteran Intern Program offers student veterans a way to gain work experience and valuable skills to add to their résumés and assist them in finding employment upon graduation. Internships last between three and four months. Students must be enrolled in a trade school, vocational school, community college, or four-year college or university at a minimum of half time. Student veterans participate in programs related to their course of study.

CBS Veterans Network
https://www.cbsvetnet.com/internship

The CBS Veterans Network internship program is run by veterans already employed with the organization. The program has positions open across the country and is for eligible college students who are attending an accredited university fulltime. CBS states on its website that the company is, "committed to supporting the career development of our veterans by offering hands-on experience, career-building workshops, professional development courses and the opportunity to network with the best in our business."[33]

Positions are posted here: https://cbscorporation.jobs/. The organization requires a commitment of approximately twenty to thirty hours per week. Make sure to check the openings for specific requirements as they can vary based on the needs of the position. Also, check with your college to see if it might be possible to earn college credit for your work. For example, MiraCosta College in California offers Business 299, "Occupational Cooperative Work Experience," which students may take to earn credit for their paid or nonpaid experience as long as it is applicable to their learning.

Oracle
https://www.oracle.com/corporate/careers/diversity/veterans-programs.html

This is for transitioning service members who have been injured during training or during a military campaign. Internships are paid and are in career areas such as IT, data, logistics, HR, and sales.

Michigan Department of Transportation (MDOT)

https://www.michigan.gov/mdot/0,4616,7-151-9623_38029_61350—,00
.html

https://www.michigan.gov/documents/mdot/MDOT_WoundedVeterans
Flyer_385954_7.pdf

This internship is for honorably discharged or discharging veterans. A
DD214 must be supplied prior to placement. Areas available for placement depend on the veteran's skills, knowledge, and training and also on
available openings with MDOT. Job areas include, but are not limited to,
aeronautics, engineering, finance, project management, and administration. Participants are paid at a rate commensurate to the skill set needed
for the position.

Federal Bureau of Investigation (FBI)

https://www.fbijobs.gov/veterans

The FBI internship is for wounded warriors. It provides career development and preparation to a wounded warrior during his or her recovery.
The program includes support with résumés, career path development,
determining career interest areas, and providing recovering warriors
federal work experience. Internship positions may be available at head-
quarters or in field offices, and participants should view placement as a
working interview.

Federal Aviation Administration

https://www.faa.gov/jobs/working_here/veterans/

Three internship programs, the New Sights Work Experience Program,
the Vet-Link Cooperative Education Program, and the Veterans Training
Program, are designed to assist transitioning service members with ser-
vice-connected disabilities or those who have pending medical retirements.
These programs are considered work-experience programs. Department of
Veterans Affairs career counselors can provide more information.

Mount Adams Institute, VetsWork

https://mtadamsinstitute.org/vetswork-environment/
https://mtadamsinstitute.org/vetswork-greencorps/

Mount Adams Institute offers veterans two internship programs:
VetsWork Environment and VetsWork Greencorps. The Environment

program is a twelve-month internship that places veterans in local, state, and federal land-management agencies. The GreenCorps program is a twelve-week internship program for veterans who are interested in wildfire landscape management.

Federal Energy Management Program

https://www.energy.gov/eere/femp/federal-energy-management-program
-veteran-internships

Run by the Department of Energy, the internship offers opportunities in areas such as accounting and finance, business policy and program management, and law and communications. This is a paid internship for undergraduate and graduate students.

Chapter Six

Franchise/Business Opportunities

So you want to be a small-business owner or a franchisee, but you are unsure whether you have the right qualities to be successful, and you don't know the type of business you should start. This chapter will walk you through the basics of business ownership and help you begin to organize your thoughts. The following topics are covered:

- Business Ownership Information

  ○ Personality Profiling
  ○ Transferable Skill Set
  ○ Hiring Others to Help
  ○ Business Models
  ○ Finding Franchise Opportunities
  ○ Developing an Entrepreneurship
  ○ Financing a Business

INTRODUCTION

Many service members are interested in starting a franchise or business once they separate from the service. Some even plan to start their businesses while still on active duty. One concern that many share is in finding the best pathway for their needs, especially since many don't know what their needs are!

For those trying to find the best fit and interested in the option to franchise, working with a franchise consultant may offer direction when it's needed. Working with a consultant can open up new avenues that many interested in business ownership might not be aware existed, such as the different types of business ownership a person might consider. Some businesses don't require a tremendous amount of hands-on work by the franchise owner. They are more of a manage-the-manager type of business. This is a flexible option for those still on active duty or in the process of separating/retiring.

As you are transitioning and considering all of your options, business ownership may be an employment opportunity that is appealing to you. One of the authors of this book has been involved in franchise consulting for twelve years. She states that it is extremely rare that someone comes to her 100 percent sure they want to own a business. Her recommendation is to take the time to do some research to investigate your options. It is hard to cross something off your list if you do not fully research it. Franchising is complex, and you will never learn everything you need to know or get all of the information you need simply by researching on the internet. There is so much to this process that you need to engage and speak with the franchise companies as well as the franchisees to learn what it is like, boots on the ground. How else can you determine what it would be like for you to run a particular type of business? Only then will you truly understand whether this is something that will fit your lifestyle and your employment needs. The same goes for entrepreneurship. Unless you attend workshops and take real steps at creating a business model, you will never know if your ideas have merit. Taking these steps can either lead you in the direction of business ownership or help you cross this off your list so that you can focus on your other options. Then you can move on without doubting yourself or constantly wondering whether business ownership would have been a better option.

BUSINESS OWNERSHIP INFORMATION

Personality Profiling

What types of businesses are you best suited for?

Taking a personality-profile assessment is a great way to determine if you may be a suitable franchise owner, and if so, what type of franchise might be best for you. If you skipped chapter 1, you may want to consider going back to view the information on assessments. For those of you who are more interested in business ownership, these assessments can be beneficial in giving you a place to start your search. There are several free assessments available on the internet, such as at https://www.franchise opportunities.com/resources/self-survey. The company the author works for uses an exclusive assessment, developed specifically for FranNet. The science behind the assessment is based on the DiSC profile. The DiSC personality assessment is commonly used for insight into people's behavioral differences. The assessment asks participants to answer a series of questions; their responses produce a story about the participants' personalities and behavior. The results can offer insight into the type of work you may be best suited for and also the types of people your personality may fit in with best. Working with someone who can translate the results can also help groups of people within a company learn how to better communicate with one another through gaining insight into their different personality, communication, and problem-solving styles. If you use a company like FranNet, you will most likely take one of these tests, but you won't need to translate the results on your own. The tests have been modified to be more relevant to the industry, and consultants have been trained to interpret the results.

There are several similar, more widely used tests, like the Myers-Briggs and the Gallup Strengths Finder. The Myers-Briggs has a college version that some of you may have already taken. Often, when you work with an advisor or counselor at your school, if you are undecided on a future career, they will send you to the career-services department for further research. The Myers-Briggs is a common assessment that the counselor/advisor gives to gather more information about the type of work you might find most satisfying in terms of factors that are important to you, such as work environment and salary. More information on these assessments can be found in chapter 1 and on the following websites:

- https://www.myersbriggs.org/my-mbti-personality-type/
- https://www.gallupstrengthscenter.com/home/en-us/strengthsfinder

When author Roxanne Rapske works with a client who decides to begin the process of looking for a business, her first step is to give a personality-profile assessment. This gives me the background I need to learn more about the types of businesses that may be best suited for my client. It is not an exact science, and the profile is not the sole source of information, but it's a tool to support us through the process and to use to find direction.

For example, Rapske's personality profile states the following:

> Roxanne is a hands-on practical business owner focused on long-term relationships and customer satisfaction. People in this group are motivated by the need to feel secure, harmonious, and contributory to their family and community. Security and community involvement define success for the Belonger-Societal. They favor proven, practical service or solution-based concepts. They are conservative, conventional people with concrete beliefs and deeply held morals. They follow established routines, organized in large part around home, family, community, and social organizations to which they belong. Roxanne is hardworking and committed in order to provide security for loved ones and service to others. They live lives of simplicity, harmony and integrity.
>
> Roxanne highly values agreements. She adheres to finances, schedules and plans with only incremental adjustments as necessary. She likes it best when she can work with family, friends, and associates she has come to trust. She is a business builder with realistic expectations. As a Belonger-Societal, she would find a business that is high-touch and low-tech attractive.

Once a client's profile is visible to a consultant, she can look through her portfolio to come up with a long list of franchises she thinks will be a good fit for the client, solely based on the client's results. The next step in the process is building a business model. This is a very important piece of the puzzle and takes about two hours. Consultants ask a lot of questions to learn as much as possible about the client. In this step, consultants are able to ascertain important information that will help them narrow down the initial long list of franchises. Building the business model usually helps consultants to render a good portion of the original list as no longer valid. The clients leave this meeting with three or four choices that the consultant feels are the best fit, based on the information she has about them at this point. This is just the starting point in the process of figuring out what the best fit will be.

Transferable Skill Set

Organizing, defining, and understanding your aptitude (skill set) and your areas of interest and choosing a business based on these factors will help maximize your success. When considering your transferable skill set, ask yourself *"What is my highest and best use?"* and *"What am I good at?"* Chances are that the areas in which you excel are also the areas you enjoy the most, since you usually practice enjoyable activities more often and become better at them by default.

So, now you need to determine the area in which you excel. Consider the following questions:

- Are you an operations person? Do you enjoy rolling up your sleeves and being involved in the day-to-day operations?
- Are you a manager?
- Are you a strategic thinker focused on the big picture?
- Do you enjoy mentoring and/or delegating?
- Do you prefer sales and business development?
- Do you enjoy being out in the community meeting with potential clients?

This is the time to conduct some real soul searching about the role you want to play in your business and what that role will look like. If this is not the role you have the most experience or strength in, then it will provide an opportunity for growth and learning and typically require some additional training, classes, workshops, education, and/or college degrees.

Hiring Others to Help You

Determining areas of weakness and contracting with professionals will help you to maximize business benefits. It is just as important to be aware of your weaknesses as of your strengths. Everyone has blind spots or areas of deficiency they need to fill in to be successful in owning a business, as none of us have the ability to wear all of the hats required to be successful in business ownership. So, consider the following two questions:

- What is your lowest and/or worst area in running a business?
- What are you absolutely horrible at doing, and what tasks do you loathe performing in a business?

For Rapske, it is anything that ties her to a desk or forces her to sit still. She loves being out and about and meeting with clients and being active in the community. The worst possible place for her in running a business is sitting at her desk crunching numbers, shuffling papers, and organizing receipts. When she first went into business, she tried building her own website. Biggest mistake and waste of time ever! We all try to economize because we don't want to spend any extra money. In hindsight, we actually hold ourselves back from quicker growth by focusing so much time and energy on trying to do what we should have hired someone else (an expert) to do in the first place. It usually takes much more time and effort to perform the tasks that we are not good at than it should or that the business can allow.

The people we hire do not have to be actual employees of our company. There are many independent contractors available who have their own businesses in their areas of expertise; we can simply hire someone for a job, then move on, or hire someone regularly. Rapske has a CPA, a bookkeeper, and an administrative assistant. They all have their own companies and bill her for the work they perform. This is helpful if you don't want the responsibility of having an employee or don't have enough work for them to put them on your payroll.

Business Models

There are three main types of business-ownership options: owner-operator, executive, and semi-absentee models. Knowing the type of owner you want to be up front will help you choose your option.

Owner Operator Model

An owner operator is involved full time and is hands-on in the business. There are a few reasons some people prefer an owner-operator model:

- They like what they are doing, want to work with their hands, or personally deliver the services of the business to the customer or end user.
- They want to keep costs down by not hiring any employees initially. They are willing to perform the service of the business until they have enough customers to validate hiring an employee. They may have a

revenue goal or a bottom-line income goal before they hire their first employee. The goal may be to grow the business to the break-even point before hiring an employee.

- They want to learn the role or roles in the business themselves so they can fill in later if needed. Having the training and knowledge will potentially help them hire, train, and manage better. Rapske has had clients tell her they don't want to be held hostage by their employees. Learning the roles of the business as a hands-on owner operator can prevent this from happening.

A side note of caution in an owner-operator model: some people in this type of role will have tremendous passion for what they are doing. This can be bad and good. If you enjoy what you are doing too much, you will spend too much time focusing on performing the work and not enough time overseeing the business. You cannot spend all your time working in your business. At some point, you have to work on your business. It's important as an owner-operator to plan your time in advance, dictating how much time you will spend working on projects and how much you will spend on business development each week. This will take discipline and may be challenging for you.

Executive Model

In this model, you start out as the manager or CEO of your new business. You hire technicians or employees right from the start. Your role is to oversee the business in a big-picture way. You may be in charge of business development, overseeing projects, hiring, training, scheduling, quality control, or all of the above. Let's say you buy a residential-cleaning-service franchise. Your role is not in the actual cleaning. Instead, your daily tasks will most likely be:

- Hiring, training, and managing employees. The owner's relationship-building and organizational skills are very important in this area.
- Meeting in person with customers for in-home estimates.
- Executive-management responsibilities, including tracking profit and loss, executing a marketing plan, and building management infrastructure.

- As the business grows, the owner will primarily function at the executive-management level, as most owners hire office staff to handle the routine aspects of running the business.

The franchise company would most likely be looking for a candidate for this type of business who would have:

- Management, leadership, or team-building experience
- Business aptitude, a great attitude, and well-developed communication skills
- A desire to contribute, an aptitude for ownership, and a knack for putting people first

Many franchisees in these types of businesses have management experience; they include former executives, those with PhDs, and high-level technology professionals. Many other successful owners are retired military service members, individuals who are active in the community, and other professionals who have developed high-level interpersonal skills throughout their lives.

Many owners of this type of business have in common a desire to contribute, an aptitude for ownership, and a knack for demonstrating an attitude that puts people first. Most businesses like this will start with two home-service professionals or residential cleaners. If only one owner will be involved (no spouse or partner), then an hourly receptionist/office manager may be hired. The employee base will grow as the business grows with additional teams of two home-service professionals at a time. This type of business, when it's fully established, may have approximately eight to ten full-time teams of home-service professionals, two part-time home-service professionals or "floaters," and two to three administrative staff members.

Semi-Absentee Model

This model is suitable for someone who needs or wants to keep their day job or for someone who wants to be a consultant in their area of expertise. This model is also appropriate for someone who wants to build their own empire or own multiple businesses. Examples of this type of business are

Supercuts, Great Clips, Massage Envy, or a frozen yogurt store. There are many more examples, but we will start here. In the hair salon example, owners do not need to have any experience with hair. They will hire a licensed cosmetologist who has managerial experience to manage their store.

Depending on the phase of the business, franchisees can spend as little as ten to fifteen hours per week on the business, if they like. When opening your first business (or salon, as in our example), it may feel as though you have a second full-time job. Once a franchisee has opened multiple locations, the franchisee can either hire a general manager to manage the salons or they can quit their day job and run the business from a home office or another location. This may only require checking the daily reports, and/or checking in on the salon on a weekly basis to be the coach (or cheerleader!) for the managers and stylists at the salon. In the hair salon model, the average franchisee owns five salons.

The ideal candidate for this type of business is usually someone who has a corporate job and who wants to build a legacy on the side. Those likely to have the most success have strong leadership skills, great people skills, and an interest in building a multi-unit business. Prior business and management experience is a definite asset for franchisees, as their primary function is developing people, not cutting and styling hair.

In addition to a store manager, each salon would typically have an assistant manager and could have a number of stylists, something in the range of eight to twelve. In many of these types of businesses, the owner hires the store manager, then the store manager hires the stylists. This is a great way to scale into many units over time but still maintain coverage in the units already owned.

Finding Franchise Opportunities

There are many ways to find franchise opportunities. Many people search the internet and visit the vast numbers of websites available, such as https://www.franchise.org/ or https://www.franchisegator.com/. There are many more to peruse. If you search "franchise opportunities," you will find an overwhelming amount of information. There are about 4,000 different franchises in the market, in many different industries, with over 700,000 operating units in the United States. To learn more about the franchise industry in general, visit http://atourfranchise.org/.

Typically, most people look for franchise or business opportunities backward. They get online and start looking for businesses they think they might like to own without considering all of the factors that may impact the process. It's important to understand yourself and build a business model based on all of your wants and needs in a business first, before you go out and look for businesses. There are many things to consider, such as the types of businesses, the investment, the number of employees, the customer, the market, and the demographics of your potential customers. It's important to find a business that lines up with your lifestyle and income goals as well as your skill sets. Laying the groundwork with a business model is key. As you look at different businesses, you can keep referring back to your business model to make sure the business is aligned with the goals you are trying to accomplish.

So, how does one narrow down the list? Try finding a franchise consultant or an expert in your geographic area whom you trust and would like to work with. This should be someone who does not charge you an up-front fee for services. Most consultants in this business have a model where they:

- Are compensated at the backend by the franchisor only if their clients move forward and purchase a franchise
- Work just like an executive recruiter—franchise companies pay the consultants to recruit good candidates for their particular models
- Work with hundreds of franchises in many different industries

Be careful contracting with a franchise consultant whom you find online and who doesn't have a local office. Many franchise consultants buy franchise leads online and work from a home office. This will not result in the best working relationship. Also, be cautious about completing any online forms. There are companies that have designed landing pages to make it appear that you are on a franchisor's website. They capture your information and sell it (called an "internet lead") to multiple consultants. Many consultants who work from a home office buy these leads and sit all day dialing for dollars. Once someone completes one of these forms, their phone will start blowing up because it becomes a race for these consultants to get to the lead first so that they can win the business. This type of consultant spends all of their time on the phone talking to potential clients all over the country. I don't believe that it is in your best interest to have someone who lives in another state or city help with your local search. Find someone in your area that understands the market. You'll want someone who has a presence and an office where you can go and meet them face-to-face. Higher-level franchise consultants will be active in the community. They will offer local events and workshops you can attend. You'll want the opportunity to meet them in person or see them in action to see if they are someone you are interested in working with. Most people want to work with consultants they know, like, and trust. If you stay local and work with a consultant face-to-face, you can develop a more in-depth relationship. Most likely, your consultant will have ties to the local business community and will want to maintain a stellar reputation within the community. Plus, you get the added benefit of the consultant better understanding the environment and the market for business in your area.

Okay, so now that you have found a consultant to work with, he or she should take you through a thorough thirty- to ninety-day, step-by-step process to find the right franchise for you. The process typically follows this pattern:

- Attend a webinar or a seminar.
- Take an assessment or personality profile.
- Build a business model with your consultant.
- Identify three to four franchisors you would like to speak with.
- Interview franchise companies.
- Receive and review the franchise disclosure document (FDD).
- Interview franchise owners within the concepts you are considering—I would recommend speaking with a minimum of ten from each concept.
- Start the financial process—speak with lenders, and so on. (Sometimes, I have my clients start this process up front to get a better understanding of what they are qualified to do and what type of project dollar amount makes sense so we are on the right track from the very beginning.)
- Attend a discovery or meet-the-team day. This is where you get to meet the franchisor, support staff, and maybe some current franchisees, and they get a chance to meet you.
- Consult with a franchise attorney to review your franchise agreement, and have a CPA look at your business plan/pro forma statement if you have not done so already.

- Finalize financing.
- Awarding process with the franchisor. This is when you sign the franchise agreement and pay the franchise fee.
- You are now onboard with the franchise, and your training will begin.

You'll want to speak to several different franchise companies in different industries. The International Franchise Association's website offers many resources to help you begin to conduct research. The organization's Frequently Asked Questions page offers answers to many questions that arise when many people begin to consider franchising. The information can be found here: https://www.franchise.org/faq. Read through the entire page before moving forward.

While you can conduct research online, you can also begin working with a consultant who can help you navigate the process. Franchise consultants can be very informative and offer you direction when you need support. You will never be able to learn everything you need to know about a particular franchise by only researching it online. To truly understand a franchise concept, it's important to engage with the companies you are considering and allow them to take you through their discovery process. Franchises worth joining are going to be selective about whom they bring into their franchise family. It's important that this be a good fit on both sides for it to be a successful partnership. In other words, you must feel the franchise is a good fit for you, and the company must be comfortable with you as well. After all, you will become a part of their brand. So the process should feel as if you are accepting an award as opposed to purchasing a business.

After the franchisor has one or a few phone conversations with you, they will send you their FDD for review. Franchises are heavily regulated by the Federal Trade Commission. By law, the franchisor is required to provide you with this document early on in the process. They will provide it at different times, as each company has its own process, but will usually share it with you after the first few phone conversations. For more on the FDD, visit https://www.entrepreneur.com/article/254051 for a breakdown of what it must contain.

The franchisor will usually set up a phone call with you to review the FDD and answer any of your questions and concerns. Once you understand the franchise's business model, and both you and the company are still interested in moving forward in the process, the next step is to speak to franchisees. You will have an opportunity to interview the franchisees of that system to ask them questions about their struggles and successes in building a business. You can ask them anything you'd like to help you learn about their business and to ultimately help you decide whether this is the right business for you. You should speak to enough franchisees to feel comfortable that you've gotten all of your questions answered. I recommend speaking to at least ten to fifteen franchisees. You'll also want to speak with them in different stages of development: those just starting, those who have been in business for a few years, and some in business longer (depending on how long the franchise has been operating). You'll want to speak with franchisees who are doing well, some who are doing about average, and some who are struggling. All of them have something to teach you, and these conversations will help you determine how you might perform in the system, based on their personal information, such as their backgrounds and personalities.

You'll want to build a pro forma statement or spreadsheet to figure out income and expenses, based on everything you've learned. This is done to give you the clearest picture possible of the finances for your business for the first, second, third, and further years. You'll also want to understand the market you will be in and what you think will be a good territory for you, based on where you live and where you think you'd like to build your business. The franchisor will help you with this process.

Once this portion of the process is complete and you are still interested in learning more, it's time for you to visit the franchise company. On a scale of one to ten, you should be at least a seven when considering your interest in moving forward before you take the next step. The franchise company will usually invite you to a discovery or meet-the-team day. This will give you an opportunity to meet the executive team and the staff that will be supporting you as you build your new business. Sometimes there will also be local franchisees participating in this event, or you may have the chance to go out and visit some of the franchisees local to the corporate office. This is usually the final step in the decision-making process. It's important for you to make sure this franchise is also a cultural fit for you once you've completed your research.

When you return from this trip, the franchisor will typically be looking for an answer from you—either yes or no—in the next week to ten days. If you have not done so already, you'll want to meet with a CPA to review the numbers you put together. You'll also want to have a franchise attorney review your franchise agreement to make sure you understand exactly what you are signing and will need to abide by. It's important to use a franchise attorney specifically, so that a regular business attorney isn't learning franchise law on your dime. Also, it is important to use a franchise attorney in your state. Each state has its own quirks and requirements. It will be a cleaner process if your attorney practices law in the state in which you will open the business.

Now, the perfect business does not exist. There will always be parts of your business that you find challenging. The goal is to try to find a business you believe will be a good fit, that will meet your lifestyle and income goals, and that you will enjoy doing. It's important to do enough research to believe that you can do this and you will not fail. You will always feel fear about moving forward, and conducting thorough research is of the utmost importance, but taking a leap of faith is required to get started.

Developing an Entrepreneurship

Franchising is not for everyone. Starting an independent business from scratch may be the right path for you, especially if you don't want to follow someone else's rules. Another reason may be that you are creative and want to build your own brand or carve your own path. This is the riskiest way of going into business, and it can be an intimidating process. Working with a life or business coach or at least taking an assessment may help point you in the right direction for the type of business ownership that is best for you.

Once you've come up with an idea, you should consider the following:

- Seek out a mentor or mentors to guide you—Who is someone you know who is successful in business ownership and whom you can ask for help?
- Conduct a market assessment—Who else is doing what you want to do? How many competitors do you have in your market?
- Look for leaders in the industry within the community whom you can learn from.
- Write a business plan—What will your business provide and whom are you selling to?

- What are your end goals, including your exit strategy?
- Who is your demographic—your target customer, and how will you get them in your door to buy this product or service from you versus your competitors?
- How will you do this better or set yourself apart from your competition?
- Choose your branding/logo.

This website offers an online guide to conducting this type of research: https://www.business.com/articles/guide-to-market-research/?_ga =2.53791976.1508915217.1567979608-1411513594.1567979606.

What do your finances look like? Do you have enough money to start this business on your own or do you need help financially? If you need help, where will you find that help? (See the heading, "Financing a Business.")

- Experts state that the number-one reason a business will fail is undercapitalization—running out of money before the business can break even or be profitable.
- Overestimating the amount of startup capital you will need is a very good idea. I would recommend being conservative when putting together your business plan.
- Many businesses will also spend money on unnecessary things. You can be conservative with how much space you might need when leasing a place. It's better to be a little cramped and be forced to grow into something bigger than to have way too much space, wasting precious cash on your lease for that extra space. The same goes for buying too much inventory or going overboard with high-end equipment, furniture, and other similar items.
- Speak with an attorney or a CPA on how to structure your business. Will you form a C-Corp, and S-Corp, or an LLC, or will you be a sole proprietor to start? What type of registration is required with the IRS for your business?
- Research your state, county, and city to see what kind of licensing you need to run your operation. Make sure you have all of the proper licenses and permits in place.
- Speak with an insurance agent regarding liability insurance, and to see if other types of coverage are needed.
- Hire your team.
- Research any vendors you may need for your operation.

- Create a website and get your social media lined up to announce your grand opening.

If going the independent business/entrepreneurial route, I would recommend arming yourself with as many resources as possible. Start doing some research about the types of resources that are available in your area. It is important to engage with these organizations early on, even before you have an idea about what you want to do.

Learn about the SBA and the services they offer at the local level. This support organization is paid for by our tax dollars and hosts valuable resources. Visit the following websites to get started:

- https://www.sba.gov/
- https://www.sba.gov/local-assistance
- https://americassbdc.org/
- https://www.score.org/, https://www.score.org/find-location
- https://americassbdc.org/small-business-consulting-and-training/find-your-sbdc/

If possible, sign up for the SBA, Score, and SBDC newsletters so you will learn about local events and workshops that may be of interest to you. Workshops offered by the SBDC and SCORE will review topics like conducting market research, building a business model, determining your demographics, putting a business plan together, financing options and sources, legal assistance, completing applications for business licenses, QuickBooks, etc. Once you get your business up and running, these organizations' consultants will continue to work with you at every step of the way. For more resource information, see chapter 5.

Financing a Business

This process is very personal and will be different for each candidate. In addition to needing money to finance a business, it is important to develop a budget for your living expenses. Someone looking into buying a franchise should have a minimum of twelve months of living expenses saved, plus the business investment. If you are starting a business from scratch, I recommend a minimum of twenty-four months' living expenses, plus the investment. If you've been banking with the same bank for years and have a working relationship with someone there, that may be a good place to start. Meet with this person to discuss your desire to own a business. Find out if the bank finances start-up businesses or the purchase of a franchise. If they don't, start researching other banks in the area that loan money for business start-ups.

One of the most popular types of financing for a business is an SBA loan, although there are other options, but many banks only offer SBA loans to current operating businesses looking for additional capital. So, be sure to specifically ask if that particular bank offers SBA loans to start a brand-new business or franchise. Most banks offering SBA loans will look for a 25 to 30 percent cash injection from the borrower. This means that if your total project amount is $300,000, the bank would typically require approximately $75,000 to $90,000 from you in available funds; the rest of the project money would come from a bank loan. You can learn more about SBA loans here: https://www.sba.gov/funding-programs/loans.

Another popular option is the ROBS (Rollover as Business Start-Ups) program. This is a way to roll pre-tax retirement funds into a new business and pay no penalties or taxes. This program is part of the Employee Retirement Income Security Act (ERISA). More information regarding this program can be found here: https://www.dol.gov/general/topic/retirement/erisa. This program is highly regulated by the IRS, so it's important to use a financial company that has a lot of experience with these programs. There are many available. For informational purposes, the following three websites are reputable options to reference. They are not in any particular order of preference.

- Benetrends: https://www.benetrends.com/
- Guidant Financial: https://www.guidantfinancial.com/
- FranFund: https://www.franfund.com/

Not only have these companies been around for decades, they offer a one-stop option for funding. They take a look at each client's financial picture, then give him or her all of their funding options, as well as the costs of each option. Then the client can make an informed decision about the manner in which he or she would like to proceed.

It isn't unusual to see clients use multiple forms of financing, depending on the amount they need. Most typically use the rollover funds for the cash injection piece required for the SBA loan. Some clients will use all rollover funds to avoid the burden of financing. Each client is unique and needs to find what works best for them and their family. The following list offers other options for financing a business:

- Personal savings
- Angel investors
- Friends, relatives, or business partners
- Home equity line of credit
- Financial institutions
- Seller financing, if you decide to buy an existing business
- Self-Directed 401K or IRA

Many people are aware of those choices except for this last bullet point. Look for grants in your area as well as city or county funds. For example, a friend recently opened a winery. Part of his construction was paid for by the city because they were doing a large improvement project.

An industry colleague, who worked for the Small Business Development Center for years helping entrepreneurs identify funds for start-ups, recently wrote *Target Funding*, a book that may offer you interesting insights. You can find the book here: https://www.amazon.com/Target -Funding-Proven-Resources-Business/dp/1260132366/ref=sr_1_1?key words=book+by+kedma+ough&qid=1567982969&s=gateway&sr=8-1.

Chapter Seven

Cost and Payment Resources

Cost is often a major factor for students when picking a college or vocational program to attend. Active-duty service members should try to attend institutions that fall within the parameters of TA. Veterans should consider GI Bill coverage while researching potential schools. Why pay for school when you have coverage? If you can stay within these parameters, you might come out of your educational experience completely debt free.

The following topics will be covered in this chapter:

- Financial Assistance
- Montgomery GI Bill (MGIB)
- Post-9/11 GI Bill
- GI Bill Activation
- Transfer of GI Bill Benefits
- Yellow Ribbon Program
- VA GI Bill Feedback System
- Federal Student Aid
- State-Based Veteran Education Benefits
- Scholarships (Including Dependents)
- Textbook-Buying Options

INTRODUCTION

Transitioning from the military is difficult enough without you also having to worry about finances. Veterans who prepare in advance will have less stress during the process and will be able to focus on their studies more effectively. Having minimal distractions during school will enable veterans to achieve a higher degree of academic success. Successfully educated or trained veterans will be more productive in their future endeavors and be able to enrich their surrounding civilian communities.

Bypassing the work option, veterans have three main sources of income while attending school. These sources include:

- GI Bill housing stipend
- Federal student aid (Pell Grant)
- Unemployment benefits

If a veteran is able to maximize benefits under each of these three options, he or she will have a good starting base and hopefully not have to worry about daily stressors, such as paying for rent, gas, and food.

The housing stipend on the Post-9/11 GI Bill typically is not enough to take care of an individual's personal needs, especially because "break pay" money is not paid while the student is not physically in school. The "Post-9/11" section in this chapter explains that the housing allowance is prorated, and veterans will most likely not be receiving as much money as they expect.

Federal Student Aid Pell Grant money can be a great benefit for veterans attending school. Think about having an extra $6,000 per academic year to help with education-related expenses and beyond the GI Bill. How much better off would you be for spending thirty minutes to fill out the Free Application for Federal Student Aid (FAFSA)? The time will be well spent, especially if you are awarded assistance.

Your previous year's tax information is required to fill out the FAFSA, so you need to pay attention upon your initial separation from active duty. If you have recently separated from the military, your tax information may not reflect your current financial situation. For example, if you separated in July 2019 and began college in August 2020, you would submit your 2018 taxes on the FAFSA that reflect your military pay. The main problem is that you are no longer working and receiving this level of pay. In most cases, a veteran's pay is drastically reduced upon separation. If you do not receive an award or do not receive the full amount, you would need to visit your financial aid counselor to have your listed income level readjusted. Hopefully, upon readjustment of your income, you will be eligible for the maximum Pell Grant award. Be aware that Pell Grant money is based on your tax information, so it will fluctuate from person to person depending upon household finances.

The Unemployment Compensation for Ex-Servicemembers (UCX) program may help eligible separating service members rate some level of unemployment. Unemployment will vary by state because state laws determine how much money an individual can receive, the length of time they remain eligible, and any other eligibility conditions. Veterans must have been honorably separated in order to be eligible. Information on unemployment can be located on the DoL's website (https://workforce security.doleta.gov/unemploy/uifactsheet.asp).

Contact your local State Workforce Agency (http://www.servicelocator .org/OWSLinks.asp) upon separation to determine eligibility and apply. Make sure to have a copy of your DD-214.

Some military members may receive a service-connected disability percentage; others may not. When you separate from the military, you will be screened by the VA to determine whether you sustained any injuries or diseases while on active duty, or if any previous health-related issues were made worse by active military service. If you receive a minimum rating of 10 percent or higher, you may be eligible to receive a tax-free stipend from the VA every month. Zero percent ratings do not have a monetary stipend attached; however, in the "State-Based Veteran Education Benefits" section of this chapter, you will see that many states offer benefits that are tied to these disability ratings. For example, in California a zero percent rating equals free schooling for your children at state-supported institutions. If you receive a percentage rating, this may help with your expenses. Be aware that ratings can take as long as twelve months to be determined, and there is such a thing as "no rating."

Make sure to be screened prior to exiting the military. If you are not sure where to find your local VA office, it might be on the base where you are stationed. The Disabled American Veterans (DAV) and the VFW maintain offices at several Marine Corps bases and may assist you as well. Many academic institutions have visiting representatives from these organizations. They will help you with your initial claim if you did not make it while still on active duty. They can also help you submit for a claims adjustment if your medical situation has changed.

MONTGOMERY GI BILL (MGIB)

Not all service members have MGIB. When you entered the service, if you opted in to MGIB and paid $100 per month for your first year of service, to total $1,200, you might rate MGIB. You must be separated with an honorable discharge as well; that goes for most benefits. Double check your eligibility on the GI Bill website (http://www.gibill.va.gov).

As of October 1, 2019, MGIB will pay $2,050 per month for up to thirty-six months for school. MGIB can be used for academic degrees, certificate programs, on-the-job training (OJT), correspondence classes, apprenticeship programs, and flight training. Benefits are good for ten years after separation from the military.

Some service members participated in the $600 Buy-Up program under MGIB. For those who did, an extra $150 per month will be added to their MGIB payments. That amount per month pays you back your $600 investment in four months. Every month after that, you are making money. If you cannot remember if you paid for the optional Buy-Up program, check with the section of your branch tasked with managing personnel administration, such as IPAC in the Marine Corps and PSD in the Navy. For those who did not pay the money, check with the veterans' representatives at the school you are interested in attending before paying it. If you select Post-9/11, you forfeit the $600 that it takes to fully fund the Buy-Up. Smaller Buy-Up packages can be bought for prorated amounts. If you rate it and decide to stay under MGIB, you will most likely want to pay the Buy-Up for increased monthly payments. Your personnel department can make the unit diary entry prior to your EAS.

There are only a few situations where it makes more sense for the veteran to remain under MGIB instead of opting for Post-9/11. Here are two big ones: first, online-only schools, which isn't the best option because you might be missing out on the full housing stipend under Post-9/11, and, second, when veterans attend school in a state with a full state-based benefit, such as Illinois. But even in this case, it depends on which part of the state you are attending school in. The state-based benefit section in this chapter will review both of these circumstances and demonstrate why a veteran might elect to remain under MGIB. Prior to selecting either GI Bill, it is best to discuss all available options. Contact your state VA to determine your available state benefits and learn how to use them.

Contact the veterans' department at the institution you would like to attend and request guidance. Typically, the veterans' representatives can offer great advice pertaining to the best benefit pathway. They have already blazed the trail and learned for themselves. The VA also offers guidance and can be reached at 1-888-GIBILL-1.

POST-9/11

Post-9/11 is truly an amazing educational benefit for veterans who rate it. To determine your eligibility, visit the website (http://www.gibill.va. gov). Basically, to rate 100 percent of Post-9/11, you need to meet these criteria:

- Served thirty-six consecutive months after September 11, 2001
- Received an honorable discharge

There are other categories for approval, but, as we have stressed at other points in this book, always check to determine your specific eligibility. In this case, contact the VA at 1-888-GIBILL-1.

The Post-9/11 GI Bill has three financial components built into the program: for books and supplies, housing, and tuition.

Books and Supplies

Post-9/11 has a books and supplies stipend. The stipend is prorated at $41.67 per credit hour for a maximum of $1,000 per academic year. A regular full-time student (a minimum of twelve credits per semester) would receive the full $1,000. Anything less than that is prorated until the veteran drops below the 50 percent rate of pursuit mark. At that point, the GI Bill stops paying. The stipend is broken into two payments per academic year and lumped in with the first month of the housing stipend for each semester.

You should take note that $1,000 is not actually a great amount for books. Often, books can run more than $200 per class. Many universities list the approximate costs of textbooks for the school year on their website. For example, California State University, Long Beach, estimates books at $2,058 for the 2019–2020 academic year. According to the institution's calculations, $1,000 won't suffice for books. You definitely need to check into other options. The "Textbook-Buying Options" section in this chapter is dedicated to helping you find used or rental books.

Housing

The housing stipend is slightly more complicated. Referred to as the Monthly Housing Allowance (MHA), it is equivalent to the salary for an E-5 with dependents and applies to everyone. That is great if you separated anywhere near E-5, but if you separated as a general, you will need to adjust your budget (sorry—that is my bad sense of humor!). Use the GI Bill Comparison Tool website (https://www.va.gov/gi-bill-comparison-tool) to look up the current housing stipend of the school you are interested in attending. The MHA is based on the zip code of your school, not your residence. There is an exception for schools on foreign territory. The MHA for schools on foreign territory is the average of the forty-eight contiguous states' MHA, currently $1,789 per month.

Tuition

Tuition under the Post-9/11 GI Bill can be complicated to explain. Let's keep it simple. If you follow the most basic of parameters, you will not pay a dime for your schooling. Go outside of these parameters and you run into technical billing questions; in this case, you should contact the school you are interested in attending for further information.

If you are pursuing an undergraduate or graduate degree, plan to attend a state school in the state where you have residency, and finish your degree within the thirty-six months of your benefit allotment, your schooling should be covered. The thirty-six months is enough for most bachelor's degrees if you stay on track because it equates to nine months of school per year over the course of four years. Traditionally, we do not usually attend school in the summer, although you may if you want to, and many veterans do. If one of these factors changes, so might your GI Bill benefits.

Veterans who choose to attend private school received $24,476.79 for the academic year 2019–2020 (https://www.benefits.va.gov/GIBILL/resources/benefits_resources/rates/ch33/ch33rates080119.asp). Anything above that amount, and you run the risk of having to pay out of pocket. However, many schools participate in the Yellow Ribbon Program (https://www.benefits.va.gov/gibill/yellow_ribbon.asp), which may help cover private school costs that come in above the maximum VA-allotted threshold or out-of-state tuition charges. What about out-of-state tuition? Because of past changes in the GI Bill, in most cases, you should not be charged out-of-state tuition and fees. For more information on the corresponding rules, visit https://www.benefits.va.gov/gibill/post911_residentraterequirements.asp.

As stated earlier, the VA will pay you the full-time housing allowance if you attend school full time. The VA considers twelve credit hours to be full time over the course of a traditional four-month semester. However, if you have no previous college credit and intend to pursue a bachelor's degree, twelve credits per semester will not suffice. Most bachelor's degrees require students to complete 120 semester credit hours of specific subject matter in order to earn the degree. That equates to fifteen credit hours each semester, or five classes. Academic subjects such as engineering may require longer school attendance. Some veterans and Fry Scholars may be eligible for the Edith Nourse Rogers Science Technology Engineering Math (STEM) Scholarship, which, in certain cases, may extend their benefits for an extra nine months or $30,000. Exclusions apply, and the Yellow Ribbon Program cannot be used in tandem. For further details, visit https://benefits.va.gov/gibill/fgib/stem.asp.

The college year runs similarly to the high school year: two semesters each year over the course of four years. So, 120 semester hours breaks down to 15 semester hours each semester to total 30 credits each year (freshman year, 30; sophomore year, 30; junior year, 30; and senior year, 30—total: 120). If you follow the VA's minimum guidelines of 12 credits each semester, or four classes, you will run out of benefits at the end of your senior year but will only have earned 96 semester credit hours, or 24 credits shy of the 120 required. You will be out of benefits but will not have obtained your degree. The academic counselors/advisors at the school you attend will help you with your degree plans. If you need to make changes or have questions, contact them for further advice.

If a service member attending school while on active duty chooses a school that costs more than the amount allotted under TA, GI Bill Top-Up can be used to top off the TA. The service member would activate his or her GI Bill and tap into it as a funding resource for the portion of the class not covered by TA. This would affect the individual's overall remaining benefit amount upon separation from the military.

Using Top-Up may be necessary in some cases, but, generally, I would avoid the recommendation. Tapping into Top-Up will pull on the service member's available GI Bill months, thereby reducing the amount of benefits remaining after separation from the military.

Many institutions across the country cost less than or equal to the amount covered under TA. If the institution you are planning to attend is over the $250-per-credit-hour threshold and recommending GI Bill Top-Up, please speak to an academic counselor/advisor for advice prior to making any final decisions.

Three situations come to mind when discussing using Top-Up for service members.

1. If the individual is about to run out of TA money, is at the end of his or her degree, and is separating from active duty soon, it is important to report that he or she will obtain the degree prior to separating and will be able to list the accomplishment on his or her résumé. This enables the veteran to get into the workforce faster.
2. The cost of most master's degree programs is above and beyond the $250 per credit hour that TA can cover. Completing an advanced degree while still on active duty will be an enormous benefit to separating service members.
3. If the service member is looking to attend a prestigious university and cannot cover the costs out of pocket, I would typically recommend attending a local community college (many have fully online, fast-paced programs available) for as long as possible prior to transferring to the university. At least this way, the individual would not be drawing from his or her GI Bill for such an extended period.

For undergraduate study, try all possibilities prior to looking into Top-Up. Often, the Pell Grant is a viable option (see the "Federal Student Aid" section). Some states, such as California, have state-based benefits that may assist in payment. In California, the California Promise Grant program is available through the state community colleges. If you are stationed in California, contact the financial aid department at the local community college for more information. Ultimately, the decision to use Top-Up must be the service member's, but the guidelines included here are solid and should be considered prior to making a move.

Last, the GI Bill can be used for entrepreneurship training; however, only programs sponsored/offered by the SBDC are approved. Training courses must have been specifically approved by the VA in order for your benefits to work. More information can be found here: https://www .benefits.va.gov/GIBILL/docs/factsheets/Entrepreneurship_Training.pdf.

GI BILL APPLICATION/CONVERSION PROCESS

The application process for the GI Bill is not complicated; however, it does take approximately thirty days to receive the Certificate of Eligibility (COE) statement. Make sure to allot time for the wait prior to starting school. If you find yourself in a time crunch, check with your school to see if the institution might take a copy of the submitted application and let you begin your studies.

If you have MGIB and you are positive you want to convert to Post-9/11, the process can be done at the same time you activate the benefit. Although there is no need to do so prior to this point, some service members are more comfortable making the switch while still on active duty. To activate the GI Bill, you will need to access the application (vets .gov). Scroll down to "Education." Click on the tab "Apply for education benefits." Then click on the green tab, "Find your education benefits form." Answer the questions appropriately. For veterans, this will take you to the VA 22-1990 form. You will need three pieces of information before you proceed:

1. Your school's name and address
2. A bank account and routing number (VA is direct deposit)
3. An address where you will be in the next thirty days

The easiest way to prepare for the application process is to be accepted at your intended institution prior to applying to activate your benefit, but you can change the required information later by contacting the VA at 1-888-GIBILL-1. The VA no longer sends hard checks. Inputting your bank account and routing numbers enables the VA to directly deposit your MHA and book and stipend money. You may change this information later if you change your bank.

Your COE will be delivered to the address you list. Service members living in the barracks might want to have their COEs sent to their parents' or another reliable family member's address. Just make sure that the individuals located at the listed address keep their eyes open for the document and inform you when it arrives. You will need to take that document to your school's certifying officials as soon as you receive it along with your DD-214, because it is the school's ticket to receive payment from the VA, and part of the process for you to be certified and to receive the housing allowance. If you are transferring to a new school or changing your program of study, you will need to fill out the 22-1995 form. It can be found on the vets.gov website, or check with your school certifying officials.

If you are concerned about the questions on the 22-1990 or whether you are making the correct choices, contact the VA at 1-888-GIBILL-1. The veterans' representatives at your intended school are usually good sources of information as well.

POST-9/11 TRANSFERABILITY TO DEPENDENTS

Active-duty service members may be eligible to transfer their Post-9/11 GI Bill benefits to dependents. The transfer process requires a four-year commitment to stay in the military, and as of July 12, 2019, a service member who has completed more than sixteen years of service is no longer eligible to transfer the benefit (https://www.benefits.va.gov/gibill/ post911_transfer.asp). If benefits are successfully transferred, certain rules apply while the service member remains on active duty.

To be eligible to transfer benefits, a service member must be eligible for Post-9/11 and:

• Have completed six years of active-duty service and agree to four more years;
• Have four years remaining on contract (enlisted) or commit four more years (officer); or

- Be precluded by standard policy or statute from serving an additional four years (must agree to serve maximum time allowed by such policy).

The transfer must be approved while the service member is still in the armed forces. In a nutshell, active-duty service members need to have completed the required time in service and have four years left on contract. The best time to complete the process is at the time of a reenlistment or extension package that gives the individual the required amount of payback time. To transfer benefits, follow these steps:

- Verify your time in service.
- Visit the milConnect website: https://milconnect.dmdc.osd.mil/mil connect/.
- Click on the "Transfer of Entitlement" option.
- Follow the directions.
- Click on the "Go to Transfer of Eligible Benefits" link on the right-hand side.
- Enter the needed information and submit—but you are not finished.
- Obtain a Statement of Understanding from the website.
- Fill in all required information and take the form to the administrative personnel.
- Once the transfer is approved, eligibility documents for each individual will be found on the Transfer Education Benefits website (https://www.dmdc.osd.mil/milconnect/help/topics/transfer_of_education _benefits_teb. htm).

Service members may revoke transferred benefits at any given time. Designated months may also be changed or eliminated through the website while on active duty or through a written request to the VA once separated. Dependents who have received transferred benefits will need to apply to use the benefits through the VA website (https://www.va.gov/). Once the questions are answered, dependents should find themselves on the VA Form 22-1990e.

Eligible dependents include:

- A spouse;
- A service member's children; or
- A combination of spouse and children.

Dependents must be in the Defense Enrollment Eligibility Reporting System. Spouses may use the benefit immediately. However, they:

- Are not entitled to the MHA while the service member remains on active duty, but are entitled once the service member separates.
- Are entitled to the book stipend.

Children use the benefits under the following rules:

- They may use the benefit only after the service member has attained ten years on active duty.
- They may use the benefit while the parent is on active duty or after separation.
- They must have obtained a high school diploma or equivalency certificate, or have turned eighteen.
- They may receive the MHA while a parent remains on active-duty status.
- They are entitled to the book stipend.
- They must use the benefits prior to turning twenty-six.

Service members can commit the required payback time of four years after separating from active duty and dropping into the Reserves.

YELLOW RIBBON PROGRAM

The Yellow Ribbon Program (YRP) (https://www.benefits.va.gov/gibill/yellow_ribbon.asp) is designed to help cover tuition over the maximum allowable rate for private schools. The program is not automatic, and there are many stipulations to watch out for prior to determining if the benefit will work for your particular purpose. YRP does not pay the student any money.

Eligibility

- Participants must rate 100 percent of the Post-9/11 GI Bill.
- Active-duty members of the military are not eligible, nor are their spouses; however, children of active-duty parents may qualify (if the active-duty parent is eligible for 100 percent of Post-9/11).

YRP potentially enables veterans to cover costs above and beyond the Post-9/11 GI Bill parameters. Not all schools participate, and a school's participation for one year does not guarantee participation in subsequent years. You do not need to maintain full-time status to be eligible for YRP. Summer terms may be eligible as well, but check with your particular institution.

Schools must reestablish their YRP program with the VA every year. This means, and it has happened, that a school may participate one year but not the next. You could be left hanging. For example, a Marine corporal attended a well-known private school in Georgia. The school participated during her first year but not the following years. She was out roughly $22,000 per year for her school at that point. . . . Ouch!

Schools may participate on different levels by limiting the number of YRP spots available and the amount of money they offer. This can restrict veterans from considering certain institutions based on financial constraints. Here is a hypothetical breakdown:

- School A participates in YRP with unlimited spots and unlimited money. Therefore, you shouldn't pay out of pocket. But you still run the risk of the school choosing not to participate in upcoming years.
- School B participates with twenty spots and $4,000 per student. Therefore, you may or may not get one of those twenty spots (remember that it is first come, first served!), and the VA will match the $4,000, effectively giving you an extra $8,000 toward tuition (this is a rough explanation of how it works).

You must also check to see how the program at your school is participating. Consider the following hypothetical situations:

- School C: This graduate-level business program participates with seventeen spots and $11,000 per student.
- School D: This graduate-level education program participates with four spots and $6,000 per student.

Notice that different programs within the same school may participate with different amounts of money and numbers of available spots.

Last, a school may participate differently at the graduate level than it does at the undergraduate level. See the following examples:

- School E participates at the undergraduate level with five spots and $8,000 per student.
- School F participates at the graduate level with three spots and $1,000 per student.

Although it can be complicated to determine the benefit you may be eligible for, the vet reps at the school can usually offer sound advice. You can search YRP participating schools by state (https://www.benefits .va.gov/gibill/yellow_ribbon.asp). However, I always recommend contacting the VA directly for solid confirmation that the school you are applying for does participate and to what degree.

If you intend to transfer, you must speak with your new school regarding YRP eligibility. Eligibility at one school does not guarantee eligibility at another. If you take a hiatus from the school where you were enrolled in YRP, you may be dropped for subsequent semesters. Before you make any decisions, talk with your academic adviser and/or veterans' department. The more informed you are, the better you can plan.

VA GI BILL FEEDBACK SYSTEM

The VA implemented a new system (http://www.benefits.va.gov/GI BILL/Feedback.asp) to handle complaints pertaining to issues involving the Principles of Excellence program. Educational institutions that abide by the specific guidelines of the program agree to:

- Inform students in writing (should be personalized) about all costs associated with education at that institution
- Produce educational plans for military and veteran beneficiaries
- Cease all misleading recruiting techniques
- Accommodate those who are absent due to military requirements
- Appoint a point of contact that offers education-related and financial advice
- Confirm that all new programs are accredited before enrolling students
- Align refund policies with Title IV policies (Federal Student Aid)

If a school participates in the Principles of Excellence program, this information will be included on the GI Bill Comparison Tool website: (https://www.va.gov/gi-bill-comparison-tool).

Complaints should be submitted through the GI Bill feedback website (http://www.benefits.va.gov/GIBILL/Feedback.asp) when institutions participating in the program fall below the set of standards listed above. Complaints can be filed on subjects such as recruiting practices, education quality, accreditation issues, grade policies, failure to release transcripts, credit transfer, financial topics, student loan concerns, refund problems, job opportunities after degree completion, and degree-plan changes and subsequent requirements. For more information, visit https://gibill.custhelp.va.gov/app/answers/detail/a_id/1557/~/how-do-i-submit-a-complaint-about-my-school-or-employer%3F.

FEDERAL STUDENT AID

TA money and GI Bills are a source of funding, but they are not the only source available. Active-duty and veteran service members can apply for Federal Student Aid and should be encouraged to do so, in order to cover any extra costs they are unable to get funded. For example, TA cannot cover books or supplies. Under the Post-9/11 GI Bill, a student attending school full time will receive $1,000 per academic year toward books and supplies. In most cases, this is not enough to cover book expenses. Federal Student Aid is a viable option to help in these circumstances. Student aid can come from the federal government, states, schools, and nonprofit organizations. Student aid money is usually provided on a first-come, first-served basis. Most students elect to apply for Federal Student Aid through the U.S. Department of Education, but not everyone qualifies. Prior to applying for Federal Student Aid, it is important to understand what it is, how it works, and what you would want to accept.

Federal Student Aid comes in three forms: work-study, loans, and grants. Work-study might be an option upon separation from the service, but it is not a feasible option for active-duty service members. VA Work-Study is a great option for veterans who are interested in making extra money while attending school and keeping their work activity on their résumé full at the same time.

Active-duty and veteran students using their GI Bills should not need loans in most cases. In fact, it is best to avoid them at all costs. Typically, active-duty service members have access to TA money, and veterans have access to their GI Bills. Loans have to be repaid with interest, and you should think carefully before accepting them. The much-discussed federal Pell Grant is the target for most. Pell Grant money does not need to be paid back. The award must be used for education-related expenses, and only undergraduate students who do not already possess a bachelor's degree are eligible. The maximum award amount for the 2019–2020 academic year is $6,195.

Not everyone rates Pell Grant money. The award is based on financial need, the cost of the school, and the rate of educational pursuit. The Pell Grant award amount can change yearly, and the FAFSA must be reapplied for every academic year. When you reapply, your personal information will automatically be filled in to help expedite the process.

If a student is awarded Pell Grant money, the amount is sent to the school, and the school pays the student. Federal Pell Grant money is paid in at least two disbursements. Most schools pay students at least once per semester. If any money is owed toward tuition and fees, schools deduct that amount from the Pell Grant award prior to turning the money over to the student. Award money is typically turned over to students as a check, cash, or a bank deposit. Most veteran students' tuition is covered by the GI Bill, so most veterans should get to keep the full amount of the award.

Remember this prior to choosing an institution that may not be fully covered under Post-9/11 or MGIB. In order to be eligible to apply for Federal Student Aid, borrowers must:

- Demonstrate financial need (required by most programs)
- Be a U.S. citizen or eligible noncitizen
- Have a valid Social Security number (exceptions apply)
- Be registered with the Selective Service (if male)
- Be enrolled or accepted, at a minimum of half time, as a regular student
- Be enrolled in an eligible degree or certificate program

Federal Student Aid applicants will also need to sign statements stating that the student:

- Is not defaulting on any federal student loans
- Does not owe money on any federal grants
- Will only use aid money for educational-related expenses
- Can demonstrate evidence of eligibility by having a high school diploma, GED, or a completed home-school program approved by state law

Be sure to research and understand where a student loan is coming from prior to accepting any money. Student loans can be federal or private, depending on the source. Federally backed loans and private loans have many differences. Here are just a few of the reasons that federally backed loans can offer greater flexibility than loans from private sources:

- Federal loans can offer borrowers fixed interest rates that are typically lower than private sources.
- Borrowers are given a six-month grace period upon completion of the degree to begin repayments. Often, private school loans will require payments to be made while the student is still attending school.
- Only federally backed loans are subsidized, meaning the government pays the interest for a period of time.
- Interest may be deductible; this is not an option for private loans.
- Federal loans can be consolidated into a Direct Consolidation Loan; private loans cannot.

Private lenders might demand that the individual borrowing the money already have a credit record, but most lenders of federal student loans will not perform a credit check.

Federal loans offer more options for forbearance or deferment. Federal student loans come in three shapes and sizes:

- Direct Subsidized Loans
- Direct Unsubsidized Loans
- Direct PLUS Loans (for advanced education)

According to the U.S. Department of Education, Direct Subsidized Loans have slightly better parameters for students with financial need. Direct Subsidized Loans are only available for undergraduate students, and the amount awarded cannot exceed the financial need. Interest on this type of loan is covered by the U.S. Department of Education while students remain in school at a minimum of half time and for the first six months after graduation (the grace period).

Direct Unsubsidized Loans demand a demonstration of financial need and are available for undergraduate and graduate school. The amount borrowed is regulated by the school and is based upon the school's costs. Interest is the responsibility of the borrower at all times. If the borrower chooses not to pay interest while in school, the amount accrues and is added to the overall loan and will be reflected in payments when they come due.

Federal PLUS loans are available for graduate- or professional-degree-seeking students and parents of dependent undergraduate students. Schools must participate in the program for students to be eligible. Loans are fixed at 7.9 percent, and borrowers must not have an adverse credit history. PLUS loans do not require financial need and have payback options in case the student has needs above his or her available benefit levels and resources of parents who will help. For more specific information regarding the types of loans available, see the U.S. Department of Education's Federal Student Aid website (http://studentaid.ed.gov/types/loans/federal -vs-private). The federal Perkins Loan program did offer options, but on September 30, 2017, was not renewed by Congress and thus expired.

If you plan to apply for Federal Student Aid, you will need access to your taxes from the previous year. For example, if you are applying for student aid for the 2019–2020 school year, you will need your 2018 taxes. The FAFSA (http://www.fafsa.ed.gov/) application period opens in January of each year and must be reapplied for each year. Check with your state for possible state-based financial awards and potential deadline dates. For example, California has the CalGrant award. The award is applied for while completing the FAFSA; however, the deadline is March 2 of each year. If you are eligible and do not fill out the FAFSA and submit required documents prior to this point, you will not be eligible for any state-based assistance if attending a school in California.

If you do not rate any money one year, do not let it deter you from applying in subsequent years. You may rate it at another time because finances can change. If you are under age twenty-four but have already served on active duty (or are currently serving), you will not need to enter your parents' tax information on the FAFSA (per the Higher Education Reconciliation Act of 2005). You will enter your personal tax information only.

If you are interested in applying for Federal Student Aid but are unsure how to proceed, contact your school's financial aid office for further guidance. Here is a quick checklist for applying for federal financial aid:

- Have your tax information from the previous year on hand.
- Apply on https://studentaid.ed.gov/sa/fafsa/filling-out/fsaid for your FSA ID number.
- Apply for Federal Student Aid through FAFSA (http:// www.fafsa.ed .gov); you will need to list your school.
- Verify your submission with your school's financial aid office.
- Keep an eye out for your financial aid award letter, and monitor your student account on your school's website.
- Hopefully, receive a payment!
- The http://www.fafsa.ed.gov website offers many helpful hints if you get stuck while filling out the FAFSA. The application should take twenty to thirty minutes to complete online.

STATE-BASED VETERAN EDUCATION BENEFITS

Aside from the federal GI Bills available for honorably discharged veterans, many states also have state-based benefits to help with education. Some of the benefits work quite liberally; others have stricter guidelines. In some cases, it is possible to double-dip off MGIB and a state-based benefit to maximize monetary intake. Potentially, this can mean more money in the student's pocket or longer-lasting education benefits.

It is extremely important to figure out whether you rate a state-based benefit and how that benefit works before you sign up for your federal GI Bill. In some cases, you can bring in more money monthly by staying under MGIB instead of opting for Post-9/11. If you opt for Post-9/11 and activate your GI Bill, then find out later that you could have made more money under MGIB, it is too late. Once the Post-9/11 GI Bill is selected and activated, you cannot go back.

In order to determine what benefits your state offers and whether you are eligible, check with your state's Department of Veterans' Affairs

Office (http://www.va.gov/statedva.htm). Oftentimes, the school's veterans' representatives have information on their particular state's education benefits, but always check with the state VA to verify all available benefits, including possibilities other than education.

We list and describe many of the state-based benefits later in this chapter. Remember that states may cancel, change, or add benefits over time. Although we strive to be as accurate as possible, this book was compiled and written in 2019, and things change. Because you are the veteran, you need to double check what is available at any specific time.

There are typically two situations where MGIB might be a better choice than Post-9/11, and they are explained next. Remember that you can always visit with an education counselor on your base for further advice, and a quick phone call to the veterans' representatives at the school can usually tell you which GI Bill veterans are opting for in the same situation.

There are two groups of veterans who sometimes prefer to remain under MGIB: those who come from a state that has a full state-based education benefit, and, in a few rare cases, those who choose to attend school fully online. I do not recommend a fully online school because it usually means forgoing a good chunk of the housing stipend.

An example of a veteran who did better by staying under MGIB instead of selecting Post-9/11 is Sergeant Smith, who enlisted in Illinois. In 2019, after serving four years of honorable service in the Marine Corps, he is about to separate and return home. Sergeant Smith is interested in attending Southern Illinois University at Carbondale and needs to determine his available education options.

Sergeant Smith learns about the two federal GI Bills and the Illinois Veteran Grant (IVG) from this book. He needs to determine whether he paid into MGIB, which would have been $100 per month for the first year of his enlistment to total $1,200. He believes he did, but he cannot remember for sure. He will double check with the local Admin Office to clarify, but he continues to plan as if he did pay the $1,200 into MGIB.

Sergeant Smith might also be eligible for IVG. Only the Illinois state VA can determine his eligibility and notify veterans of the availability for the program, and he will need to verify with them whether he will be able to use the benefit prior to following through with the details. Make note that the program may not consistently be funded every year.

IVG will cover the cost of tuition and certain fees for eligible veterans at state-supported universities and community colleges within the state of Illinois. If Sergeant Smith does rate IVG, he might do better financially by using it in tandem with MGIB rather than opting for Post-9/11.

Here is the IVG eligibility list from the Illinois State VA (also at https://www2.illinois.gov/veterans/benefits/pages/education.aspx) that Sergeant Smith reviewed (remember: things change!):

- The veteran must have received an honorable discharge.
- The veteran must have resided in Illinois six months prior to entering the service.
- The veteran must have completed a minimum of one full year of active duty in the U.S. Armed Forces (this includes veterans who were assigned to active duty in a foreign country in a time of hostilities in that country, regardless of length of service).
- The veteran must return to Illinois within six months of separation from the service.

Sergeant Smith falls within those parameters, feels confident that he will rate the IVG, and proceeds accordingly. Looking up the MHA stipend for the Post-9/11 GI Bill (https://www.va.gov/gi-bill-comparison -tool), Sergeant Smith finds the MHA stipend for the academic year 2019 is $1,194. Carbondale, Illinois, is located in a rural, southern portion of the state; hence, the housing allowance under Post-9/11 is on the low side. Sergeant Smith feels that this amount is too low and that he could do better if he elects to stay under MGIB instead of choosing Post-9/11.

Here are his calculations:

- Post-9/11 MHA: $1,194.
- MGIB payments (as of October 1, 2018): $2,050.
- Sergeant Smith will rate IVG, which will pay most of his public university's tuition and fees.
- If Sergeant Smith pays the $600 buy-up to MGIB prior to separation, it will increase his monthly MGIB payments by an extra $150 per month, so his monthly take-home amount would be $2,200, or $1,006

more than the $1,194 he would receive under Post-9/11. If none of the amounts change over the thirty-six months Sergeant Smith has allotted, he would take home $36,216 more under MGIB than he would under Post-9/11 over the course of the thirty-six months of benefits.

- One drawback is that IVG can be used for a master's degree as well. If Sergeant Smith uses both his federal and state-based benefit at the same time, he may not retain any benefits that could have been used for graduate school. That is a personal decision.

Sergeant Smith reviews his calculations and realizes that he still needs to verify his IVG with the Illinois state VA and his GI Bill eligibility with the federal VA. He also needs to contact the veterans' representatives at Southern Illinois University to discuss which GI Bill the veterans already attending the school have chosen and any recommendations that the vet reps may have for him. Sergeant Smith must decide whether he does not mind depleting both of his benefits at the same time because tapping into them simultaneously will result in that outcome.

Illinois veterans who meet IVG requirements must decide if the extra payoff they obtain by depleting both benefits at the same time is worth it. Many veterans may want to pursue a graduate degree with that benefit later, whereas others may be more interested in maximizing their benefits immediately. Also remember that Sergeant Smith is going to attend a school in a rural area. If you are from Illinois and select an institution closer to Chicago, your MHA amount will be much higher than the listed amount for Southern Illinois University at Carbondale. In this case, double-dipping is not necessary.

The second instance in which some veterans have opted for MGIB is for online-only school. Under the Post-9/11 GI Bill, veterans only receive $825 in MHA (as of academic year 2019–2020) for strictly online school because you must attend a minimum of one face-to-face class every semester in order to rate the full MHA assigned to the Zip code of the school. In a few cases, veterans who decide that they can only attend online school may do better by remaining under MGIB and paying the $600 buy-up prior to separation. In the case of strictly online school, it is difficult to run the numbers in this book because too many factors are unknown. Examples of this include tuition charges, MHA attached to the school's zip code, and fluctuations in GI Bill payouts.

Here is a hypothetical example: Sergeant Smith decides to attend a fully online academic program. The cost of the school per credit hour is $250. He is taking two classes over an eight-week semester. The total cost for his two classes will be $1,500. The MHA for strictly online school at this time is $894.50 per month. Sergeant Smith paid the $600 buy-up program at Admin before separating. His combined monthly payout under MGIB and the buy-up program for academic year 2019–2020 is $2,200 per month. In the span of his eight-week classes, he will take in $4,400. After paying $1,500 for his two classes (two classes on an eight-week semester schedule is considered full time), he is left with $2,900, but remember that this does not include fees. That is roughly $1,138 more than what he would take home if he had selected Post-9/11 and only received the $1789 that is allotted for strictly online school ($2,900 − $1,789 = $1,111). MGIB, in this case, looks like the better choice.

Other state-based benefits can be a bit trickier. Right now, only some states offer in-state tuition to out-of-state residents. The Student Veterans of America maintains a website where you can check to see whether the state where you plan to attend school offers this benefit (https://studen tveterans.org/32-media-news/latest-news-2013/178-sva-s-interactive-map -illustrates-fight-for-in-state-tuition). Some university systems will also grant in-state tuition for veterans. There are always qualifying criteria you must abide by, so, as I keep saying throughout this book, always check with the state VA or with the vet reps at the school to verify your eligibility.

As a veteran, it is important for you to follow through with your own research on state and federal benefits. States are often updating and adding benefits for veterans. The monetary amounts attached to the federal GI Bills change as well. The only way to stay current with the information is to become fluent with the websites and check back regularly.

Legislation was passed that gives veterans and eligible dependents the in-state tuition rate at all state-based colleges and universities that continue to accept the GI Bills (https://www.va.gov/opa/choiceact/documents/ choice-act-summary.pdf. The benefit took effect on July 1, 2015.

What if you are trying to save your GI Bill benefits for graduate school, or you transferred them to a child? Twenty states currently have state laws that waive the in-state residency requirement for veterans: Alabama, Arizona, Colorado, Idaho, Illinois, Indiana, Kentucky, Louisiana, Maryland, Minnesota, Missouri, Nevada, New Mexico, North Dakota, Ohio, Oregon,

South Dakota, Texas, Utah, and Virginia. In the following list are the websites for the states that currently offer in-state residency to veterans. Some of these states offer other veteran benefits as well. There are specific steps (such as registering to vote or getting a driver's license) tied into eligibility for the in-state tuition, and sometimes it is up to the school to participate. Check with the veterans' representatives at the institution you wish to attend to determine how to begin the process for that particular state.

Alabama

https://registrar.ua.edu/academics-policies/residency-for-tuition -purposes/#accordion

In-state tuition for veterans who reside in Alabama and were honorably discharged within the five years immediately preceding their enrollment at a state institution of higher learning. Reservists and service-connected disabled veterans are eligible as well.

Arizona

https://dvs.az.gov/state-tuition

In-state tuition for veterans who registered to vote in the state and meet at least one of the following parameters: have an Arizona driver license or motor vehicle registration, demonstrate employment history in Arizona, transfer their banking services to Arizona, change their permanent address on all pertinent records, or provide other materials (any kind or from any source) relevant to domicile or residency status.

California

https://www.calvet.ca.gov/VetServices/Pages/Non-Resident-College -Fee-Waiver.aspx

Currently, the state of California offers honorary residency to veterans who were stationed in California for one year prior to separation from the military, separate, and stay in the state to attend an institution of higher education.

Colorado

https://financialaid.colostate.edu/residency-exceptions-veterans-and -dependents/

In-state tuition for qualifying veterans and dependents. Veterans must be honorably discharged and maintain a permanent home in Colorado.

Enlisted service member who are stationed in Colorado and receiving the resident-student rate (themselves or their dependents will be able to maintain that rate upon separation from the military if they continue to reside in the state.

Florida
http://www.flsenate.gov/Session/Bill/2014/7015/BillText/er/PDF
In-state tuition for honorably discharged veterans at state community colleges, state colleges, and universities.

Idaho
http://www.margbva.org/News_and_resources/State%20Benefits%20PDF/ID-2017.pdf
In-state tuition for qualified veterans and qualifying dependents. Veterans must have served at least two years on active duty, have received an honorable discharge, and enter a public school within one year of separating from the service. Dependents must receive at least 50 percent of their support from the qualifying veteran.

Illinois
https://veterans.illinois.edu/
All veterans using the Post-9/11 GI Bill will be billed as in-state residents at state-supported institutions.

Indiana
http://www.in.gov/legislative/bills/2013/SE/SE0177.1.html
Veterans enrolled in undergraduate classes no more than twelve months after honorably separating from the Armed Forces or Indiana National Guard are eligible for in-state tuition.

Kentucky
https://www.uky.edu/veterans/content/active-duty-military
In-state tuition for qualifying veterans.

Louisiana
http://legiscan.com/LA/text/HB435/id/649958
In-state tuition for veterans who served a minimum of two years on active duty and received an honorable discharge. Veterans who have

been assigned service-connected disability ratings and are either already enrolled or are applying to a state institution are eligible as well.

Maine

www.mainelegislature.org/legis/bills/getDoc.asp?id=39934

Honorably discharged veterans enrolled in a program of education within the University of Maine system, the community college system, or the Maritime Academy are eligible for in-state tuition.

Maryland

http://www.mdlegion.org/Forms/VetBrochure%5B1%5D.pdf

In-state tuition for honorably discharged veterans of the armed forces. Veteran must reside in Maryland and attend a state institution of higher learning.

Minnesota

https://www.revisor.mn.gov/statutes/?id=197.775&format=pdf

In-state tuition at the undergraduate rate for veterans.

Missouri

www.senate.mo.gov/13info/BTS_Web/Bill.aspx?SessionType=R&Bill ID=17138567

In-state tuition for veterans who received honorable or general discharges from the service. The benefit can be used at the state two-year or four-year institutions. Two-year institutions also offer the in-district rate.

Nebraska

https://veterans.nebraska.gov/education

Honorably discharged veterans receive in-state tuition within two years of their date of separation from service. Dependents are eligible as well. Not applicable if the service member is eligible for the YRP.

Nevada

http://leg.state.nv.us/Session/77th2013/Bills/AB/AB260_EN.pdf

In-state tuition for veterans who were honorably discharged and matriculated within two years of their date of separation from the Armed Forces.

New Mexico

http://www.nmdvs.org/state-benefits/

In-state tuition for qualified veterans, their spouses, and their children.

North Dakota

www.legis.nd.gov/cencode/t15c10.pdf?20131106152541

In-state tuition for veterans who served 180 days or more on active duty and received an honorable discharge. Dependents who received transferred Post-9/11 benefits may also be eligible.

Ohio

https://www.ohiohighered.org/veterans

In-state tuition for qualified veterans.

Oregon

https://olis.leg.state.or.us/liz/2013R1/Measures/Text/HB2158/Enrolled

Honorably discharged veterans who establish a physical presence in Oregon within twelve months of enrolling in school may be eligible for in-state tuition and fees.

South Dakota

http://legis.state.sd.us/statutes/DisplayStatute.aspx?Type=Statute&Statute=13-53-29.1

In-state tuition for honorably discharged veterans with at least ninety days of service.

Tennessee

http://www.capitol.tn.gov/Bills/108/Bill/SB1433.pdf

In-state tuition for veterans discharged within the last two years who did not receive a dishonorable discharge.

Texas

http://www.statutes.legis.state.tx.us/Docs/ED/htm/ED.54.htm#54.241

In-state tuition for veterans who qualify for federal education benefits. Dependents may qualify as well.

Utah
(https://veterans.utah.gov/state-education-benefits/
In-state tuition for qualifying veterans at certain schools.

Virginia
https://www.schev.edu/index/students-and-parents/student-type/military
-education/veterans-and-families
Veterans released or discharged under conditions other than dishonorable are eligible for in-state tuition.

Washington
http://apps.leg.wa.gov/documents/billdocs/2013-14/Pdf/Bills/Senate%20
Passed%20Legislature/5318.PL.pdf
Veterans (and their dependents) who served a minimum of two years in the military and received an honorable discharge will be granted in-state tuition as long as they enroll in school within one year of their date of separation from the service.

A few state-based university systems across the country may also offer veterans in-state tuition without a state-based benefit in place. The following is a current list:

- University of Alaska system: https://www.alaska.edu/studentservices/military/veterans-residency/
- Mississippi institutions of higher learning: http://www.ihl.state.ms.us/board/downloads/policiesandbylaws.pdf
- University of Wisconsin system: https://docs.legis.wisconsin.gov/statutes/statutes/36/27/2/b/4
- Kentucky public universities: http://www.lrc.ky.gov/record/11rs/HB 425.htm
- University of Iowa system: https://registrar.uiowa.edu/veteran-education-transition-services-vets-previously-gi-bill-services
- University system of Georgia: http://www.usg.edu/policymanual/section7/C453/
- University of Rhode Island: https://web.uri.edu/admission/residency-policies/

Many institutions of higher learning have adopted scholarships for disabled veterans. For example, the University of Idaho has the Operation Education scholarship that may provide financial assistance for eligible service-connected disabled veterans and their spouses (http://www.uidaho .edu/operationeducation). Check with the institutions you are interested in attending to obtain information regarding policies or programs that may benefit you.

The following are states with state-based education benefits at this time. Most of the information is taken from the state VA websites.

Alabama: "For children and spouses of certain disabled veterans, tuition may be waived at state supported colleges and vocational/technical schools. The veteran must meet certain residency requirements prior to entering active service and after leaving active duty. The minimum disability rating eligible for the scholarship program returns to a 40 percent service-connected disability rating in most cases. Veterans with at least a 20 percent service-connected disability rating but less than 40 percent who file for scholarship benefits prior to July 31, 2023, may qualify under certain criteria. Veterans who have a disability claim currently pending prior to May 23, 2017, may still qualify if their claim results in a rating of at least 20 percent and they file for scholarship benefits within six months of the final decision."[1]

Arkansas: "The Arkansas Department of Higher Education has the authority to provide free tuition and fees at any state-supported college, university, technical school, or vocational school to the spouse and children of any Arkansan who has been declared to be prisoner of war or placed on missing-in-action status since January 1, 1960. The same provisions apply to the surviving spouse and children of any Arkansas resident killed in action since 1960."[2]

California: "Children who are California residents may qualify for a tuition waiver at state colleges and universities if a parent is a veteran with a disability rating of zero percent or higher."[3] Note: Zero percent is an actual disability rating with the VA, the lowest disability rating. It is not the same as not having a disability rating.

Connecticut: Tuition waiver: "Veterans may attend Connecticut public colleges and universities tuition free. Connecticut statutes provide that tuition may be waived for qualified veterans attending the University of Connecticut, Connecticut State Universities and the twelve community-technical colleges. Waivers cover only the cost of tuition for credit-bearing undergraduate and graduate programs. Other charges, such as for books, student activity and course fees, parking, and room and board, are not waived. To be eligible for veterans' tuition benefits at any college or university, a veteran must:

- have been honorably discharged or released under honorable conditions from active service in the U.S. Armed Forces. National Guard members, activated under Title 10 of the United States Code, are also included;
- have served at least 90 days or more cumulative days active duty in time of war (see Periods of Service) except if separated from service earlier because of a U.S. Department of Veterans Affairs–rated service-connected disability or if the war, campaign, or operation lasted less than ninety days and service was for the duration;
- have been accepted for admission at a Connecticut public college or university;
- have been living in Connecticut at the time of acceptance, which includes domicile for less than one year."[4]

Delaware: "Delaware provides educational benefits for the children of deceased veterans of the military services of the United States, military service personnel held prisoner of war and military service personnel officially declared to be missing in action. In order to qualify for this entitlement an applicant shall be: the child of a member of the armed forces who was killed while on active duty or who died from disease, wounds, injuries or disabilities arising or resulting from performance of duty; a member of the armed forces who is being held, or who was held prisoner of war; or a member of the armed forces officially declared missing in action; a person who at the time of application for benefits is at least 16 years of age, but not more than 24 years of age, and a resident of the State for at least three years prior to the date of application; attending or admitted for attendance at an educational institution beyond the high school level in a program not to exceed four years in duration. Benefits are administered by the Delaware Postsecondary Education Commission."[5]

Florida: "Florida waives undergraduate-level tuition at state universities and community colleges for Florida Purple Heart recipients and other combat-related decorations superior in precedence to the Purple Heart. In 2014, legislation was signed expanding the waiver program to include the state's career and technical training facilities. In 2016, legislation was passed expanding the eligibility for this earned benefit. Call (850) 245–0407 for more information."[6]

Illinois: "Waiver of tuition at state colleges and universities for veterans who served during a time of hostilities (whether actually involved in the hostilities or not)."[7]

Indiana: "Free tuition at state colleges and universities for children of veterans with a zero percent disability rating or higher if the veteran served during a time of hostilities. They must meet certain Indiana residency requirements."[8]

Kentucky: "A waiver of tuition is an education benefit provided by the Commonwealth of Kentucky in recognition of military service of certain Kentucky veterans. The tuition waiver is provided for children, stepchildren, adopted children, spouses, and un-remarried widows & widowers. An approved tuition waiver means a student may attend any two-year, four-year or vocational technical schools that are operated and funded by the Kentucky Department of Education." Refer to https://veterans.ky.gov/Pages/HidPages/TuitionWaiver.aspx. "You may qualify if one of the following is true of the veteran:

- Died on active duty.
- Died as a direct result of a service-connected disability as determined by the U.S. Department of Veterans Affairs.
- 100% service-connected disabled.
- Totally disabled (non-service connected) with wartime service as deemed by the U.S. Department of Veterans Affairs or Department of Defense.

- Is deceased and lived in KY at time of death and served during a wartime period.
- Award from Social Security Administration is not acceptable."[9]
- Kentucky residency is a requirement for both the veteran and the applicant. A deceased veteran must have been a Kentucky resident at the time of death.

Maine: "The Veterans Upward Bound program helps Maine military veterans prepare for and pursue the attainment of a degree. More information is available at https://usm.maine.edu/trioprograms/veterans-upward -bound. Maine provides a 100 percent tuition waiver and all related fees for spouses and dependents of veterans as defined in Title 37B, Chapter 7, Section 505(2). Specifically, veterans must meet the following criteria:

- Have a 100% total permanent disability rating resulting from service-connected disability.

Or who:

- Was killed in action;
- Died from a service-connected disability as a result of service;
- At the time of death was totally and permanently disabled due to a service-connected disability, but whose death was not related to the service-connected disability; or is a member of the Armed Forces on active duty who has been listed for more than 90 days as missing in action, captured or forcibly detained or interned in the line of duty by a foreign government or power. 'Veteran' means any person who served in the military or naval forces of the United States and entered the service from this State or has been a resident of this State for 5 years immediately preceding application for aid and, if living, continues to reside in this State throughout the duration of benefits administered under the educational benefits program." "Schools covered under this program include the University of Maine System, Maine Community Colleges, and Maine Maritime Academy."[10]

Maryland: "The Edward T. Conroy Memorial Scholarship is designed to provide aid for tuition and other educational expenses to veterans and their family members who are attending an institution of higher learning within the borders of the State of Maryland. You must be:

- The son or daughter of a member of the United States Armed Forces who died, or is 100 percent disabled as a direct result of military service;
- A veteran who suffers, as a direct result of military service, a disability of 25 percent or greater and has exhausted or is no longer eligible for federal veterans educational benefits;
- The son, daughter or surviving spouse of a victim of the September 11, 2001 terrorist attacks, who died as a result of the attacks on the World Trade Center in New York City, the attack on the Pentagon in Virginia, or the crash of United Airlines Flight 93 in Pennsylvania;
- A POW/MIA of the Vietnam Conflict or his/her son or daughter;
- Or a state or local public safety employee or volunteer who was 100 percent disabled in the line of duty.
- You must be a Maryland resident at the time of the application."[11]

Massachusetts: "For all veterans of the state, there is a tuition waiver at state-supported colleges and universities on a space-available basis."[12]

The Veterans Upward Bound program is a free pre-college program to help veterans develop the academic and personal skills necessary for success in a program of post-secondary education. There are two Veterans Upward Bound locations in Massachusetts: UMass Boston and Suffolk University.[13]

Michigan: "The Children of Veterans Tuition Grant provides undergraduate tuition assistance to the child of a veteran who died while on active federal duty or who has been awarded a total and permanent disability rating from the VA. The grant is administered by the Michigan Department of Treasury. Call 888-447-2687 for more information."[14]

Minnesota: "The Minnesota GI Bill program provides assistance to eligible Minnesota Veterans, currently serving military, National Guard and Reserve members who served after September 11, 2001 and eligible spouse and children. The Program provides a maximum benefit of $10,000, up to age 62. Eligible participants can use the benefit in Higher Education, On-the-job training (OJT)/Apprenticeship or License and Certification." Eligibility requirements include:

- Veteran who is serving or has served honorably in any branch of the United States armed forces at any time, or;
- Surviving spouse or children of a person who has served in the military at any time on, and who has died or has a 100% VA determined permanent and total disability as a direct result of that military service and must be eligible to receive federal education benefits under Chapter 33 Fry Scholarship, or Chapter 35 and provide a certificate of eligibility."[15]

Missouri: The Missouri Returning Heroes' Education Act limits tuition to no more than $50 per credit hour at public colleges and universities while a veteran is enrolled in an undergraduate certificate or degree program after all other financial aid is taken into account. Veterans who served after September 11, 2001, are eligible. The veteran remains eligible for ten years after honorable discharge. The War Veteran's Survivor Grants are available annually to children and spouses of veterans whose deaths or injuries were: a result of combat action or were attributed to an illness that was contracted while serving in combat action, or who became 80 percent disabled as a result of injuries or accidents sustained in combat action since September 11, 2001. The veteran must have been a Missouri resident when first entering the military service or at the time of death or injury. The total number that may receive a grant in any year is limited by statute to 25 recipients.[16]

Montana: "The Veterans' Upward Bound Program is offering free statewide classes that prepare veterans for college and other post secondary training. If you are a military veteran," the state of Montana "can assist you in achieving your educational goals. Veterans' Upward Bound is offering free classes in math, algebra, grammar, writing, computers, college survival, and Spanish."[17]

Nebraska: "Waiver of Tuition is a state program . . . available to dependents of an eligible veteran that may be used to waive 100% of a student's tuition charges and tuition-related fees to the University of Nebraska campuses, Nebraska state colleges, and Nebraska community colleges. Waiver of Tuition can be used to receive ONE degree, diploma, or certificate from a community college and ONE baccalaureate degree from the university or a state college." The dependent must be a resident of Nebraska. Dependents of veterans in the following categories may qualify:

- "be rated permanently and totally disabled as a result of military service; or
- have died of a service-connected disability; or
- have died subsequent to discharge as a result of injury or illness sustained while a member of the armed forces; or
- have been classified as missing in action or a prisoner of war during armed hostilities while a member of the armed forces."[18]

New Hampshire: "The child of a missing person who was domiciled in this State serving in or with the U.S. armed forces after February 28, 1961, is entitled to free tuition at vocational-technical college so long as said missing person is so reported/listed as missing, captured, etc. . . . Children of military members who die in service during wartime, and children of certain wartime veterans who die from a service-connected disability, may qualify for free tuition at New Hampshire public institutions of higher learning. A scholarship for board, room, rent, books and supplies up to $2500 per year for a period of no more than 4 years at such educational institutions may be furnished to these children if they are in need of financial assistance."[19]

New Mexico: "Wartime Veteran Scholarship Fund can be used by any veteran who has served in combat since 1990 and who has exhausted all available federal GI Education Benefits options. An eligible combat veteran who has served since 1990 will thus no longer have to worry about utilizing their GI Education Benefit bill under a deadline which may not fit their time frame.

The fund reimburses state-supported educational institutions for the cost of tuition and books. This scholarship is available to veterans who have been residents of New Mexico for a minimum of ten years and who were awarded the Southwest Asia Service Medal, Global War on Terrorism Expeditionary Medal, Iraq Campaign Medal, Afghanistan Campaign Medal, or any other medal issued for service in the Armed Forces in support of any U.S. military campaign or armed conflict as defined by Congress or presidential executive order for service after August 1, 1990."[20]

New York: "Veterans Tuition Awards (VTA) are awards for full-time study and part-time study for eligible veterans matriculated in an approved program at an undergraduate or graduate degree-granting institution or in an approved vocational training program in New York State (NYS). For full-time study, a recipient receives an award of up to undergraduate tuition for NYS residents at the State University of New York (SUNY), or actual tuition charged, whichever is less. Fulltime study is defined as 12 or more credits per semester (or the equivalent) in an approved program at a degree-granting institution, or 24 or more hours per week in a vocational training program. To be eligible, the recipient must be a legal resident of NYS and have resided in NYS for 12 continuous months prior to the beginning of the term. More eligibility criteria:

- Be discharged under honorable conditions from the U.S. Armed Forces and:
- A Vietnam Veteran who served in Indochina between February 28, 1961 and May 7, 1975; or
- A Persian Gulf Veteran who served in the Persian Gulf on or after August 2, 1990; or
- An Afghanistan Veteran who served in Afghanistan during hostilities on or after September 11, 2001, or
- A Veteran of the United States Armed Forces who served in hostilities that occurred after February 28, 1961, as evidenced by receipt of an Armed Forces Expeditionary Medal, Navy Expeditionary Medal, or a Marine Corps Expeditionary Medal. For part-time study, awards will be prorated by credit hour. Part-time study is defined as at least three but fewer than 12 credits per semester (or the equivalent) in an approved program at a degree-granting institution, or six to 23 hours per week in a vocational training program. Tuition payments received by a veteran under the Chapter 33 Program and Yellow Ribbon component will be considered duplicative of any VTA award a student may have received. However, payments received under the Montgomery GI bill do not duplicate the VTA award."[21]

North Carolina: "Scholarship for Children of Wartime Veterans. North Carolina's Scholarship Program was created to show its appreciation for the services and sacrifices of its war veterans. The scholarship program applies to North Carolina schools. The scholarship is for eight academic semesters and the recipient has eight years to utilize the eight academic semesters. The Scholarship program has been established for the qualifying natural or an adopted child (if adopted before the age of 15) children of certain class categories of deceased, disabled, combat, or POW/MIA veterans. Applicant must be under the age of 25 at the time of application. The veteran's qualifying criteria must have occurred during a period of war. At time of application, applicant must be domiciled and a resident of North Carolina."[22]

North Dakota: "Dependent Tuition Waiver for any dependent of a resident veteran who was killed in action or died from wounds or other service-connected causes, was totally disabled as a result of service-connected causes, died from service-connected disabilities, was a prisoner of war, or was declared missing in action, upon being duly accepted for enrollment into any North Dakota state-supported institution of higher education or state-supported technical or vocational school, must be allowed to obtain a bachelor's degree or certificate of completion, for so long as the dependent is eligible, free of any tuition and fee charges if the bachelor's degree or certificate of completion is earned within a forty-five-month or ten-semester period or its equivalent and if tuition and fee charges do not include costs for aviation flight charges or expenses."[23]

Ohio: "The Veterans Upward Bound program, funded by the U.S. Department of Education, is designed to motivate and assist veterans in the development of academic and other requisite skills necessary for acceptance and success in a program of postsecondary education. The program provides assessment and enhancement of basic skills through counseling, mentoring, tutoring and academic instruction in the core subject areas. The primary goal of the program is to increase the rate at which participants enroll in and complete postsecondary education programs. Currently, Ohio is home to two Veteran Upward Bound Programs:

- Cuyahoga Community College—Veterans Upward Bound Program
- Cincinnati State Technical and Community College—Veterans Upward Bound Program"[24]

"The Ohio War Orphans Scholarship Program awards tuition assistance to the children of deceased or severely disabled Ohio veterans who served in the armed forces during a period of declared war or conflict. To receive War Orphans Scholarship benefits, a student must be an Ohio resident and enrolled for full-time undergraduate study and pursuing an associate or bachelor's degree at an eligible Ohio college or university. Applicants must apply between the ages of 16–24. Scholarship benefits cover a portion of instructional and general fee charges at two and four-year public institutions and a portion of these charges at eligible private colleges and universities."[25]

Rhode Island: "Free tuition for veterans with disability rating of 10 percent or higher."[26]

South Carolina: "Children of certain categories of wartime veterans may attend state supported universities, colleges, and technical schools with free tuition. For the child to qualify for free tuition, the veteran parent must meet certain state residency requirements, have served during time of war, and fall into one of the following categories: KIA, Died during service or from a service-connected disease or disability, POW, permanently and totally disabled (VA), awarded the Congressional Medal of Honor, MIA, or awarded the Purple Heart. Child must not have reached twenty-six years old."[27]

South Dakota: "Certain veterans are eligible to take undergraduate courses at a state-supported university without the payment of tuition, provided they are not eligible for educational payments under the GI Bill or any other federal educational program. To qualify the veteran must:

- Have been discharged under honorable conditions; and
- Be a current resident of South Dakota and qualify for in-state tuition or meet one of the following criteria:
  - Have served on active duty at any time between August 2, 1990, and a date to be determined;
  - Have received an Armed Forces Expeditionary medal or other U.S. campaign or service medal for participation in combat operations against hostile forces outside the boundaries of the United States; or
  - Have a service-connected disability rated 10 percent or more.

Eligible veterans may receive one month of free tuition for each month of 'qualifying service' with a minimum of one, up to a maximum of four, academic years. Qualifying service is defined as: the amount of time served on active duty between the beginning and ending dates of the particular period of conflict or hostilities during which, the veteran earned eligibility for this program. South Dakota provides free tuition for children of veterans who were killed in action and for dependents who are prisoner of war or missing in action."[28]

Texas: "The Hazlewood Act is a State of Texas benefit that provides qualified Veterans, spouses, and dependent children with an education benefit of up to 150 semester hours of tuition exemption, including most fee charges, at public institutions of higher education in Texas. This does NOT include living expenses, books, or supply fees. The benefit is reduced or eliminated while the participant is drawing benefits under a federal program such as the GI Bill or vocational rehabilitation."[29]

Utah: "Purple Heart recipients are eligible for a tuition waiver at all public institution of higher learning in Utah. This benefit can be used toward a degree up to and including a master's degree. Surviving dependents of service members killed in action on or after September 11, 2001 are eligible for a tuition waiver at state schools."[30]

Virginia: "The Virginia Military Survivors and Dependents Education Program (VMSDEP) provides education benefits to spouses and children of military service members killed, missing in action, taken prisoner, or who served in covered military combat and has been rated by the United States Department of Veterans Affairs as totally and permanently disabled or at least 90 percent permanently disabled as a result of such service. NOTE: A Veteran's 90–100 percent permanent disability must have been directly caused by the Veteran's involvement in military operations: 1) against terrorism; 2) on a peacekeeping mission; 3) as a result of a terrorist act; 4) an armed conflict. The service-connected disability cannot have incurred during active duty that coincides with, but was not the direct result of, one of the listed events or missions."[31]

Washington: "The governing boards of the state universities, the regional universities, The Evergreen State College, and the community and technical colleges, may waive all or a portion of tuition and fees for a military or naval veteran who is a Washington domiciliary, but who did not serve on foreign soil or in international waters or in another location in support of those serving on foreign soil or in international waters and who does not qualify as an eligible veteran or national guard member under subsection (8) of this section. However, there shall be no state general fund support for waivers granted under this subsection. Tuition may be waiver for a child and the spouse or the domestic partner or surviving spouse or surviving domestic partner of an eligible veteran or national guard member who became totally disabled as a result of serving in active federal military or naval service, or who is determined by the federal government to be a prisoner of war or missing in action."[32]

West Virginia: "Since fiscal year 1997, the West Virginia legislature has included in the annual budget various amounts of funding for postsecondary education. This program offers up to a $500 per semester stipend to veterans who are enrolled in a certified postsecondary class. Additionally, this program can assist veterans with vocational and non-traditional education endeavors on a case-by-case basis. All public institutions of higher education waive tuition and mandatory fee charges for West Virginia residents who have been awarded the Medal of Honor or Purple Heart. Students who qualify for the War Orphan Education Program will not be charged tuition and fees by a West Virginia post-secondary education or training institution. Award amounts administered by the West Virginia Department of Veterans Assistance are to cover costs associated with room, board, books and other living expenses. This amount fluctuates according to the number of applications received each semester. No more than $1,000 will be awarded to a student in any one semester and no more than $2,000 will be awarded to a student in any one year."[33]

Wisconsin: "The Wisconsin GI Bill remits (forgives) full tuition and segregated fees for eligible veterans and their dependents for up to eight full-time semesters or 128 credits, whichever is greater, at any University of Wisconsin System or Wisconsin Technical College System school. The Wisconsin GI Bill is a state program that is entirely separate from the Federal GI Bill. The Veterans Education (VetEd) grant program provides a reimbursement grant based on a credit-bank system that is based on length of active duty military service to eligible veterans who have not yet been awarded a bachelor's degree for the reimbursement of tuition and fees following successful course completion at an eligible UW, technical college, or approved private institution of higher learning. Veterans may currently receive federal VA Chapter 30 Montgomery GI Bill benefits and VetEd for the same semester. Individuals eligible for Wisconsin GI Bill benefits must apply for, and use those benefits in order to be eligible for VetEd reimbursement. VetEd reimbursement will be reduced to the extent that tuition and fees have already been paid by other grants, scholarships, and remissions provided for the payment of tuition and fees, including federal VA Chapter 33 Post-9/11 GI Bill tuition benefits."[34]

SCHOLARSHIPS

For some reason, service members are loathe to apply for scholarships, but military dependents are always ready and prepared to. We have helped veterans apply for scholarships many times, and many times they were awarded large and small sums of money. One veteran even paid for his first two years of community college with only scholarship money. This helped him save his GI Bill benefits, which he needed because he is a civil engineering student with many more classes to take! That was a large pot of easy money to help with school. Sound good? If so, read on.

Although quite a bit of scholarship money is available for veterans, you must be proactive in your pursuit. No one is going to hand you the money without your making an effort. Applying for scholarships is not as difficult as it seems. Often, you can reuse information, so keep everything you write down. Most education centers have financial aid packets available for you to pick up or posted on their websites (e.g., Camp Pendleton, http://mccscp.com/bec). These packets offer a good place to start your search.

Try to remember that the active-duty TA money only goes so far. TA does not cover books, tools, computers, and so on. You should run the numbers before you start to determine what you need the money for: books, housing, tuition?

Scholarships come in all shapes and sizes. You will need to determine which scholarships may apply to you. Do not narrow yourself to veteran-based possibilities. You can apply for civilian scholarships as well. Most break down into specific categories, such as pursuit of study, age, gender, race, disability, state based, or school based. When you begin your search, remember that it will take some time to find and determine eligibility. Start by making a quick search on your school's website. Many schools list scholarships specific to their institution there. Check with your school's veterans' representatives, the financial aid department, and the local education center for possible scholarship opportunities. Libraries are an underused resource for scholarship opportunities. Check opportunities based on options outside your military experience; then, check opportunities based on options within the military community. Prepare the best essay possible, then see if someone in the education center is willing to proofread it for you. Always start far, far in advance. Most scholarships are due during the spring semester in order to pay out for the following fall.

Be very careful of organizations demanding that you pay to be eligible for a scholarship. Scholarship information is widely available, and you should not have to pay to find, receive, or complete an application. Most certainly, never give any credit card information. If you need help, contact your school's financial aid department.

MILITARY SERVICE–RELATED SCHOLARSHIPS

The following are just a few of the scholarships available to service members. See what might be relevant to you. At the end of the section, several scholarship search sites are listed.

Pat Tillman Scholarship

http://www.pattillmanfoundation.org/tillman-military-scholars/apply/
(480) 621-4074
info@pattillmanfoundation.org

Award amount varies every year. Awards average around $11,000 per scholar. That would be money above and beyond your GI Bill. Active duty, veterans, and spouses of both categories are eligible to apply. Applicant must be attending school full time at a four-year university or college (public or private) at the undergraduate or graduate level. This scholarship is a great opportunity for graduate school students, because options at that level are more difficult to find. Applicant must apply for Federal Financial Aid (FAFSA). Digital files of the applicant's DD-214 or personal service record and résumé will be required in order to submit, as well as responding to the two essay prompts. Those who proceed further will need to turn in their financial aid award letter (from attending institution), SAR report from FAFSA, and a photo highlighting the applicable individual's military service. Application opens in January and closes the following month. Check the website for more information.

American Veterans AMVETS
https://amvets.org/scholarships
(877) 726-8387

Award amount is $4,000 over four years. Applicant must be pursuing full-time study at the undergraduate, graduate, or certification level from an accredited institution. Three scholarships awarded annually. Application is due by April 15. Applicant must be a veteran, be a U.S. citizen, and have financial need. Required materials include the veteran's DD-214, official school transcripts, a completed (and signed) 1040 form, a completed FAFSA application, an essay of fifty to one hundred words addressing a specific prompt (see website), a résumé (see website), and proof of school-based expenses.

American Veterans AMVETS National Ladies Auxiliary
http://amvetsaux.org/scholarships/
(301) 459-6255

Two scholarships at $1,000 each and up to five scholarships at $750 each may be available. In order to be eligible, applicant must be a current member of the AMVETS Ladies Auxiliary; a son or daughter; stepchild; or grandchild or step grandchild of a member. Application can be filled out starting in the eligible individual's second year of undergraduate study at an eligible institution. Required documents include a personal essay of two hundred to five hundred words (see website for more information), three letters of recommendation, official transcripts, a copy of the member's membership card, and all required paperwork from the Ladies Auxiliary. Applications are due by July 1.

Military Order of the Purple Heart MOPH

https://www.purpleheart.org/military-order-of-the-purple-heart-scholarship
-program/

(703) 642-5360

scholarship@purpleheart.org

Be aware that this scholarship demands a $15 payment at time of submittal. Applicant must be a Purple Heart recipient and a member of the Military Order of the Purple Heart, or the spouse, widow, child (step and adopted), or grandchild. Student must currently be a high school senior or attending college as an undergraduate student full-time (or attending trade school), and have a minimum 2.75 GPA on a 4.0 scale. Applicant must submit an essay of two hundred to three hundred words (see site for prompt), two letters of recommendation, all other required materials, and the $15 fee (check or money order).

American Legion Auxiliary

https://www.alaforveterans.org/Scholarships/Non-Traditional-Student
-Scholarship/

Approximately five scholarships at $2,000 each are awarded to applicants who are members of the American Legion, American Legion Auxiliary, or Sons of the American Legion. Members must have paid dues for a minimum of two years prior to applying. Applicants must be nontraditional students (going back to school after an absence or starting later in life). Applications are due by March 1.

Veterans of Foreign Wars VFW

http://www.vfw.org/Scholarship/

816-756-3390, ext. 220

Twenty-five annual scholarships for VFW members who served or are currently serving in one of the branches, or members of their immediate family. Five scholarships per branch will be awarded at $3,000 apiece. If already separated, the EAS date must have been within thirty-six months before the December 31 annual deadline.

Armed Forces Communications and Electronics Association AFCEA

http://www.afcea.org/education/scholarships/undergraduate/military.asp

(703) 631-6100

Three scholarships are available to eligible veterans through the AFCEA: the Military Personnel/Dependents Scholarship, the Afghanistan and Iraq War Veterans Scholarship, and the Disabled War Veterans Scholarship (Afghanistan or Iraq). The Military Personnel/Dependents Scholarship awards $2,000. Active duty, veterans, dependents, and spouses may apply, but they must be attending a four-year institution (no community college) full time. Active duty and veterans can apply in their first year of school; however, spouses and dependents must be in their second year at minimum. AFCEA scholarships require certain fields of study, such as electrical, chemical, systems, or aerospace engineering; mathematics, physics, science, or mathematics education; technology management; management information systems; or computer science. Majors of study that support U.S. intelligence initiatives or national security may be eligible as well, if the subjects are applicable to the purpose of AFCEA. Transcripts and two letters of recommendation from faculty members are mandatory.

Disabled American Veterans Auxiliary

https://auxiliary.dav.org/membership/programs/
(877) 426-2838 ext. 4020

Life members with the DAV Auxiliary who are attending a college or vocational school full time can participate in the scholarship program. The scholarship maxes out at $1,500. Part-time pursuit of study may be eligible for $750. Applicants must maintain a minimum of twelve credit hours per semester to remain eligible. Renewals are not guaranteed.

Society of Sponsors of the United States Navy Centennial Scholarship

http://societyofsponsorsofusn.org/scholarship-program/

Applicant must be combat-wounded Iraq or Afghanistan veteran (or spouse) with an associate degree (or equivalent credits), pursuing a bachelor's degree (full time) leading to a teacher credential. Five $3,000 scholarships will be awarded annually. Applications can be submitted throughout the academic year (August–May) for open enrollment.

Navy and Marine Corps Relief Society
Navy and Marine Corps Wounded Veterans

http://www.nmcrs.org/pages/education-loans-and-scholarships

Navy and Marine Corps wounded veterans of OIF, OEF, Operation New [6.780] Dawn, or those wounded in operational deployments, major training exercises, or operational mishaps may be eligible for $3,000 scholarships. Applicant must be pursuing a degree in a teaching profession. Spouses of wounded warriors may be eligible as well (teaching profession, medical, or medical-related fields only).

MECEP or MECP Programs-LOAN

http://www.nmcrs.org/pages/education-loans-and-scholarships

Active-duty (Marines and sailors) accepted into the Marine Enlisted to Commissioning Program (MECEP) or Medical Enlisted Commissioning Program (MECP) may be eligible to apply for a $500–3,000 loan per year through NMCRS. The interest-free loan must be paid back within forty-eight months of commissioning.

SCHOOL-BASED SCHOLARSHIPS

Many schools offer internal scholarships. Speak to the financial aid department of your chosen institution to find out about opportunities. This section points out just a few of the scholarships available around the country.

Florida

Santa Fe College

Jeffrey Mattison Wershow Memorial Scholarship

https://sfcollegefoundation.scholarships.ngwebsolutions.com/scholarx_scholarshipsearch.aspx

Applicant must have received an honorable discharge (but can still be on active duty) and must maintain a 2.5 GPA for award renewal. Award amount is $1,600 per year, or $800 per semester. Application demands a thousand-word essay pertaining to student's education (see website) and three letters of recommendation (see website).

Idaho

Idaho State University

Iwo Jima Scholarship

https://isu.academicworks.com/opportunities/11128

The Iwo Jima Scholarship may be available to a descendant of World War II veterans (preference for those who served at Iwo Jima). Applicant must have a 3.0 GPA to be eligible, and preference is given to engineering majors. Personal statement and discharge papers are required (see website).

Kansas

Johnston County Community College

Veterans Scholarship

https://www.jccc.edu/admissions/veterans/payment/scholarships.html

This scholarship is designed to assist veterans who are reentering the work force or higher education after being discharged from active duty or deployment. Funding is available to veterans who have been discharged within six months of the first day of classes of the semester they plan to enroll at JCCC. The scholarship will be applied to tuition and book costs, with no cash going directly to the student. Books must be purchased at the JCCC bookstore.

Dixon Memorial Veterans Scholarship

https://www.jccc.edu/admissions/veterans/payment/scholarships.html

913-469-3840

Veteran applying for scholarship must have completed a minimum of nine credit hours prior to submitting application. Applicant must demonstrate need and have at least a 2.5 GPA. Student must be enrolled in a minimum of nine credit hours to receive the $500 award and must have submitted all required documents (see website), including a FAFSA application.

Maryland

Wor-Wic Community College

Salisbury Optimist Scholarship

https://worwic.academicworks.com/opportunities/1002

Applicant must be a resident of Wicomico County, Maryland; must enroll at [6.809] the college within two years of returning from the military; and must demonstrate financial need. A GPA of 3.0 is necessary to apply.

Michigan

Michigan State University

MSU Disabled Veteran's Assistance Program
http://finaid.msu.edu/veterans.asp

New and returning undergraduate veterans with a military-related disability who are Michigan residents and working on their first baccalaureate degree potentially qualify for an aid package that covers all costs.

Minnesota

University of Minnesota Duluth
LaVerne Noyes Scholarship
http://www.d.umn.edu/onestop/student-finances/financial-aid/types/scholarships/umd-current.html

This scholarship is available to students attending the University of Minnesota Duluth. Applicant must be a direct blood descendant of a military member who served in the U.S. Army or Navy in World War I and died in service or received an honorable discharge. Applicant must demonstrate financial need. Award is $1,000.

New York

Cornell University Law School
Dickson Randolph Knott Memorial
http://www.lawschool.cornell.edu/alumni/giving/endowed_funds/scholarships_g-l.cfm

Applicant must be a military veteran enrolled in the law school (see website for more information).

Monroe Community College
Donald W. Holleder Endowed Scholarship
https://www.monroecc.edu/tuition-aid/types-of-aid/scholarships/

Applicant must demonstrate financial need, and preference is given to Vietnam veterans and their dependents. Award is for $600 per year.

Texas

Angelina College
Disabled American Veterans Scholarship
http://www.angelina.edu/financialaid/scholarship.html

Applicant must be a descendant of a member of the DAV. Award is $500 per semester for full-time study.

Texas Christian University
Adrienne Miller Perner Scholarship
https://tcu.smartcatalogiq.com/en/current/Undergraduate-Catalog/Material
-Resources/Endowed-Scholarships
(817) 257-7615

Amount varies. Applicant must be a child or grandchild of a career military service member. Applicant must also be female and majoring in ballet. Scholarship is based on talent or community work.

TEXTBOOK-BUYING OPTIONS

Who knew books could be so expensive? Welcome to college! The cost of books can be out of control. The Post-9/11 GI Bill maxes out at $1,000 per academic year for books and supplies, and often that does not begin to cover the bill. If you are still on active duty, you already know that TA does not cover books.

College books are notoriously expensive. Unlike high school, a year of college requires an incredible number of books. Professors have to find supplemental materials to feed your brain and back up information with proof. Books are still the most common and easiest way of accomplishing this. Now you know why you need them, but not why college books are so expensive. A few reasons come to mind: for example, copyrighted material, specialized material, and online supplements. College books can hold an incredible amount of copyrighted material. Publishers have to cover the copyright fees, as well as all other fees, in the cost of the book. Information in college books is usually quite specialized and often not found elsewhere. This means that the books do not have another avenue for sales, which contributes to a highly competitive market, driving up the cost. Many books also have online supplements attached to them, and those fees must be included in the cost.

Last—we hate addressing this reason, but feel we must—many professors have written books. Can you guess which books could be included in your reading list? Terrible, we agree . . . because professors get royalties just like other authors. Let's think more positively about the situation. These books can be among your most informative and easily organized reference materials. Professors often write books based on the knowledge they have derived from their years in the classroom and field experience to help themselves or others teach. Many schools take pride in having such accomplished professors on staff. Speaking from personal experience, being published is no easy feat. This practice may sometimes help a professor cut down on the book expenses for his or her students because the book follows along closely with the class's learning expectations, thereby allowing the student to purchase one book, or at least fewer books than previously necessary.

Although many other factors contribute to book costs, this cost is the reason you are reading this section: how to pay for them. The first trip to the bookstore can be excruciating as reality sets in. Do not stress; other options may exist. Because many books top the $100 range (sometimes closer to $200), students should spend as much time as feasible trying to find books from alternate sources.

We still recommend checking the campus bookstore first. Some schools maintain significant used-textbook sections. You will need to get to the store as early as possible to take advantage of this possibility; discounted books will be the first ones to leave the shelves. See if you can sell back your books at the end of the semester. Most likely, the store will offer you a greatly reduced price. Think of it as "a little cash is better than none," and you can roll that money into your textbooks for the following semester.

Next, you can try either renting or buying used books online. Which path you choose depends on whether you want to keep the books. Personally, because books change every few years, and the information in them becomes outdated at such a fast pace, I only kept my French books. The language was not changing, so I figured I would keep them for future reference.

An astounding number of sites on the internet sell or rent used textbooks. Even some bigwigs have gotten into the game. Amazon has a used-textbook section (www.amazon.com/New-Used-Textbooks-Books/ b?ie=UTF8&node=465600) that may suit all of your needs. It enables users to refer friends and earn five-dollar credits. Although five dollars may not seem like much, if you are the first in your group to start referring friends, you could end up with a stash of extra money to help cover your own textbook expenses.

Amazon also allows users to sell back books for Amazon gift cards. If you would prefer to rent (yes, for a full semester!), the site has that option available to users. If you are an Amazon Prime member (payment required: join as a student and receive a discount), you can receive your shipment in two days; otherwise, orders over twenty-five dollars receive free shipping but will run on regular shipment time frames. Last, you can rent or buy Kindle textbooks for Kindle Fire Tablets, or put the Kindle application on your iPad, Android tablet, PC, or Mac, and read them on your own device. You can rent the eTextbooks for an amount of time you specify. When you pick a book, Amazon lets you set the return date, although the price goes up the longer you keep the book.

Barnes & Noble offers the same services as Amazon (https://www.barnesandnoble.com/b/textbooks/_/N-8q9). You can receive a check from the store and even get a quick quote by entering some easy information on the website. The eTextbooks offered through B&N can be viewed with a seven-day free trial before purchase on your PC or Mac (not available for the actual NOOK device or mobile phones). This may come in handy if you are looking for an older version to save money. Make sure you compare the older version with a new version before purchasing. The eTextbooks are viewed through NOOK Study (free app). You can highlight, tag, link, and conduct searches on textbooks downloaded with this app.

If I were currently attending school, I would ask for gift certificates to these two stores for every single holiday. The generosity of family could keep me going with school textbooks for quite some time.

Now, these are not the only two sites to rent or purchase textbooks from. Below are a few other possible sources. Always compare prices at different sites to make sure you are getting the best deal possible before you proceed.

- Amazon Student Website: http://www.amazon.com/New-Used-Text -books-Books/b?ie=UTF8&node=465600
- Barnes and Noble: https://www.barnesandnoble.com/s/textbooks+college• textbooks/_/N-8q9

Compare book prices:

- http://www.bookfinder4u.com/
- https://www.textbookrentals.com/

Rent, sell, or buy back books:

- https://www.chegg.com/
- https://www.campusbookrentals.com/
- https://www.valorebooks.com/

Here are my last few ideas on this subject. You may be incredibly shocked to learn that sometimes the library is a good place to start. Check out both your college's library and your community library. A book may not be available for rental for the full semester, but if you only need a section or two, copy machines will work nicely, and some campus libraries let you scan free copies if you email them or save them to an external storage drive, and many professors leave their books in the library each semester for short-term checkout, for around two to three hours at a time. Or befriend someone who has already taken the class and has not returned his or her book, and offer that individual a decent price. Check with the college's bookstore for class reading lists, or send a nice email to the professor to find out the reading list in advance, and then double down on your mission.

Veterans Attending School with GI Bill Tutoring Available

Veterans attending school on a GI Bill at one-half time or more in a postsecondary program at an educational institution may be eligible for an extra tutoring stipend from the VA. The VA will pay up to $100 per month for tutoring on top of your regular GI Bill payments. The subject must be mandatory for program completion. Total amount cannot exceed $1,200. Students must need help in the subject, and even if currently receiving a passing grade, can receive the assistance if the current grade will not count toward program completion.

Under Post-9/11, there is no entitlement charge (deduction of remaining months of benefit). Under MGIB, there is no entitlement charge for the first $600: https://www.benefits.va.gov/gibill/tutorial_assistance.asp.

Notes

CHAPTER ONE: IS A CAREER IN
BUSINESS RIGHT FOR YOU?

1. University of Wisconsin, Madison. "Career Center." Accessed August 21, 2019. https://careercenter.education.wisc.edu/career-exploration/holland-personality-code/.

2. Utah Department of Workforce Services. Accessed August 21, 2019. https://jobs.utah.gov/jobseeker/smartstart/choosecareer.pdf.

3. National Association of Colleges and Employers. "About NACE." Accessed August 21, 2019. https://www.naceweb.org/about-us/.

4. National Association of Colleges and Employers. "MIS Projected as Class of 2019's Top-Paid Business Majors." Accessed August 21, 2019. https://www.naceweb.org/job-market/compensation/mis-projected-as-class-of-2019s-top-paid-business-majors/.

5. National Association of Colleges and Employers. "M.B.A.s Projected as Top-Paid Business Majors at Master's Level." Accessed August 21, 2019. https://www.naceweb.org/job-market/compensation/mbas-projected-as-top-paid-business-majors-at-masters-level/.

6. National Association of Colleges and Employers, "The Four Career Competencies Employers Value Most," Accessed April, 27, 2020. https://www.naceweb.org/career-readiness/competencies/the-four-career-competencies-employers-value-most/.

7. Antwan Gibson, email message to author, August 27, 2019.

CHAPTER TWO:
INFORMED DECISIONS

1. Babson University. "Arts and Humanities/History and Society Foundations (AHS)." Accessed August 22, 2019. https://www.babson.edu/academics/undergraduate-school/core-experiences/arts-and-humanities/.

2. University of Wisconsin. "Undergraduate Certificate." Accessed August 22, 2019. https://guide.wisc.edu/undergraduate/business/management-human-resources/entrepreneurship-certificate/.

3. University of Wisconsin. "Undergraduate Certificate." Accessed August 22, 2019. https://guide.wisc.edu/undergraduate/business/management-human-resources/entrepreneurship-certificate/.

4. University of Wisconsin. "MS in Business Analytics." Accessed August 22, 2019. https://wsb.wisc.edu/programs-degrees/masters/business-analytics.

5. University of Wisconsin. "MS in Supply Chain Management." Accessed August 22, 2019. https://wsb.wisc.edu/programs-degrees/masters/supply-chain.

6. Babson College. "Undergraduate Courses." Accessed August 22, 2019. https://www.babson.edu/academics/academic-divisions/entrepreneurship/curriculum/undergraduate-courses.

7. Babson College. "Undergraduate Courses." Accessed August 22, 2019. https://www.babson.edu/academics/academic-divisions/entrepreneurship/curriculum/undergraduate-courses.

8. Babson College. "Undergraduate Courses." Accessed August 22, 2019. https://www.babson.edu/academics/academic-divisions/entrepreneurship/curriculum/undergraduate-courses.

9. Babson College. "Undergraduate Coursework in Entrepreneurship." Accessed August 22, 2019. https://bus.wisc.edu/centers/weinert/wave/undergrad-coursework-entrepreneurship.

10. Babson College. "Undergraduate Coursework in Entrepreneurship." Accessed August 22, 2019. https://bus.wisc.edu/centers/weinert/wave/undergrad-coursework-entrepreneurship.

11. University of Wisconsin. "Morgridge Entrepreneurial Bootcamp (MEB). Accessed August 22, 2019. https://bus.wisc.edu/degrees-programs/non-business-majors/morgridge-entrepreneurial-bootcamp.

12. Honolulu Community College. "Automotive Technology." Accessed August 24, 2019. https://www.honolulu.hawaii.edu/amt.

13. Rio Hondo College. "Automotive Technology Bachelor of Science Program." Accessed August 24, 2019. https://www.riohondo.edu/autotechbachelor/program/#description-tab.

14. Marine Corps COOL. "MOS 3537 Motor Transport Operations Chief." Accessed August 24, 2019. https://www.cool.navy.mil/usmc/enlisted/3537.htm.

15. Marine Corps COOL. "Motor Transport Operations Chief." Accessed August 24, 2019. https://www.cool.navy.mil/usmc/enlisted/3537.htm.

16. Navy COOL. "CS-Culinary Specialist Navy Rating." Accessed August 24, 2019. https://www.cool.navy.mil/usn/enlisted/cs.htm.

17. Antwan Gibson, financial data analyst, email interview with the author, April 23, 2019.

18. Antwan Gibson, financial data analyst, email interview with the author, April 23, 2019.

19. James Hawthorne, branch manager, ABC Supply Co., email interview with the author, April 23, 2019.

CHAPTER THREE:
EDUCATION AND TRAINING

1. Judith Eaton, "An Overview of U.S. Accreditation," Council for Higher Education Accreditation. http://www.chea.org/pdf/Overview%20of%20US%20Accreditation%202012.pdf, last modified August 2012.

2. Barbara Brittingham, Mary Jane Harris, Michael Lambert, Frank Murray, George Peterson, Jerry Trapnell, Peter Vlasses, Belle Wheelan, Ralph Wolff, Susan Zlotlow, and Judith Eaton, "The Value of Accreditation," Council for Higher Education Accreditation, June 1, 2010. https://www.chea.org/sites/default/files/other-content/Value%20of%20US%20Accreditation%2006.29.2010_buttons.pdf.

3. Arizona State University, "Benefits of AACSB accreditation." Accessed September 5, 2019. https://wpcarey.asu.edu/about/accreditation.

4. Pepperdine University, "WSCUC and AACSB Accreditation." Accessed September 5, 2019. https://bschool.pepperdine.edu/about/at-a-glance/accreditation/.

5. Barbara Brittingham, Mary Jane Harris, Michael Lambert, Frank Murray, George Peterson, Jerry Trapnell, Peter Vlasses, Belle Wheelan, Ralph Wolff, Susan Zlotlow, and Judith Eaton, "The Value of Accreditation," Council for Higher Education Accreditation, June 1, 2010. http://www.chea.org/pdf/Value of US Accreditation 06.29.2010_buttons.pdf.

6. College Board, "Trends in Higher Education." Accessed September 5, 2019. https://trends.collegeboard.org/college-pricing/figures-tables/average-published-undergraduate-charges-sector-2018-19.

7. National Association of Independent Colleges and Universities, "Independent Colleges and Universities: A National Profile." Accessed April 8, 2016. https://www.naicu.edu/docLib/20110308_NAICU_ profiles.pdf.

8. Marine Corps COOL, "MOS 0431 Logistics/Embarkation Specialist." Accessed September 5, 2019. https://www.cool.navy.mil/usmc/enlisted/0431.htm.

9. Bureau of Labor Statistics Occupational Outlook Handbook, "How to Become a Logistician." Accessed September 5, 2019. https://www.bls.gov/ooh/business-and-financial/logisticians.htm#tab-4.

10. University of Colorado College of Business, "About International Business Seminars." Accessed September 5, 2019. https://www.uccs.edu/business/programs/international/ibs/about.

11. University of Wisconsin School of Business, "Outgoing Study Abroad Students." Accessed September 5, 2019. https://bus.wisc.edu/current-student-resources/bba/study-abroad/outgoing-study-abroad-students.

12. University of San Diego International Center, "Double Degree Programs." Accessed September 5, 2019. https://www.sandiego.edu/international/study-abroad/programs/dual-degree-programs.php#accordion-panel1.

13. National Center for Education Statistics, "Income of Young Adults." Accessed September 5, 2019. https://nces.ed.gov/fastfacts/display.asp?id=77.

14. Livescribe, "How Smartpens Help Students with Learning Disabilities." Accessed September 5, 2019. http://www.livescribe.com/en-us/solutions/learningdisabilities/.

15. Georgetown University, "Graduate Career Center." Accessed September 5, 2019. https://grad.georgetown.edu/gradcareer#.

16. Ibid.

17. Ibid.

18. Virginia Tech, "Internships and Co-ops: What's the Difference?" Accessed September 5, 2019. https://career.vt.edu/experience/ceip/ceip-internship-coop.html.

19. MiraCosta College, "Student Resources." Accessed September 5, 2019. http://www.miracosta.edu/instruction/careerservices/forstudents-career-exploration-resources.htm.

20. MiraCosta College catalog. Accessed September 5, 2019. http://miracosta.edu/officeofthepresident/pio/downloads/catalog.pdf.

21. MiraCosta College catalog. Accessed September 5, 2019. http://miracosta.edu/officeofthepresident/pio/downloads/catalog.pdf.

22. Student Veterans of America, "National Veterans Education Success Tracker." Accessed September 5, 2019. https://nvest.studentveterans.org/.

23. Veterans Transition Support, "Lean." Accessed April 24, 2018. https://www.veteranstransitionsupport.org/.

24. Marine Corps Credentialing Opportunities Online. "COOL Overview." Last updated January 9, 2016. https://www.cool.navy.mil/usmc/overview/index.htm.

25. University of California, Irvine, "Transfer Credit to Partner Colleges." Accessed September 5, 2019. https://ce.uci.edu/resources/academic/transfer_credit/.

26. HR Certification Institute, "Professional in Human Resources." Accessed April 11, 2018. https://www.hrci.org/our-programs/our-certifications/phr.

27. Society for Human Resources Management, "Why Seek SHRM Certification?" Accessed April 11, 2018. https://www.shrm.org/certification/about/about -shrm-certification/Pages/keybenefits.aspx.

28. Catherine Blue, email message to author, June 28, 2018.

29. Army COOL, "Credential Snapshot: Council of Supply Chain Management Professionals (CSCMP)—SCPro Level One—Cornerstones of Supply Chain Management." Last modified February 28, 2018. Accessed April 11, 2018. https://www.cool.osd.mil/army/search/CERT_COSCMSLO6968.htm.

30. Council of Supply Chain Management Professionals, "SCPro™ Certification." Accessed April 11, 2018. http://cscmp.org/CSCMP/Certification/SCPro _Certification_Overview/CSCMP/Certify/SCPro__Certification_Overview.aspx.

31. Ibid.

32. Career One Stop Credentials Center, "Find Certifications." Accessed April 11, 2018. https://www.careeronestop.org/Credentials/Toolkit/find-certifications -help.aspx#ansi.

33. Navy COOL, "Credential Snapshot: Institute for Supply Management (ISM)—Certified Professional in Supply Management (CPSM)." Accessed April 11, 2018. https://www.cool.navy.mil/usn/search/CERT_CPSM4494.htm. Last updated January 4, 2018.

34. Institute for Supply Management, "CPSM® Requirements." Accessed April 11, 2018. https://www.instituteforsupplymanagement.org/certification/ content.cfm?ItemNumber=30608&SSO=1.

35. Purdue University, "Six Sigma vs Lean Six Sigma." Accessed April 11, 2018. https://www.purdue.edu/leansixsigmaonline/blog/six-sigma-vs-lean-six -sigma/.

36. Project Management, "Project Management Professional." Accessed April 11, 2018. https://www.pmi.org/certifications/types/project-management-pmp.

37. Project Management Institute, "Earning Power: Project Management Salary Survey 10th Edition." Accessed April 24, 2018. https://www.pmi.org/-/ media/pmi/documents/public/pdf/learning/salary-survey-10th-edition.pdf.

38. Rick Cassoni, professor of computer studies and information technology (CSIT) at MiraCosta College, email message to author, July 5, 2019.

39. Occupational Safety and Health Administration, "Q & A's for Small Business Employers." Accessed June 4, 2018. https://www.osha.gov/Publications/ OSHA3163/osha3163.html.

40. Ibid.

41. Syracuse University EBV, "Programs and Schedules." http://ebv.vets.syr
.edu/veterans/program-schedule/.

42. Ibid.

CHAPTER FOUR: INTERNATIONAL BUSINESS
DEGREES AND STUDY ABROAD

1. Amos Owen. "Is It True Only 10% of Americans Have Passports?" BBC
News, January 9, 2018. Accessed September 7, 2019. http://www.bbc.com/news/
world-us-canada-42586638.

2. Amelia Friedman. "America's Lacking Language Skills." *The Atlantic*, May
10, 2015. Accessed September 7, 2019. https://www.theatlantic.com/education/
archive/2015/05/filling-americas-language-education-potholes/392876/.

3. Scott Jaschik. "Foreign Language Enrollments Drop Sharply." *Inside Higher
Ed*, March 7, 2018. Accessed September 7, 2019. https://www.insidehighered
.com/news/2018/03/07/study-finds-sharp-decline-foreign-language-enrollments.

4. J. Batalova and J. Zong. "Immigrant Veterans in the United States," *Mi-
gration Policy Institute*, May 16, 2019. Accessed September 7, 2019. https://
www.migrationpolicy.org/article/immigrant-veterans-united-states.

5. Skye Schoole. "Lost in Translation: 10 International Marketing Fails,"
Business News Daily, August 12, 2019. https://www.businessnewsdaily.com/
5241-international-marketing-fails.html.

6. Ibid.

7. San Diego State University. "Aztecs Abroad." Accessed September 7,
2019. https://sdsu-sa.terradotta.com/index.cfm?FuseAction=Programs.ListAll.

8. *U.S. News and World Report*. "Best Undergraduate International Business Programs." Accessed September 27, 2019. https://www.usnews.com/best
-colleges/rankings/business-international.

9. University of South Australia. Accessed September 27, 2019. https://
www.unisa.edu.au/Student-Life/Support-services/Student-administration/
Academic-calendars/Academic-calendar-2018/.

10. World Atlas. "Countries Hosting the Most Foreign Students." Accessed
September 8, 2019. https://www.worldatlas.com/articles/countries-hosting-most
-foreign-students.html.

11. Rick Noack. "7 Countries Where Americans Can Study at Universities,
in English, for Free (or Almost Free)," *Washington Post*, October 29, 2014.
https://www.washingtonpost.com/news/worldviews/wp/2014/10/29/7-countries
-where-americans-can-study-at-universities-in-english-for-free-or-almost-free/
?noredirect=on.

CHAPTER FIVE: PREPARATION AND RESOURCES FOR CAREER PLANNING

1. National Association of state Boards of Accountancy. Accessed September 8, 2019. https://nasba.org/.

2. Bureau of Labor Statistics Occupational Outlook Handbook, "OOH Facts." Accessed September 10, 2019. https://www.bls.gov/ooh/about/mobile/ooh-faqs.htm#growth3.

3. O*NET OnLine, "Browse by Career Cluster." Accessed September 8, 2019. https://www.onetonline.org/find/career.

4. NH Works, "NH Works Center." Accessed September 8, 2019. http://www.nhworks.org/job-seekers/nh-works-centers/.

5. U.S. Small Business Administration, "Organization." Accessed September 8, 2019. https://www.sba.gov/about-sba/organization.

6. U.S. Small Business Administration, "Veteran-Owned Businesses." Accessed September 8, 2019. https://www.sba.gov/business-guide/grow-your-business/veteran-owned-businesses#section-header-0.

7. Department of Veterans Affairs, "Office of Small & Disadvantaged Business Utilization." Accessed September 8, 2019. https://www.va.gov/osdbu/entrepreneur/.

8. USAGov, "Start Your Open Business." Accessed September 8, 2019. https://www.usa.gov/start-business?source=busa.

9. Marine Corps Community Services Camp Pendleton, "Transition Readiness Program." Accessed September 8, 2019. http://www.mccscp.com/transition/.

10. Marguerite Ward, "The Best Fonts to Use on a Resume, According to Typographers and Designers," CNBC. https://www.cnbc.com/2017/08/08/the-best-fonts-to-use-on-a-resume-according-to-designers.html. Last updated August 9, 2017.

11. University of North Carolina, "Informational Interview Guide." Accessed September 10, 2019. https://career.unca.edu/sites/default/files/documents/Job_Search_PDFs/Informational%20Interview%20Guide.pdf.

12. University of California, Berkeley, "Informational Interviewing." Accessed September 10, 2019. https://career.berkeley.edu/Info/InfoInterview.

13. Champlain College, "The Importance of Networking." Accessed September 12, 2019. https://www.champlain.edu/online/blog/importance-of-networking.

14. Top Resume, "The Importance of Networking (and How to Do It Well)." Accessed September 12, 2019. https://www.topresume.com/career-advice/importance-of-networking-for-career-success.

15. T. Casciaro, F. Gino, and M. Kouchaki. "Learn to Love Networking," *Harvard Business Review*, May 2016. https://hbr.org/2016/05/learn-to-love-networking.

16. Bonnie Marcus, "The Networking Advice No One Tells You," *Forbes Women*, May 22, 2018. https://www.forbes.com/sites/bonniemarcus/2018/05/22/the-networking-advice-no-one-tells-you/#9e7370077726.

17. CareerOneStop, "Networking Is a Key Part of Job Hunting." Accessed September 12, 2019. https://www.careeronestop.org/JobSearch/Network/why-network.aspx.

18. John Simmons, "How to Craft the Perfect Elevator Pitch," Monster.com. Accessed September 12, 2019. https://www.monster.com/career-advice/article/how-to-do-an-elevator-pitch.

19. Ibid.

20. Ibid.

21. CareerOneStop, "Contact Potential Employers." Accessed September 12, 2019. https://www.careeronestop.org/JobSearch/Network/contact-potential-employers.aspx.

22. Rotary, "Who We Are." Accessed September 12, 2019. https://www.rotary.org/en/about-rotary.

23. Ibid.

24. Ibid.

25. Undercover Recruiter, "Five Tips for Successful Career Fair Networking." Accessed September 12, 2019. https://theundercoverrecruiter.com/5-tips-successful-career-fair-networking/.

26. Ibid.

27. LinkedIn, "About LinkedIn." Accessed September 12, 2019. https://about.linkedin.com/?trk=homepage-basic_directory.

28. Entrepreneur, "The 5 Types of Business Networking Organizations." Accessed September 12, 2019. https://www.entrepreneur.com/article/302630.

29. Ibid.

30. Business Network International, "Local Business-Global Network." Accessed September 12, 2019. https://www.bni.com/.

31. Colleen Deere, email correspondence to author, April 20, 2019.

32. Jake Henne, email correspondence with author, April 29, 2019.

33. CBS Corporation, "Veterans at CBS." Accessed August, 12, 2019. https://cbscorporation.jobs/pittsburgh-pa/summer-2019-veteran-intern-pittsburgh/9DD6F182482A4A249EEF55D123CDB8E3/job/.

CHAPTER SEVEN: COST AND PAYMENT RESOURCES

1. Alabama Department of Veterans Affairs. "GI Dependent Scholarship Program." Accessed January 27, 2020. https://va.alabama.gov/dependents-scholarship.

2. Arkansas Department of Veterans Affairs. "Educational Benefits." Accessed January 27, 2020. http://www.veterans.arkansas.gov/benefits/state-benefits.

3. California Department of Veterans Affairs. "College Fee Waiver." Access January 27, 2020. https://www.calvet.ca.gov/VetServices/Pages/College-Fee-Waiver.aspx.

4. Veterans Affairs and Military Programs. "CT Veterans Tuition Waiver." Retrieved January 27, 2020. https://veterans.uconn.edu/ctveteranswaiver/.

5. Office of Veterans Affairs. "Veterans Benefits. Retrieved January 27, 2020. https://veteransaffairs.delaware.gov/veterans-benefits/.

6. Florida Department of Veterans Affairs. "Education." Retrieved January 27, 2020. http://floridavets.org/benefits-services/education/.

7. Illinois Student Assistance Commission. "Illinois Veterans Grant (IVG) Program. Retrieved January 27, 2020. https://www.isac.org/students/during-college/types-of-financial-aid/grants/IVG-program.html.

8. Indiana Commission for Higher Education. "Tuition and Fee Exemption—Children of Disabled Veterans." Retrieved January 27, 2020. https://www.in.gov/che/4517.htm.

9. Kentucky Department of Veterans Affairs. "Tuition Waiver." Retrieved January 27, 2020. https://veterans.ky.gov/Pages/HidPages/TuitionWaiver.aspx.

10. Bureau of Veterans Services. "Veterans Dependents Educational Benefits." Retrieved January 27, 2020. https://www.maine.gov/veterans/benefits/education/dependents-educational-benefits.html.

11. Maryland Department of Veterans Affairs. "Scholarships." Retrieved January 27, 2020. http://veterans.maryland.gov/education-supports-and-scholarships/.

12. Massachusetts Department of Higher Education. "Categorical Tuition Waiver for Veterans and Active Duty." Retrieved January 27, 2020. https://www.mass.edu/forstufam/veterans/financialaid.asp.

13. National Resource Directory. "Massachusetts Veterans Upward Bounds Programs." Retrieved January 27, 2019. https://nrd.gov/resource/detail/21076358/Massachusetts+Veterans+Upward+Bound+Programs.

14. Michigan Student Aid. Retrieved January 27, 2020. https://www.michigan.gov/mistudentaid/0,4636,7-372—481212—,00.html.

15. Minnesota Department of Veterans Affairs. "Veteran Education Assistance." Retrieved January 27, 2020. https://mn.gov/mdva/resources/education/vea.jsp.

16. Department of Education Workforce and Development. "Wartime Veteran's Survivors Grant Program." Retrieved January 27, 2020. https://dhewd.mo.gov/ppc/grants/wartimevetsurvivor.php.

17. Department of Military Affairs. "Montana University System Veterans Services Website." Retrieved January 27, 2020. http://montanadma.org/montana-university-system-veterans-services-website.

18. Nebraska Department of Veterans' Affairs. "Waiver of Tuition Program." Retrieved January 27, 2020. https://veterans.nebraska.gov/waiver.

19. New Hampshire State Office of Veterans Services. "Education Benefits." Retrieved January 27, 2020. https://www.nh.gov/nhveterans/benefits/education.htm.

20. New Mexico Department of Veterans Services. "State Benefits." Retrieved January 27, 2020. http://www.nmdvs.org/state-benefits/.

21. New York State Division of Veterans' Services. "State Education and Scholarships." Retrieved January 27, 2020. https://veterans.ny.gov/content/state-education-scholarships.

22. North Carolina Department of Military and Veterans Affairs. "Scholarships." Retrieved January 27, 2020. https://www.milvets.nc.gov/services/scholarships.

23. North Dakota Department of Veterans Affairs. "ND Dependent Tuition Waiver." Retrieved January 27, 2020. http://www.nd.gov/veterans/benefits/nd-dependent-tuition-waiver.

24. OhioHigherEd. "Education Opportunities for Veterans and Service Members." Retrieved January 27, 2020. https://www.ohiohighered.org/veterans.

25. Ohio Higher Ed. "Ohio War Orphan and Severely Disabled Veterans' Scholarship." Retrieved January 27, 2020. https://www.ohiohighered.org/ohio-war-orphans.

26. State of Rhode Island Office of Veterans Services. "Disabled Veterans Tuition Waiver." Retrieved January 27, 2020. http://www.vets.ri.gov/.

27. South Carolina Division of Veterans Affairs. "Application for Tuition Assistance for Certain War Veterans' Children. Retrieved January 27, 2020. http://va.sc.gov/documents/2015_free_tuition_application.pdf.

28. South Dakota Department of Veterans Affairs. "Benefits." Retrieved January 27, 2020. https://vetaffairs.sd.gov/benefits/State/State%20Education%20Programs.aspx.

29. Texas Veterans Commission. "Hazlewood Act." Retrieved January 27, 2020.https://www.tvc.texas.gov/education/hazlewood-act/.

30. Utah Veterans and Military Affairs. "State Benefits." Retrieved January 27, 2020. https://veterans.utah.gov/state-benefits/.

31. Virginia Department of Veterans Services. "Virginia Military Survivors and Dependents Education Program." Retrieved January 27, 2020. https://

www.dvs.virginia.gov/education-employment/virginia-military-survivors-and
-dependents-education-program-2-2.

32. Washington State Department of Veterans Affairs. "Education and Training. Retrieved January 27, 2020. http://www.dva.wa.gov/benefits/education-and
-training.

33. State of West Virginia Department of Veterans Assistance. "State Benefits
and Programs." Retrieved January 27, 2020. https://veterans.wv.gov/Benefits/
Pages/default.aspx.

34. State of Wisconsin Department of Veterans Affairs. "Wisconsin GI Bill."
Retrieved January 27, 2020. https://dva.wi.gov/Pages/educationEmployment/
Wisconsin-GI-Bill.aspx.

Resources

ACCREDITING BODIES WEBSITES

- Middle States Association of Colleges and Schools: http://www.msche.org/
- New England Association of School and Colleges: http://cihe.neasc.org/
- North Central Association of Colleges and Schools: http://www.ncahlc.org/
- Northwest Commission on Colleges and Universities: http://www.nwccu.org
- Southern Association of Colleges and Schools: http://www.sacscoc.org/
- Western Association of Schools and Colleges, Accrediting Commission for Community and Junior Colleges: http://www.accjc.org
- Western Association of Schools and Colleges, Accrediting Commission for Senior Colleges and Universities: http://www.wascweb.org/

RESOURCE WEBSITES

- American Corporate Partners (ACP): http://www.acp-usa.org/, www.acp-advisornet.org
- American Council on Education: http://www.acenet.edu
- Austin-Bergstrom International Airport: http://austintexas.gov/department/veteran-fellowship-program-austin-bergstrom-international-airport
- Benetrends: https://www.benetrends.com/
- Board of Governors Waiver, California: http://www.icanaffordcollege.com/?navId=10

- Bunker Labs: https://bunkerlabs.org/our-impact/
- Bureau of Labor Statistics: http://www.bls.gov/ooh/
- California Career Zone: https://www.cacareerzone.org/
- California Employment Development Department: https://www.edd.ca .gov/
- California Promise Grant: https://home.cccapply.org/money/california -college-promise-grant/terms
- CareerOneStop: https://www.careeronestop.org/
- CareerScope: https://va.careerscope.net/gibill
- CBS Veterans Network: https://www.cbsvetnet.com/internship
- College Navigator: http://nces.ed.gov/collegenavigator/
- Council for Higher Education Accreditation (CHEA): https://www.chea .org/directories
- Credentialing Opportunities Online (COOL) sites:

  - Army: https://www.cool.army.mil/
  - Navy: https://www.cool.navy.mil/
  - USMC: https://www.cool.navy.mil/usmc/index.htm
  - Air Force: https://afvec.us.af.mil/afvec/Public/COOL/

- DANTES Kuder: https://dantes.kuder.com/landing-page
- Defense Intelligence Agency, Wounded Warriors Internship: http://www .dia.mil/Careers-and-Internships/Veterans/
- Department of Veterans Affairs First Contracting Program: https://www .va.gov/osdbu/verification/
- Dog Tag, Inc. (DTI): https://www.dogtaginc.org/our-mission
- Federal Aviation Administration: https://www.faa.gov/jobs/working_here /veterans/
- Federal Bureau of Investigation (FBI): https://www.fbijobs.gov/veterans
- Federal Energy Management Program: https://www.energy.gov/eere/ femp/federal-energy-management-program-veteran-internships
- Federal Student Aid: http://www.fafsa.ed.gov/
- FranFund: https://www.franfund.com/
- GI Bill Comparison Tool: https://www.vets.gov/gi-bill-comparison-tool
- GI Bill information: https://benefits.va.gov/gibill/post911_gibill.asp
- Glassdoor: https://www.glassdoor.com/
- Guidant Financial: https://www.guidantfinancial.com/
- Hiring Our Heroes: https://www.hiringourheroes.org/

- Illinois workNet: https://www.illinoisworknet.com/
- Indeed: https://www.indeed.com/
- Informational Interviewing:

  ○ University at Buffalo: http://mgt.buffalo.edu/career-resource-center/students/networking/mentorlink/40-questions-to-ask-in-an-informational-interview.html
  ○ University of California, Berkeley: https://career.berkeley.edu/Info/InfoInterview
  ○ CareerOneStop: https://www.careeronestop.org/JobSearch/Network/informational-interviews.aspx
  ○ Indeed: https://www.careeronestop.org/JobSearch/Network/informational-interviews.aspx
  ○ Penn State: https://studentaffairs.psu.edu/career/resources/networking/informational-interviewing
  ○ Live Career: http://www.miracosta.edu/instruction/careerservices/for students-career-exploration-resources.html and https://www.livecareer.com/career/advice/interview/information-interview

- Internal Revenue Service (IRS): https://www.jobs.irs.gov/resources/equal-opportunity/veteran-hiring
- Internships:

  ○ Career Builder: https://www.careerbuilder.com/
  ○ Idealist: https://www.idealist.org/en/?type=JOB
  ○ Internship Programs: http://www.internshipprograms.com/
  ○ College Recruiter: https://www.collegerecruiter.com/
  ○ After College: https://www.aftercollege.com/
  ○ U.S. Chamber of Commerce: https://www.uschamber.com/about/careers/internship-program
  ○ Los Angeles Chamber of Commerce: https://lachamber.com/about/employment-internships-with-the-chamber/

- Joint Services Transcript: https://jst.doded.mil/
- LinkedIn: https://www.linkedin.com/
- Los Angeles County Veterans Internship Program: https://hr.lacounty.gov/veterans-internships/
- Make the Connection: http://maketheconnection.net/

- Michigan Department of Transportation (MDOT): https://www.michigan .gov/mdot/0,4616,7-151-9623_38029_61350—,00.html
- Military Digital Library Program:

  ○ Army: https://www.myarmyonesource.com/EducationCareersand Libraries/Libraries/default.aspx
  ○ Navy: https://www.navymwrdigitallibrary.org/
  ○ USMC: https://mccs.ent.sirsi.net/client/en_US/default
  ○ Air Force: https://libguides.nps.edu/portals/afdigital
  ○ Coast Guard: https://www.navymwrdigitallibrary.org/

- Mount Adams Institute, VetsWork: https://mtadamsinstitute.org/vets work-environment/
- My Next Move for Veterans: https://www.mynextmove.org/vets/
- National Career Development Association (NCDA): https://www.ncda .org/aws/NCDA/pt/sp/credentials_cmcs
- National Center for Veteran Institute for Procurement: https://national vip.org/Home/Home
- National Veteran Small Business Coalition: https://www.nvsbc.org/
- Navy COOL: http://www.cool.navy.mil
- New Hampshire Works: http://www.nhworks.org/
- O*NET OnLine: https://www.onetonline.org/
- Oracle: https://www.oracle.com/corporate/careers/diversity/veterans -programs.html
- Payscale: https://www.payscale.com/
- Projections Central: https://projectionscentral.com/
- San Diego Airport Veterans Fellowship Program: https://sdcraa-careers .silkroad.com/Careers/Interns—-Vets.html
- SCORE: https://www.score.org/
- Service-Disabled Veteran-Owned Small Businesses Program (SDVOSB): https://www.sba.gov/federal-contracing/contracting-assistance-programs /service-disabled-veteran-owned-small-businesses-program
- Small Business Administration (SBA): https://www.sba.gov/
- Small Business Development Centers (SBDC): https://americassbdc.org/
- States' Departments of Veterans Affairs Offices: http://www.va.gov/ statedva.htm
- State workforce agencies: http://www.servicelocator.org/OWSLinks.asp
- Student Veterans of America: http://www.studentveterans.org

- Study Abroad Programs:

  ○ University of California, San Diego (UCSD): https://studyabroad.ucsd.edu/
  ○ The State University of New York (SUNY): https://www.suny.edu/studyabroad/
  ○ University of Alabama (UA): http://international.ua.edu/educationabroad/
  ○ Washington Community College Consortium for Study Abroad (WCCCSA): http://wcccsa.com/
  ○ British Council: https://study-uk.britishcouncil.org/
  ○ Australian Government: https://www.studyinaustralia.gov.au/english/home
  ○ New Zealand Government: https://www.studyinnewzealand.govt.nz/
  ○ Enterprise Ireland: http://www.educationinireland.com/en/
  ○ Canadian Government: http://www.cic.gc.ca/ENGLISH/study/index.asp

- Syracuse University Institute for Veterans and Military Families (IVMF): http://vets.syr.edu/
- Texas Career Check: https://texascareercheck.com/
- U.S. Chamber of Commerce: https://www.uschamber.com/
- U.S. Department of Defense Memorandum of Understanding: http://www.dodmou.com
- U.S. Department of Education—national accrediting agencies: http://ope.ed.gov/accreditation/
- U.S. Department of Labor's career search tool: http://www.mynextmove.org/
- U.S. Department of Veterans Affairs (VA): https://www.va.gov/
- VA Chapter 36 educational support counseling: http://www.gibill.va.gov/support/counseling_services/
- VA Vet Centers: http://www.vetcenter.va.gov/index.asp
- VA Veterans Success on Campus (VSOC): https://www.benefits.va.gov/vocrehab/vsoc.asp
- VA Vocational Rehabilitation: https://www.benefits.va.gov/vocrehab/index.asp
- VA Yellow Ribbon Program: https://www.benefits.va.gov/gibill/yellow_ribbon.asp

- Veterans Business Outreach Program (OVBD): https://www.sba.gov/business-guide/grow-your-business/veteran-owned-businesses#section-header-0
- Veterans Transition Support: https://www.veteranstransitionsupport.org/
- Vet to CEO: https://www.vettoceo.org/
- WEAMS Institution Search: https://inquiry.vba.va.gov/weamspub/buildSearchInstitutionCriteria.do (or search VA WEAMS Institution)
- Womens Business Centers: https://www.sba.gov/offices/headquarters/wbo

STATES CURRENTLY WITH STATE-BASED EDUCATION BENEFITS

- Alabama: https://va.alabama.gov/dependents-scholarship/
- Arkansas: http://www.veterans.arkansas.gov/benefits/state-benefits
- California: https://www.calvet.ca.gov/VetServices/Pages/College-Fee-Waiver.aspx
- Connecticut: https://veterans.uconn.edu/ctveteranswaiver/
- Delaware: https://veteransaffairs.delaware.gov/veterans-benefits/
- Florida: (850) 245-0407
- Illinois: https://www.isac.org/isac-gift-assistance-programs/illinois-veteran-grant/
- Indiana: https://www.in.gov/dva/2343.htm
- Kentucky: https://veterans.ky.gov/Pages/HidPages/TuitionWaiver.aspx
- Maine: https://usm.maine.edu/trioprograms/veterans-upward-bound
- Maryland: http://veterans.maryland.gov/education-supports-and-scholarships/
- Massachusetts: https://www.mass.edu/forstufam/veterans/financialaid.asp
- Minnesota: https://mn.gov/mdva/resources/education/vea.jsp
- Missouri: http://dhe.mo.gov/ppc/grants/wartimevetsurvivor.php
- Montana: http://montanadma.org/montana-university-system-veterans-services-website
- Nebraska: https://veterans.nebraska.gov/waiver
- New Hampshire: https://www.nh.gov/nhveterans/benefits/education.htm
- New Mexico: http://www.nmdvs.org/state-benefits/

- New York: http://veterans.ny.gov/state-benefits.html
- New York: https://veterans.ny.gov/content/post-911-gi-bill-other -educational-programs
- North Carolina: http://www.doa.state.nc.us/vets/scholarshipclasses.aspx
- North Carolina: https://www.milvets.nc.gov/services/scholarships
- North Dakota: http://www.nd.gov/veterans/benefits/nd-dependent-tuition -waiver
- Rhode Island: http://www.vets.ri.gov/
- South Carolina: http://va.sc.gov/documents/2015_free_tuition_applica tion.pdf
- South Dakota: http://vetaffairs.sd.gov/benefits/State/State%20Education %20Programs.aspx
- Texas: https://www.tvc.texas.gov/education/hazlewood-act/
- Utah: https://veterans.utah.gov/state-benefits/
- Virginia: https://www.dvs.virginia.gov/education-employment/virginia -military-survivors-and-dependents-education-program-2-2
- Washington: http://www.dva.wa.gov/benefits/education-and-training
- West Virginia: https://veterans.wv.gov/Benefits/Pages/default.aspx
- Wisconsin: https://dva.wi.gov/Pages/educationEmployment/Wisconsin -GI-Bill.aspx

COMMONLY USED ACRONYMS

AA: Associate of Arts
ACP: American Corporate Partners
BA: Bachelor of Arts
BLS OOH: Bureau of Labor Statistics Occupational Outlook Handbook
BS: Bachelor of Science
CC: Community College
CHEA: Council for Higher Education Accreditation
COE: Certificate of Eligibility
FAFSA: Free Application for Federal Student Aid
FSA: Federal Student Aid
FY: Fiscal Year
MGIB: Montgomery GI Bill
MOS: Military Occupational Specialty

PCS: Permanent Change of Station
SBA: Small Business Administration
SBDC: Small Business Development Center
SDVOSB: Service-Disabled Veteran-Owned Small Businesses Program
SVA: Student Veterans of America
VA: Veterans Administration
YRP: Yellow Ribbon Program

Index

317

About the Authors

Robert W. Blue has been a civilian education and career counselor for the military since 2001, working in the San Diego area on Navy and Marine Corps bases providing higher education services to Marines and sailors of all ranks, from junior enlisted to admiral. He has been responsible for setting up college programs, including classroom instruction, on dozens of U.S. Navy ships.

Julie LaCroix has been a career counselor in private practice for over a decade, based in Southern California and serving adults of all ages.

Roxanne Rapske is a franchise consultant, specializing in using the company's proven franchise matching system and her own unique experience in the business world to consult with clients and to match them to a franchise that offers the best personal and professional fit for their needs. She teaches for a transition seminar for service members held aboard the Camp Pendleton Marine Corps Base in California.

Jillian Ventrone is an adjunct veterans' counselor at MiraCosta College, which is part of the California State Community College System. She counsels military and military-affiliated students regarding their higher education and career goals. She has written five other books, also published by Rowman and Littlefield, that were designed to assist service members in the Marine Corps, Navy, Air Force, and Army, as well as dependent family members.